Durable Disorder

Understanding the Politics of Northeast India

Durable Disorder
Understanding the Politics of Northeast India

Sanjib Baruah

OXFORD
UNIVERSITY PRESS

OXFORD
UNIVERSITY PRESS

YMCA Library Building, Jai Singh Road, New Delhi 110 001

Oxford University Press is a department of the University of Oxford. It furthers the
University's objective of excellence in research, scholarship, and education
by publishing worldwide in

Oxford New York

Auckland Cape Town Dar es Salaam Hong Kong Karachi
Kuala Lumpur Madrid Melbourne Mexico City Nairobi
New Delhi Shanghai Taipei Toronto

With offices in

Argentina Austria Brazil Chile Czech Republic France Greece
Guatemala Hungary Italy Japan Poland Portugal Singapore
South Korea Switzerland Thailand Turkey Ukraine Vietnam

Oxford is a registered trademark of Oxford University Press
in the UK and in certain other countries

Published in India by Oxford University Press, New Delhi

© Oxford University Press 2005

The moral rights of the author have been asserted
Database right Oxford University Press (maker)

First published 2005

ISBN 019 5669819

Typeset in Garamond by Le Studio Graphique, Gurgaon 122 001
Printed in India by Pauls Press, New Delhi 110 020
Published by Manzar Khan, Oxford University Press
YMCA Library Building, Jai Singh Road, New Delhi 110 001

Contents

Preface

Northeast India's troubled post-colonial history does not fit easily into a standard narrative of democracy in India. A number of armed conflicts smoulder in this frontier region: the outside world is aware of a few of them, but only people living in remote war zones—and paying a price with their blood and tears—know the others. Reports of alleged brutality by security forces and private militias, and of popular protests against such brutality, make their way into the Indian media from time to time. But they do not capture national attention for long enough to provoke serious debates and soul-searching. The region seems distant from the hearts and minds of many Indians: its lush green landscape evokes the picture of another part of monsoon Asia, and the local people, in the eyes of many, look racially different. An undifferentiated picture of nameless 'insurgencies' and Indian soldiers engaged in the defence of 'the nation' dominate popular impressions of the region. This is hardly the climate for an informed and vigorous national debate on nearly four decades of failed policy.

It is difficult to reconcile the picture of dozens of low-intensity armed conflicts with the textbook idea that democracies are better able to peacefully resolve conflicts than non-democracies. While elections punctuate the trajectory of armed conflicts they do little more than confer an air of normalcy on both insurgencies and counter-insurgency operations. Yet the costs of letting armed conflicts fester have been high. As Vaclav Havel reminds us, societies pay an incalculable surcharge when following periods that history seems suspended the moment arrives for 'life and history to demand their due' (Havel 1989: 34–5). But on the scales used by India's security establishment such charges do not register.

Parts of India's human rights record in the Northeast would have put many other democracies to shame. Yet our debates appear to be stuck on a 'which came first: chicken or the egg' kind of a controversy on whether the security forces, or the insurgents bear the responsibility for the sorry state of human rights, or whether the Indian army, or insurgents are the worse violators, or on whether the region's fledgling human rights groups have a pro-insurgent bias. The Armed Forces Special Powers Act specially designed for the Northeast and that has remained in force for decades—despite popular protests—makes serious violations of human rights possible. The trouble that scholars have to go through to obtain permissions to visit many parts of the region—research visas being virtually impossible to obtain— challenges official claims that a stable peace is round the corner. The supposed imperatives of counter-insurgency provide a cover for a virtual loot of the public treasury and a corrosion of values in public life. Insurgent groups routinely perform crucial state functions such as tax collection ('extortion') and the provision of security to their ethnic constituents. These aspects of Northeast India's informal governance structure seems to have more in common with some weak and failing states of Africa than with the powerful Indian state that those who talk of a resurgent India imagine it to be.

The book has grown out of my sense of puzzlement about how democratic India tolerates the Northeast Indian exception. The region's troubles are usually framed as the 'insurgency problem.' But whatever the value of debates between academics and military generals on how best to fight insurgencies, counter-insurgency as an intellectual stance has produced neither path-breaking scholarship nor political positions that are defensible on ethical and moral grounds. Nor has it succeeded in the goal it has set for itself, that is, ending armed conflicts.

Durable Disorder is an invitation to think about the region's political troubles outside the hackneyed paradigm of 'insurgency'. It is an effort to think beyond the developmentalist mind-set that turns a blind eye to today's sufferings in the name of abstractions such as nation-building and development. I hope it is a step towards rescuing academic and policy discourse from the iron-grip of colonial ideas about castes and tribes; languages and dialects; and hills and plains—often dressed up these days as 'ethnic studies'. Many nineteenth and early twentieth century British scholar-administrators would have been astounded, and embarrassed by the appeal made more than a century later, to their often tentative ideas. *Durable*

Disorder is a call for a critical engagement with India's Northeast policy, keeping in mind Mrinal Miri's admonition that the idea of a nation having a 'policy' towards a part itself is odd (Miri 2002). Are Northeast India's troubles a sign of cracks along a racial fault line between India and its Northeast?

Much of the material in this book was published earlier, mostly as articles in journals and magazines. The primary reason for reprinting them is practical: to make them available in India, especially those that were published in European and American journals to which very few people have access. However, I could not avoid the dilemmas that all writers who gather previously published articles into a book must confront. If the articles need a lot of revision, as Clifford Geertz once said, 'they probably ought not to be reprinted at all, but should be replaced with a wholly new article getting the damn thing right.' And 'writing changed views back into earlier works' is a problematical enterprise. It is not wholly cricket, said Geertz, and it 'obscures the development of ideas that one is supposedly trying to demonstrate in collecting the essays in the first place' (Geertz 1973: viii).

In revising these articles I chose a middle path. The first end note to each chapter indicates when and where the original version was published. I left the arguments of the original articles intact (except for a change in a key term in Chapter 6 that I explain in endnote 3 of the chapter). Readers will easily recognize how my ideas have changed over time. I eliminated the background material that Indian readers would have found unnecessary. Certain articles, however, needed updating. For instance, the argument about 'Generals as Governors' in Chapter 3 would have been unpersuasive without some reference to developments since 2001. While rewriting it, I took the opportunity to expand parts of the essay, especially a section on the history of ideas that had to be kept short in the original magazine essay.

It was difficult to decide whether to include Chapters 6 and 7 because they were written prior to my last book *India against Itself*. Readers of that book will find the argument familiar. But a couple of reasons weighed in favour of including them. The articles are central to the theme of *Durable Disorder*. Written in the early 1990s, the chapters evoke the mood of the times. That section of the book aims at showing what happened over time to the politics of the United Liberation Front of Assam (ULFA) that once enjoyed significant public sympathy. There is also a practical consideration: those two articles are in considerable demand.

I have collected a lot of debt in writing this book, from the time when each chapter was conceived to preparing them for publication in their present form. The Omeo Kumar Das Institute of Social Change and Development in Guwahati, Assam, and Bard College in Annandale on Hudson, New York provided the material conditions and the intellectual space. Chapter 10 grew out of the task given to me at the OKD Institute of defining the intellectual mission of its Centre for Northeast India, South and Southeast Asia Studies [CENISEAS]. In addition, while at the institute, I wrote the introductory chapter and got the manuscript ready for publication. I am grateful to Mrinal Miri, Madan P. Bezbaruah, A.C. Bhagabati, Jayanta Madhab, Abu Naser Said Ahmed, and Bishnu Mohapatra for inviting me to the institute and for facilitating my work.

Setting up CENISEAS has given me the opportunity to interact with a new generation of talented young people working on the region. Among them are Sanjay Barbora, Anindita Dasgupta, and Boddhisattva Kar. My conversations with them and with CENISEAS Fellows Arup Jyoti Das, Bhupen Das, Uddipana Goswami, Sanjeeb Kakati, Abinash Lahkar, Mriganka Madhukaillya, Sukanya Sarma, Suranjan Sarma, Pritima Sarma, and Priyam Krishna Sinha have been a source of intellectual energy that speeded up the book. Ratna Bhuyan's assistance was invaluable in getting the manuscript ready for the publisher. Without Kalindra Dev Choudhury's competent handling of CENISEAS responsibilities and Jyoti Khataniar's conscientious work habits, I would not have been able to devote time to this book. I have been fortunate in being able to count on the support of family members—Renu Baruah, Ranjib and Deepti Baruah; Karuna and Surabhi Sarma; Papari Baruah; Prantor and Sashi Baruah—and of an old friend Pankaj Thakur.

While the book took its final shape in Guwahati, most of the chapters were first written while teaching at Bard College. Bard's innovative curriculum and the quality of its engagement with the world gave me the space to stay engaged with Northeast India. The support of Leon Botstein, Michèle Dominy, and that of my colleagues in the Political Studies and the Asian Studies programmes, have been crucial in this enterprise. Mario Bick, Diana Brown, and David Kettler have read almost every word I have written.

A number of chapters got written initially in response to invitations from various institutions. Among the individuals behind these invitations are: B.G. Karlsson of the University of Uppsala, Sweden (Chapter 1), Jürg Helbling and Danilo Geiger of the University of Zürich, Switzerland

(Chapter 2), Kanak Dixit of *Himal* magazine, Kathmandu, Nepal and Anindita Dasgupta (Chapter 3), David G. Timbermann of the Asia Foundation's project 'Separatism and Autonomy in Asia' (Chapter 8), Sandhya Goswami and Bolin Hazarika of the North East India Political Science Association (Chapter 9), and Jatin Hazarika and N.K. Das of the Assam Branch of the Indian Institute of Public Administration (Chapter 10). From their conception to their appearing as chapters of this book they have benefited from various sources such as the responses I have received at conferences and seminars where I had presented earlier versions. The suggestions of anonymous reviewers and the work of editors of publications where the chapters had come out as articles are reflected in this book.

My friendship with Jupiter Yambem had for many years nourished my interest in Northeast India. Jupiter grew up in Manipur—the most troubled of Northeast Indian states. He died on 11 September 2001 at the World Trade Center. Since then there are daily reminders of the dangers of a security-obsessed mindset, and of nationalism and patriotism, entrapping us into denying the humanity of those who do not resemble us. This book, I hope, will create some awareness that India might be faced with such a danger in its troubled relationship with the Northeast.

I am grateful to Neel Pawan Barua for permitting me to see allusions to Northeast India's durable disorder in his untitled 1997 painting and for letting me use it on the cover of this book.

In my journeys between the United States and India, Kalpana Raina and Sabyasachi Bhattacharyya, formerly of New York and presently of Mumbai, have been my soulmates. Our friendship has been a driving force in my engagement with India. Zilkia Janer left New York to be with me in Guwahati—a difficult, and even lonely, place for someone working on Latin American literature and for whom the natural language of intellectual discourse is Spanish. She has been the first reader and critic of a lot of my writings. Her companionship has made a difference to my life and in being able to write this book.

September 2004   SANJIB BARUAH

SECTION I

Introduction

1

Towards a Political Sociology of Durable Disorder[1]

The haunting *Madhavi* escapes the rustle of spring
Acrid with the smell of gunpowder.

Chandra Kanta Murasingh, 2003

These essays, originally written as journal articles, lectures and conference papers, seek to understand the causes, and the meaning and significance of a pattern of political violence in Northeast India that can no longer be seen as only temporary and aberrant. Deaths, injuries, and humiliations resulting from 'insurgencies' and 'counter-insurgency operations', as well as the hidden hurt that citizens quietly endure have become a part of the texture of everyday life in the region. They coexist, somewhat awkwardly, with elections and elected governments, a free press, an independent judiciary and investments in the name of development—in sum, the institutions and practices of a normal democracy and a developmentalist state.

For Indian democracy, maintaining a sustained capacity for counter-insurgency operations has meant the institutionalization of authoritarian practices that, though localized, is rather jarring. The book focuses on the formal and informal structures of governance and the democracy deficit—aspects of the region's political life that receives little systematic attention. Three of the chapters centre around the life and times of the United Liberation Front of Assam, and another is about the conflict between the Indian Government and the Nagas: one of the world's oldest continuing armed conflicts under suspended animation since 1997. The cultural politics that animate the militias of the region and their relationship to their constituencies and to 'mainstream' social and political forces is a theme that runs through a number of the chapters. A few chapters were originally published in journals in different parts of the world; the volume is intended to make them easily available, especially to readers in India. Since the chapters often reflect the mood of the times in which they were written, I have decided not to revise them in any substantive way except to update some of the information.

'Northeast India' As a Category

Northeast India has been known this way since a radical redrawing of the region's political map in the 1960s. It was a hurried exercise in political engineering: an attempt to manage the independentist rebellions among the Nagas and the Mizos and to nip in the bud as well as pre-empt, radical political mobilization among other discontented ethnic groups. From today's vantage point this project of political engineering must be pronounced a failure. The story of what is commonly referred to as the reorganization of Assam and the advent of what I call a cosmetic federal regional order and the introduction of the term 'Northeast India' into official usage is recounted in Chapter 2, 'Nationalizing Space: Cosmetic Federalism and the Politics of Development'.

Eight of the ten chapters were written since the publication of my book *India Against Itself: Assam and the Politics of Nationality* in 1999 (Baruah 1999).[2] That book's focus was Assam of the British colonial period and of the early post-colonial period—the 1950s and part of the 1960s—when it used to include five of the seven states of today's Northeast India, as well as the smaller Assam of the last three decades. In this volume, I explore the politics of militancy in Northeast India more widely, giving attention to areas both inside and outside the borders of what is called Assam today.

Partly in order not to fetishize a category of political engineering, I did not make 'Northeast India' the explicit focus of *India Against Itself*. However, since governments, political parties, and the media have come to view the area as a region it is useful to take it as a unit of analysis at least for certain purposes. At the same time it is important to keep in mind that an official region does not necessarily imply a regional consciousness corresponding to it.

The term Northeast India points to no more than the area's location on India's political map. Such generic locational place-names are attractive to political engineers because they evoke no historical memory or collective consciousness. Indeed it is perhaps a reflection of the lack of emotional resonance of the term that in everyday conversations one hears the English word 'Northeast' and not the available translations of the word into the local languages. People tend to use the English term even when speaking or writing a regional language. Unlike place-names that evoke cultural or historical memory, the term Northeast India cannot easily become the emotional focus of a collective political project. In that sense the term might share a political rationale not unlike that of Pakistan's North West Frontier Province and is unlike the historical regions of the subcontinent. Yet it is perhaps not impossible that the category might some day be successfully incorporated into a 'place-making strategy'[3] of an oppositional political project.

The Militias of Northeast India

The sheer number of militias in Northeast India is extraordinary. Indeed it might sometimes appear that any determined young man[4] of any of the numerous ethnic groups of the region can proclaim the birth of a new militia, raise funds to buy weapons or procure them by aligning with another militia and become an important political player. According to one count, Manipur tops the list of militias with 35, Assam is second with 34 and Tripura has 30, Nagaland has four and Meghalaya checks in with three militias (ICM 2002). However, the list lumps together militias with widely different levels of organizational strength and political influence and thus it cannot be read as a quantitative indicator of the challenge posed by militias in the different states.

Ethnic ties in Northeast India do not neatly coincide with state boundaries, especially given the nature of the boundaries between states shaped by the political logic of what, in Chapter 2, I describe as a cosmetic federal regional order. Thus while the above list suggests that there are no militias in Arunachal Pradesh and Mizoram, these states are not free from militancy with roots outside the state. Naga militias have significant influence among the Nagas that inhabit two districts of Arunachal Pradesh: Changlang and Tirap, though their inclusion in the category Naga is contested especially by Arunachali politicians. Ethnic groups based in Tripura and Manipur such as Reang, Brue, and Hmar have both a physical and political presence in Mizoram.

The number of militias in any state can change overnight and it is not proportional to the political challenge that militancy presents. The small number of militias in Nagaland, for instance, only reflects the fact that the political turf in the heartland of India's oldest insurgency is fully divided between two of the four militias that make the list.

Most, but not all insurgent groups can be described as ethnic militias. Indeed some of the names themselves loudly proclaim the names of the ethnic groups that they seek to defend, e.g. the Karbi National Volunteers, Tiwa National Revolutionary Force, Kuki National Front, Hmar Revolutionary Front or Zomi Revolutionary Volunteers. Even when they do not have such names it is quite clear that they are militias mobilized along ethnic lines. However, while the term ethnic militia may accurately describe the support base and even the agendas of many insurgent groups, the term can be misleading for militias that have a civic national project and seek to cultivate a multiethnic support base.

Often the names of militias point to agendas of liberating territories. Some of the place names used by militias can be found on a contemporary map as in the case with the United Liberation Front of Assam or National Socialist Council of Nagalim [Naga homeland], though the territories in question or the names may not coincide with the ones on a map. Sometimes the place names, that the names of militias indicate, are long lost in history, e.g. Kamatapur Liberation Army (of the Koch Rajbongshis), and the Hynniewtrep National Liberation Council (of the Khasis). At other times the names of homelands are new and have a modern ring to them, but are based on particular constructions of the past, e.g. the Bodoland Liberation Tiger Force. Manipur's United National Liberation Front and People's Liberation Army do not refer to Manipur by name, but another militia, the People's Revolutionary Party of Kangleipak (PREPAK), refers to Manipur's historical name Kangleipak. There are, in addition, a large number of Islamicist militias mostly in Assam.

Even people living in the region may not have heard of all the ethnic groups in whose names these struggles are being waged. Well-informed Indians may have heard of a couple of militias or the names of one or two of the ethnic groups whose cause militias proclaim. But to say that outsiders may not have even heard of them is to entirely miss the point of ethno-national political mobilization. If they are about what Charles Taylor calls the politics of recognition (Taylor 1994), to say that no one has ever heard of the Karbis or Tiwas of Assam or the Hmars or Zomis of Manipur may at least partly explain why their leaders feel the need to make their existence known.

The Northeast Indian Ethnoscape[5]

Considering the large number of ethnic groups that are politicized and militarized in Northeast India today, the region's ethnoscape requires some explanation. Everywhere in the world those areas that did not go through the process of standardization associated with the rise and consolidation of nation-states, e.g. the emergence of the print media, national languages, widespread literacy, and national educational systems, are perhaps significantly more diverse than areas that did. In the latter case, much of the traditional cultural and linguistic diversity has been destroyed as a result of the processes of standardization associated with nation-building and state-building. However, the notion of diversity being destroyed once for all appears theoretically more problematical today than it did a few years ago. Such notions are clearly rooted in biological metaphors of cultures and languages as forms of life and thus being susceptible to 'death'. The following summary of a debate on the 'emerging linguistics of endangered languages'— the political activism associated with the agenda of preserving endangered languages—illustrates some of the theoretical problems with which recent scholars are engaged:

> In different ways these observers all argue that 'language death' is a misnomer for what is actually a 'language shift,' the sort of cumulative process of language change that results from the self-interested, rational decisions that individuals make in the course of their lives, which happen to include choices between the transmission of one language rather than other. These arguments, founded on the premise that speakers are autonomous, knowledgeable social agents, can in turn be rebutted by calling into question easy distinctions between self-interested 'choice' and institutional 'coercion,' especially in circumstances of rapid sociolinguistic change (Errington 2003: 725).

To say that Northeast India has not gone through those processes of standardization, that accompanied the consolidation of the nation-state in Europe, is not to suggest that such a trajectory would have been desirable. Nor is it meant to take attention away from the shifts and counter-shifts in language use and the language revitalization movements that are part of today's vibrant ethnoscape. In any case, the relatively weak impact of the processes of standardization does not make Northeast India very different from other parts of India. In order to explain the region's remarkable ethnoscape of today, therefore, one would have to give closer attention to certain specificities of the region.

In Chapter 5 while discussing the Naga independentist movement, I trace Northeast India's ethnoscape to the particular ecology and the history of state formation. I draw attention to the dynamic between the hill peoples and the lowland states in pre-colonial times. From the perspective of the states in the lowlands, the hills where historically numerous cultural forms prevailed, are best seen as a non-state space to use James C. Scott's term (Scott 2000)—'illegible space' despite the existence of significant local political formations. Traditionally manpower in the region was in short supply and thus wars were not about territory, but about capturing slaves. The ethnoscape of the hills that confuses most outsiders has an affinity with the logic of slash and burn agriculture, the common mode of livelihood in these hills. The dispersed and mobile populations could not be captured for corvee labour and military service by the labour-starved states of the plains; nor could tax collectors monitor either the number of potential subjects or their holdings and income. Yet historically, the non-state space in the hills and the state space in the lowlands were not disarticulated. People continually moved from the hills to the plains and from the plains to the hills.

If wars produced movements in either direction, the attractions of commerce and what the lowlanders think of as civilization may have generated a flow of hill peoples downwards. The extortionist labour demands of the lowland states and, the vulnerability of wet-rice cultivation to crop failure, epidemics and famines produced flight to the hills where there were more subsistence alternatives. While in other parts of the world, such movements may have produced an ethnoscape of larger ethnonational formations, here what James C. Scott calls the 'lived essentialism' between the hill 'tribes' and the valley civilizations, that is their stereotypes about each other, remained powerful organizer of peoples lives and thoughts. The cultural distance between lowlanders and highlanders has been reproduced in the region's ethnoscape, though it is a continuum—no sharp line of demarcation separates them.

A Symbiosis between State and Society

A historical-institutionalist perspective that connects developments in the realm of the state with developments in society might provide some insight into Northeast India's contemporary ethnoscape. In the case of the tradition of voluntarism that plays such an important role in American political life, albeit somewhat eroded in recent years, Theda Skocpol argues that it can be understood in terms of a 'mutual symbiosis of state and society' and not as a case of society developing apart from or instead of the state, as many American conservatives like to think (Skocpol 1999: 3).

Conservatives may imagine that popular voluntary associations and the welfare state are contradictory opposites, but historically they have operated in close symbiosis. Voluntary civic federations have both pressured for the creation of public social programs, and worked in partnership with government to administer and expand such programs after they were established (Skocpol 1996: 22).

Actually existing civil society, it is now widely recognized, does not just include associations that might conform to a liberal democratic vision of the world. But many liberal analysts seem reluctant to separate their vision of a good society from their definitions of civil society.[6] However, for my purposes actually existing civil society includes organizations that liberal democrats might despise, e.g. illiberal cultural and social organizations and closely-knit ethnic solidarity networks. If ethnic militias are part of the actually existing civil societies of Northeast India the phenomenon can be explained in terms of a mutual symbiosis between state and society and not as a phenomenon that is independent of the state. To a significant extent the ethnic militias of Northeast India are responses to, and artifacts of, official policy.

The process can be illustrated by the efforts of the descendants of tea workers in Assam today to claim the status of 'Scheduled Tribes'. They seek recognition of the ethno-linguistic categories of the official census—into which tea workers and their descendants living outside tea plantations are classified—as Scheduled Tribes.[7] The term 'tea tribes', as in the name of an organization such as the Assam Tea Tribes Students Association, underscores this aspiration. A section of them call themselves *Adivasi* or indigenous people emphasizing their roots in Jharkhand and other parts of India from where their forefathers had migrated more than a century ago. Adivasi activists point out that since their ethnic kin in their original habitats are recognized as Scheduled Tribes they should have the same status in Assam. There are now ethnic militias formed to defend Adivasi, i.e. indigenous people's rights, e.g. the Adivasi Cobra Force, Birsa Commando Force—named after an Adivasi hero—and Adivasi Suraksha Samiti (Adivasi Protection Committee).

India's protective discrimination regime creates the conditions for this political demand. 'Scheduled Tribe' status is seen as a passport to educational and public employment opportunities to which the descendants of tea workers have had limited access, and political mobilization is seen as the road to securing such status. Defending basic citizenship rights—even in a physical sense—in the face of the political mobilization by a rival ethnic community for an ethnic homeland has become an added rationale for this demand.

As I have described in Chapter 9, 'Citizens and Denizens', the practice of extending institutions intended to promote tribal self-governance and autonomy to particular scheduled tribes in specified territories—legitimizing the idea of ethnic homelands—has meant a de facto regime of two-tiered citizenship. This is in line with what is happening in the transnational arena in the realm of indigenous people's rights, though the ideas and categories that have shaped these institutions in Northeast India precede the transnationalization of the politics of indigenous people's rights.

Joseph Errington describes the coalescence of transnational activism in the United Nations Working Group on Indigenous Populations as 'efforts to mobilize indigenousness as the basis of claims on behalf of communities whose members count as inheritors and stewards of particular locales and not just citizens living on segments of national territory. Aboriginality can be leveraged in this way into claims of ownership, trumping rights of access that might otherwise be claimed by and granted to encroaching "outsiders"' (Errington 2003: 724). Thus in four of the seven states of Northeast India— Arunachal Pradesh, Meghalaya, Mizoram, and Nagaland—the lion's share of public employment, business and trade licenses, and even the right to contest for elected office are reserved for Scheduled Tribes legally considered indigenous to those states and the right of others to hold and exchange property rights in land is severely restricted. The vast majority of seats in three of these state legislatures—indeed all but one seat in the case of three legislatures—are reserved for candidates belonging to Scheduled Tribes.

For all practical purposes the model entails entitlement to jobs, business licenses and political positions for members of certain ethnic groups and subordinate status for others. Whatever its rationale, this model of two-tiered citizenship obviously imposes serious disadvantages on those that are not given the status of Scheduled Tribes within those territories. In a complex ethnoscape where there is talk of turning a territory into a homeland for specified ethnic groups and there are ethnic militias to back such demands, political violence inevitably enters the picture. Political mobilization in support of homelands produces counter-mobilization by those who fear subordinate status in those homelands. This is the case with the Bodo demand for a homeland and the formation of the Bodo Territorial Council.

Ethnic assertion by Bodos and other Scheduled Tribes in Northeast India today has aspects that deserve celebration. For instance, recent years have seen a revival of Bodo language and culture. What a few years ago appeared to be an irreversible process of language loss now in retrospect seems to be only a temporary period of language subordination. The developments are nothing short of the overturning of Assamese and Bengali hegemony and the triumphant return of the language and culture of a subaltern group.[8] Yet given the two-tiered citizenship inherent in the ethnic homeland model, it is not surprising that the demand for a Bodo homeland has generated opposition by non-Bodo groups, many of them no less disadvantaged than the Bodos, and has strengthened demands for Scheduled Tribe status by some non-Bodo groups including Adivasis.

These conflicts underscore the dissonance between the ethnic homeland model and the actually existing political economy of the region. The origins of the Indian Constitution's Sixth Schedule—and implicit in it today is an ethnic homeland subtext—go back to British colonial efforts to create protected enclaves for 'aborigines' where they can be allowed to pursue their 'customary practices' including kinship and clan-based rules of land allocation. Extending a set of rules, originally meant for isolated aboriginal groups, to less and less isolated groups living along with other ethnic groups and that too in the profoundly transformed conditions of the twenty-first century can only produce a crisis of citizenship, leaving citizens with the choice of either seeking recognition as Scheduled Tribes in order to be able to enjoy ordinary citizenship rights in these ethnic homelands or accept de facto second class citizenship.

Seen through the prism of the global political economy, the migration of indentured labour to the tea plantations of Assam was part of the same nineteenth century migration that took Indian labour to plantations in various parts of the British Empire, such as Fiji, Guyana, Mauritius, and South Africa. Whether a person landed in a tea plantation of Assam or in a plantation in Guyana or Mauritius was largely a function of which labour contractor he or she had signed up with. The Indian government today officially celebrates the Indian diaspora. The Pravasi Bharatiya Divas in New Delhi since January 2003 has begun honouring descendants of those migrants to far-away shores, some who had even risen to become heads of governments of their countries. At the same time the descendants of those who had migrated to the plantations of Assam and remained within the borders of what is now India are reduced to defending their ordinary citizenship rights by organizing themselves into ethnic militias to claim tribal status. Many of them had become victims of violence committed by Bodo militants and were displaced from their homes. They remain in makeshift relief camps outside the view and care of international refugee advocacy organizations in order to save the Indian government from international embarrassment.

Whatever the transformed meaning of the term 'tribe' or 'indigenous people' in India today, efforts to claim tribal status by a community that had provided the muscle for the nineteenth century capitalist transformation of Assam, nearly a century-and-half after their forefathers had left their original habitat, is quite extraordinary. That people from this ethnic background could be physically displaced today as a result of another historically disadvantaged group's demand for an ethnic homeland, no matter how tragic the story of the latter's immiserization, is symptomatic of a crisis of citizenship that is a disturbing element in Northeast India's durable disorder.

If the demonstrated effectiveness of mobilization in support of ethnic homelands creates the conditions for the formation of rival ethnic militias, there are also examples of Indian intelligence and security agencies playing an active role in fomenting other ethnic militias. Since the activities of security agencies are not transparent it is difficult to find conclusive evidence of such complicity. However, newspapers of the region are rife with such speculations especially when ethnic militias favoured by security agencies attack rival ethnic militias that are known targets of counter-insurgency. In Chapter 8, I describe a private militia made up of former militants dependent on the government for their security, being used in vicious counter-insurgency operations against the United Liberation Front of Assam.

The saliency of ethnicity in the politics of Northeast India—the proliferation of ethnic agendas, ethnic militias, and of ethnic violence—therefore is not simply the passive reflection of Northeast India's peculiar ethnoscape, to a significant extent it is the result of a symbiotic relationship between state and society.

Beyond Militarism and Millennialism

Scholarly as well as policy-focused discussions of Northeast India today are often framed by the question of how to end insurgencies. However, counter-insurgency as an intellectual stance, with room left only for debating with military generals about differences on methods, has produced neither good scholarship nor ethically and morally defensible political positions. Rather than continuing to reinforce a false separation between 'insurgency' and the 'mainstream' of social and political life, I shall bring aspects of the ethnic militias, counter-insurgency operations, state-backed militias, developmentalist practices, and the deformed institutions of democratic governance together and suggest that for analytical purposes they can be seen as constituting a coherent whole that I will call durable disorder.[9]

A few apparent successes of counter-insurgency have permitted the assumption that each Northeast Indian insurgency could be eliminated some day by following the same old methods. But how valid is this premise? The Mizo insurgency, for example, is now a thing of the past. But there is enough happening in Mizoram and surrounding areas, where people share ethnic affinities with Mizos, that raise doubts about reading the Mizo Accord of 1986 exclusively as a success story. Mizoram's reputation vis-à-vis human rights today, in the words of a Mizo activist Vanramchuangi, 'has taken a severe beating among the world's rights activists because of the practice of mob rule in the state.' Among the examples of mob rule, he cites the role of supposed NGO activists in the forced eviction of Myanmarese refugees, the role of 'NGO vigilantes' in punishing alleged law-breakers including imposing fines and imprisoning them in steel cages. Vanramchuangi called for carrying out justice 'not by the public, but by legal means and through concerned authorities' (cited in *Telegraph* 2004a). In an important sense such practices are a legacy of the Mizo Accord and consistent with the logic of two-tiered citizenship inherent in the ethnic homeland model. The NGO vigilantism of Mizoram is often ethnically marked. The conditions for such vigilantism were to some extent inherent in the vision of an ethnic homeland that shaped the roadmap to end the Mizo insurgency a decade-and-a-half ago.

In the case of the United Liberation Front of Assam, the 'surrender' of many cadres, deaths of many in combat and the extra-judicial killing of many others, and the effects of the insurgency dividend on Assamese society have drastically cut back its size and influence. But how has it affected the quality of everyday life in Assam after ULFA? Even in official counter-insurgency circles there is recognition that the 'peace' brought about by the existing strategy is bloody and messy. Thus speaking in 2001, Lt General S.K. Sinha, the former Governor of Assam, had already pronounced that his three-pronged counter-insurgency strategy in Assam had succeeded. While there may still be a few incidents of violence in Assam, he said, 'incidents of violence occur even in Delhi.' Assam, he argued, is no longer 'in the grips of militancy' (Sinha 2002: 21). Nandana Dutta's account of life in Assam 'in the wake of militancy'[10] conveys the violence of everyday life more poignantly:

The entry in large numbers of surrendered militants ... who have brought with them this perverted education and have effected a discernible shift in the methodology of doing business or dealing with the opposition or rivals or difference—the use of brute force, the threat of guns and death, the forcible occupation of house and land. The business they are involved in is neither industry nor anything else that is remotely developmental—contracts and supply are two of the terms that have entered the linguistic stock of every individual and have become the favoured activity of unemployed youths or aspiring politicians. Each of these is a method that is peculiarly neglectful of the other—concerned purely with self. And they are ways of being that have entered mainstream society in a slow, insidious but certain fashion (Dutta 2003: 151).

Considering the conditions on the ground, Northeast India's 'insurgency problem', it can be argued, is no anathema to governance and political order. Instead the ethnic militias—those in opposition as well as those who have surrendered—can be seen as part of the evolving of actually existing governance structure of the region.

When Swedish journalist Bertel Lintner clandestinely travelled to Nagaland in the 1980s, he was struck by the contacts between mainstream political parties and the factions of the Naga underground (Lintner 1996: 53). This is not unique to Nagaland. A nexus between mainstream politicians and militants is a frequently noted dimension of the contemporary politics of Northeast India. Indeed politicians of the region are remarkably frank about these connections. In July 2003 S.C. Jamir, the president of the Nagaland State Congress and a former Chief Minister of the state said that his party 'had no quarrel with any underground organization' (*Sentinel* 2003: 10). On the same day Nagaland's present Chief Minister Neiphiu Rio explained his government's stance toward underground groups this way. While the previous government believed in 'equi-distance' from different

Naga underground factions, his policy, he said, is one of 'equi-closeness' (*Times of India* 2003: 4).

One writer even argues that the Naga insurgency persists because key mainstream political players find it profitable to continue it. For elected state governments of Nagaland, argues Udayon Misra, the insurgency is an excuse to get more resources from New Delhi. Mainstream Naga politicians do not want the insurgency to end because once that happens militia leaders would compete with them for elected office. On the other hand, the ability of the National Socialist Council of Nagalim (NSCN) to run a virtual parallel government, especially in remote areas, enables it to continue recruiting cadres. At the same time human rights violations by security forces during counter-insurgency operations help the militias extend their base by creating sympathy for their side (Misra 2000).

M.S. Prabhakara makes a similar argument about the sympathy of the Assamese middle classes for ULFA. In December 2003, when the Royal Bhutan Army cracked down on ULFA and two other militant organizations taking shelter in Bhutan, Prabhakara noted that there was 'significant support' in Assam 'to the call for an end to the crackdown in Bhutan and, by implication, an easing up, if not an end to the anti-insurgency operations in the State as well.' He interpreted a statement signed by prominent Assamese citizens as evidence of this support. While the statement did not suggest that ULFA's 'separatist ideology will once again take centre stage in the ideological discourse of the state,' Prabhakara believes that it reflects a middle class mindset. 'While not supporting ULFA's separatist ideology or other varieties of extremist violence,' this class, he writes, 'recognizes only too well that militancy has now become a necessary condition for its own prosperity and well-being' (Prabhakara 2003: 7–8).

Such instrumental explanations, i.e. arguments that insurgencies survive because they serve the class interests of the middle classes or the interests of mainstream politician, are ultimately unconvincing. The turn to such convoluted explanations perhaps illustrates the puzzle that the emotionally layered relationship between militias and their constituencies present in a context where official discourse and the pan-Indian press routinely describe the militias as anti-national extremists and terrorists.[11] This theme is developed in Chapter 6, though it was written in 1992 at a time when support and sympathy for ULFA was barely past its peak. The reservoir of sympathy for ULFA as late as December 2003, was indeed quite striking. For by then ULFA had by all account become a spent force and most people in Assam had read enough stories in the press about the supposedly affluent and corrupt life style of the ULFA's top leadership[12] and about ULFA's alleged complicity with Pakistani intelligence and with the government of Bangladesh with whom the anti-immigrant core of mainstream Assamese subnationalism is virtually at war.

Whether or not a certain convergence of interest between the insurgents and mainstream social forces can explain the capacity of the militias to persist, the condition of durable disorder is certainly not free of tensions. For instance, when ties between mainstream politicians and ethnic militias become apparent to the public they present a problem for Indian counter-insurgency officials. Indeed one of the primary purposes of the parallel governmental structure that I outline in Chapter 3 is the management of this problem. Furthermore, elected politicians of the region do not always accept the parallel structure, some of them occasionally challenge it.

The Security Dilemma and the Logic of Ethnic Militias

Aspects of Northeast India's durable disorder can be explained by its political logic. Especially away from major urban centres there are situations where it is quite apparent that institutions of the state cannot guarantee the security of life and property. Ethnic militias fill the vacuum. As ethnic loyalties are hardened and the obligation to ethnic militias increase, the space for cultivating habits of loyalty to state institutions become more constricted.

Students of international relations use the notion of a security dilemma to explain the 'anarchic' nature of global politics. According to this theoretical tradition, in the absence of an over-arching authority, sovereign states are forced to provide for their own security through self-help causing the insecurity of other states. It is not far-fetched to apply the concept of a security dilemma to those configurations in Northeastern India where rival ethnic groups form ethnic militias. In these situations when one ethnic group forms its militia, a rival ethnic group might see it as a threat to its security. Since the state is not seen as a reliable provider of security, the latter group then forms its own ethnic militia in pursuit of security through self-help.

While seen through the national security prism, an ethnic militia may be a part of a generalized threat of 'insurgency', from the perspective of its ethnic constituency a militia may be a reliable provider of security in a context where it faces a threat from an armed rival ethnic group. Indeed in an ethnically polarized situation, where the actions of Indian security forces are seen as partisan, offensives against militants who are seen as security providers by their ethnic kin, may even add to the latter's sense of insecurity and an incentive for strengthening the self-help form of security.

The perceived effectiveness of militias to provide security to their ethnic kin, at least compared to that of the State, is quite self-evident to their followers and supporters. The very proliferation and persistence of small ethnic militias, in the face of the long and bloody history of counter-insurgency, would suggest that they persist and proliferate only because they serve important functions. Their incapacity to deliver on their grandiose goals such as 'national liberation' should not obscure their function as effective provider of security in a context where the state cannot guarantee it. The Indian state's financial resources and military prowess may be a significant force to reckon with, but it remains a remote entity, of limited relevance to urgent everyday needs, except as a cash cow, and with little claim to the hearts and minds of peoples.

Ethnic Militias and Taxation

Access to finance, it has been shown, is a more significant predictor of civil conflicts than deprivation or objective grounds of injustice. The co-relation between low national income and armed civil conflicts is not necessarily because objective conditions of poverty sustain rebellion, but because poverty and unemployment provide a favourable context for militias to raise money and recruit new members at a relatively low cost (Collier 2001). For the ethnic militias of Northeast India, the major source of financing is what Indian officials term extortion but in an analytical sense should be seen as taxation by private organizations.

While there are numerous stories about fund-raising by Northeast India's ethnic militias, it is hard to separate rumours from facts. Let me therefore cite as an example an account of Manipur by an unusually authoritative source, E.N. Rammohan—a senior Indian police official, who has served as Advisor to the Governor of Manipur:

For the last couple of years the valley and hill militant groups have penetrated the state and central administration and carved out specific areas of influence. Every month when salaries are disbursed, a percentage is deducted and paid to militant groups. In effect this was a replication of what was done by the NSCN [Naga Socialist Council of Nagalim] in Nagaland, as also the Naga districts of Manipur, regular deductions are labelled as house tax and ration money. The militant groups reportedly interfere in the award of contracts and are also known to enter offices carrying files to secure signatures of officers in gunpoint (Rammohan 2002: 11).

Rammohan reported that militias had subverted even the state's public food-grains distribution system through connections with local politicians. Only the deployment of the central government's security forces in crucial state government departments eventually managed to break the penetration of government departments. He quotes government officials wryly commenting that representatives of different militias queue up at their homes every morning (Rammohan 2002: 12).

A capacity to raise money through some amount of coercion—not unlike the way states raise taxes—is not limited to ethnic militias. This form of fund-raising is a pervasive feature of political life in Northeast India today. The influential ethnic student organizations found in every part of the region, for instance, are known for this form of fund-raising. In August 2003, the Khasi commentator Patricia Mukhim reported an incident from Shillong—the capital of Meghalaya. The Khasi Students Union (KSU), according to police sources, was known to have extorted large sums of money from the traders in the city's main business district. But the KSU denied the allegation and the traders who were being extorted promptly issued a statement saying that they were not being extorted, but were voluntarily contributing for KSU's 'social activities'. The incident, in Mukhim's words, was a case of 'courage taking a backseat and the survival instinct of business rising to the fore' (Mukhim 2003: 16).

Arguably, Northeast India's ethnic militias, ethnic student associations and other political organizations have a better capacity to tax citizens than the Indian State. Government tax collectors can target only what is officially declared as income. Furthermore, the protective discrimination regime exempts wealthy scheduled tribe persons living in their 'own' states from paying income taxes. But ethnic organizations are not constrained by the taxation code of the government, and drawing on popular perceptions and rumours they are able to impose taxes based on realistic assessments of legal and illegal income. This is possible largely because of the so-called 'black economy', a sizable and growing part of the total economy that is outside the formal surveillance capacity of the state. The insurgency dividend, i.e. the leakage of government funds allocated to the region for its development, has significantly bolstered this 'black economy' in Northeast India. Indeed in 2001, the then Indian Home Minister L.K. Advani complained that money allocated for the region's development often finds its way to the coffers of the militias (*Times of India* 2001c). But the outrage about pervasive corruption in Northeast India expressed by Indian government officials and commentators misses its central political significance as oxygen to ethnic militias, and for all the Indian state's formidable strength, it does not include a capacity to cut back on, not to speak of switching off, that source of oxygen supply.

Indian officials and the media describe the fund-raising by the ethnic militias as 'extortion'. But an implied focus on coercion alone obscures the fact that the very political culture that makes ethnic groups reliant on self-help for their security, and not on the state, also sustains notions of reciprocal obligations. Those holding official positions in the Indian state, politicians as well as bureaucrats, are expected to redistribute resources acquired through those positions among people in their patronage networks that are typically founded on ethnic solidarity. Among their followers and supporters the line separating militants from non-militants is necessarily blurred. This is what ultimately explains the so-called nexus between militias, mainstream politicians and bureaucrats.

A Diminished Democracy

Apart from tolerating taxation by militias and other ethnically organized groups and allowing the substantial leakage of funds meant for development, counter-insurgency has meant the de facto suspension of the rule of law, or at least a highly selective view of legality. In Chapter 3, I suggest the phrase 'counter-insurgent constitutionalism' to explain rules that permit the official indulgence of corruption by senior politicians in exchange for supporting harsh methods of counter-insurgency—the price that Indian democracy pays for buying local legitimacy for counter-insurgency.

While democratic elections take place and the press in the region is relatively free, many aspects of political life on the ground are rather distant from the substantive values associated with democracy. In terms of respect for basic freedoms, the rule of law and principles of accountability and transparency, there is a significantly diminished form of democracy in Northeast India today.

India's human rights record in the region is unenviable. How many democracies in the world would allow security forces to 'fire upon or otherwise use force, even to the extent of causing death', then give legal immunity to security personnel for their actions and leave no room for an independent investigation of such incidents? These are some of the provisions of the Armed Forces Special Powers Act [AFSPA] that is in force in some parts of the Northeast (Government of India 1972). In 1997, a fact-finding team of Indian lawyers, journalists, and human rights activists that visited the region to examine the impact of the frequent use of the AFSPA. Their report *Where 'Peacekeepers' Have Declared War*, concluded, that 'despite denials to the contrary, the security forces have, over the last four decades, blatantly violated all norms of decency and the democratic rights of the people of the region.' Militarization, the team concluded, had become a 'way of life' in Northeast India (*Where 'Peacekeepers' Have Declared War* 1997: 53). Apart from the AFSPA there are other laws including the Terrorism and Disruptive Activities Prevention Act [TADA] and the National Security Act that apart from enabling counter-insurgency operations have been allegedly used to silence journalists and human rights activists (Amnesty International 2000: 81–6).

Annual reports of international human rights organizations confirm this sorry picture. The 1995 report of Human Rights Watch summarized the conditions during the preceding year as follows:

Indian counter-insurgency efforts in the northeastern states of Assam and Manipur in 1994 continued to be marked by reports of severe abuses of human rights, including indiscriminate attacks on residential areas, disappearances, extra-judicial killings, and torture of suspected militant sympathizers. In Assam, staged 'encounter' killings of young men detained, tortured and executed by the Central Reserve Police Force continued to be reported by human rights organizations and featured in the local press (HRW 1995).

The report also noted the increase of violence by the ethnic militias (HRW 1995) More recent reports include similar instances of human rights violations. 'Insurgency and increased ethnic violence,' according to the 2002 report, 'took a heavy toll in Assam and other northeastern states' (HRW 2002).

But reports of human rights organizations and accounts of authoritarian practices of the state as well as of the militias cannot quite capture the devastating impact on the quality of everyday life. Referring to Assam 'in the wake of militancy,' Nandana Dutta writes, 'the prevalence of terrorist/ militant violence in a society renders that society and its people immune to the other .... In articulating injustice visited upon itself a society becomes incapable of appreciating the pain of the other, or even the existence of the other' (Dutta 2003: 150).

In many ways human rights violations in Northeast India have become routine. Security forces can execute persons that they call insurgents in fake encounters and expect little effective public challenge to their version of events. Ethnic militias in many places can kidnap and kill civilians with relative impunity. Creative news management, restrictions imposed by the Indian government on visits by international human rights organizations and a compassion fatigue of pan-Indian human rights organizations, the result of the sheer persistence of the same patterns for years, have put the story of human rights violations off national and international headlines.

Credibility Gap

Yet occasional public controversies raise serious questions about the credibility of the state's version of events. For instance, in July 2003, Assam's former Chief Minister Prafulla Kumar Mahanta accused the editor of a major newspaper of Assam of masterminding what until then was portrayed as an ULFA operation: the murder in 2000 of Mahanta's ministerial colleague, Nagen Sarma. Mahanta accused the newspaper editor of having masterminded the killing in order to enable his brother to contest elections from that constituency. Mahanta was the Chief Minister of Assam when the killing had occurred. Following the murder, the editor's brother had indeed successfully contested election from the seat made vacant by Sarma's death and he had become a member of the state cabinet by the time that Mahanta made this startling allegation. Soon after the murder in 2000, the two alleged killers—routinely described by security force as ULFA militants—were killed in so-called 'encounters' with security forces. Investigating the murder three years after the extra-judicial execution of the suspected killers probably would have been difficult. Yet Mahanta's accusation in the words of a newspaper commentator was 'perhaps the gravest and the most sensational of charges made in public by a responsible person like a former Chief Minister of Assam in recent times.' Still the matter pretty much ended there. Police investigators made no attempt to reopen the investigation (Kalita 2003).

There are other examples of incidents of violence first attributed to militant groups that later have turned out to be tied to more 'mainstream' actors. Such discoveries have done significant damage to the credibility of the government's counter-insurgency posture and to the legitimacy of governmental institutions. For instance, the government and the media had routinely called incidents of pipeline blasts in Assam acts of sabotage by ULFA and other militant groups. But these standard explanation became highly suspect when the pilferage of crude oil worth crores of rupees from Assam's pipelines came to light and became a major political scandal involving government ministers, the police and officials of major oil companies. It turned out that a number of pipeline blasts had occurred during the drilling of holes in pipelines by oil thieves. There was 'a very strong possibility,' said an official close to the investigation, 'that the blasts may not have been triggered by explosives.' Instead the pipeline blasts that were described as acts of sabotage by militants were actually accidents that occurred during oil pilferage. It was easy to 'perpetuate this myth' since police officials were involved in the racket (*Telegraph* 2004c). A public counter-insurgency posture that can be seen as little more than a cover for ordinary crimes by government officials cannot exactly be expected to aid the Indian state's battle of hearts and minds vis-à-vis ethnic militants.

Insulating State from Society?

It is not surprising that organizing counter-insurgency in a context where the lines between ethnic militias and the mainstream are blurred has led to a de facto parallel political system that is authoritarian and autonomous of the formal democratically elected governmental structure. This parallel system, as I show in Chapter 3, connects New Delhi with the region with the centrally appointed governors of states as crucial nodes giving them a role that far exceeds the ceremonial functions that India's Constitution-makers had in mind. While there is limited participation of the demo-cratically elected officials of these states in this parallel system, they are seen as the weakest link in the chain and the organizational structure effectively marginalizes them and even keeps them under watch.

There is an inherent anti-democratic, militaristic and authoritarian logic to counter-insurgency, but it is especially so under these conditions. Thus Rammohan, the security official quoted earlier, in his policy recommendations focuses on ways of insulating the development projects from the interference of 'politicians and the militants'. He recommends the further strengthening of the Indian military presence in the state. He would like battalions of the Central Reserve Police Force (CRPF) to guard all government offices and the residential neighbourhoods housing central and state government officials in order to stop the penetration of the government departments by militants. In addition, he recommends that ten battalions of the Central Para-Military Force (CPMF) be deployed in the Manipur Valley in a 'counter-insurgency grid' and six to eight battalions be deployed in each hills district, where roads are few, with 'helicopter support to effectively dominate them' (Rammohan 2002: 15).

From the experience of decades of ethnic militancy and counter-insurgency it can be said that it is not difficult for the Indian State—with its significant military, financial, and other resources—to control, contain, and sometimes defeat and end 'insurgences'. Indian officials often claim that only small minorities of people are committed to an agenda of political independence from India. But arguments that posit the presumed wishes of the silent majority against the will of small militias are dangerous. They make the continuation of counter-insurgency appear inevitable: the tried tactics in the state's counter-insurgency repertoire appear as the best of a number of bad options with little convincing evidence of a way out of the logic of durable disorder.

Most political scientists these days emphasize the importance of a state being embedded in society in order for it to be able to both make and implement policy agendas. As colonial states realized long time ago, state capacity is not just a function of autonomy from societal influences; it is significantly enhanced when an autonomous state is embedded in society through networks connecting state and society (Evans 1995). Yet the thrust of India's policy in Northeast India seems to be to either create a group of local stakeholders in the Indian dispensation, primarily in terms of a share in the insurgency dividend, or de-link the institutions of the state from the local societies.

The preference for a disembedded state is, of course, the result of frustration with the ethnic militias and their penetration of state institutions. I have earlier cited the policy recommendations of a security official to increase the military presence in Manipur. Rammohan's other recommendations include (a) ensuring that officers of the All India Services assigned to the state stay in the state and (b) getting central government officers to monitor all rural development projects—that are centrally financed in any case—so that 'politicians and the militants' do not interfere in the process.

According to Rammohan, ninety per cent of the officials of all-India cadres assigned to the state are 'on deputation' and they 'continually manipulate their non-return.' Newly recruited officers of the all-India cadres to Manipur in the previous five years mostly got 'cadre transfers' to other states (Rammohan 2002: 14). The reasons why an officer of the all-India cadre may want to be away from Manipur, and by extension the Northeast are varied. The absentee bureaucrats, for instance, may include those who are themselves involved in the murky world of corruption involving nexuses of politicians, officials, and businessmen. Their positions of power in a climate where counter-insurgency dominates the policy agenda provide more than the usual opportunities for personal enrichment by staking a claim to the insurgency dividend. To some of them with a frontier mentality who use the assignments in the Northeast to make a fast buck and quit, the safety of New Delhi or a place away from the Northeast may be attractive for understandable reasons.

Officers of all-India cadres include persons from other parts of India as well as some with local roots. But irrespective of ethnicity, no matter how much security and financial incentives are provided for them to stay in the region, those who view working in the region as a hardship assignment, not unlike the way many diplomats view postings in a Third World country, or as a frontier opportunity can hardly be expected to build the sort of connections between state and society that can be the foundation of a normal, legitimate democratic state.

The challenges confronting the Indian state in the Northeast therefore are more serious than what the counter-insurgency mind-set can grasp and remedy. The Indian state may be strong in certain ways, but in Northeast India, despite the easy military victories of the security forces against some militias, the weaknesses of the state that sustain the plethora of militias have a disconcerting affinity with situations of state failure.

Imagining a Different Future

In official publications and much of Indian academic writing, Northeast India's durable disorder is often explained by the region's supposed underdevelopment and poor integration into the pan-Indian 'mainstream'. In this line of thinking it is difficult to escape the failed narratives[13] of national development and nation-building in trying to imagine an end to the current situation. In Chapter 3, I suggest a parallel between the developmentalism that is part of Indian counter-insurgency thinking and the developmentalism that characterized the intellectual defence of empire by liberal and progressive British thinkers. In both cases dealing with a place and a people in terms of their supposed future make complicity with present injustices possible.

In Chapter 2, I develop a post-structuralist critique of the theory and practice of development in Northeast India. I argue that an important subtext to the process of extending state institutions, with an in-built developmentalist bias, to what until recently were frontier areas, is that of nationalizing space. The Indian Government has pumped enormous resources into the development of Northeast India in order to remove what it apparently sees as the structural cause of insurgencies. This has had significant impact on the region's physical infrastructure, social fabric and political life: the term insurgency dividend accurately describes some of these effects. However, to date they have not significantly altered the conditions that give rise to and sustain ethnic militancy.

The idea that Northeast India is economically backward and underdeveloped and that its ties with the national mainstream are fragile, whatever their validity, lends legitimacy to today's durable disorder. The democracy deficit, for instance, can be justified as being the result of an exceptional circumstance that would disappear when the region catches up with the rest of India—economically and emotionally—whatever that might mean. Yet arguably the region's informal structures of governance, the underpinnings of the durable disorder of today, are fairly well articulated with the institutions of the Indian state especially those, through which money for the region's development is channelled. However, whether the insurgency dividend can win hearts and minds and promote Indian nationhood, apart from providing the financial foundation of durable disorder, is another matter.

The futuristic talk of economic development and of Northeast India joining the 'national mainstream', contrasts sharply with the vision of the militias that mostly hark back to history. Thus Assamese independentist intellectuals, according to one writer, 're-read, re-interpret and even re-create history' in order to make the case that 'Assam had always been a free nation' (Misra 2000: 62). Earlier I have pointed out names of ethnic militias that evoke the memory of independent old kingdoms. Such contests over history and memory underscore the inherent tensions in all national projects, including the pan-Indian project.

Continued faith in the failed narratives of national development and nation-building can be quite dangerous in the present global conjuncture. Policies that continue to be framed and legitimized by these failed narratives can also make the situation much worse. The collapse of the Soviet Union dramatically brought home the point that even states that appear all-powerful may actually be quite weak in terms of their coherence and capacity to shape society and implement policy agendas. A post-Soviet attempt at reconstructing the history of the building of the Soviet Russian state concludes that while it had impressive formal sources of power, e.g., its coercive and bureaucratic organizations, the state's capacity was constrained by the personal networks that were the informal sources of power at the regional level (Easter 2000).

Are there ways of imagining Northeast India's future outside the failed narratives of nation-building and national development? Certain developments in the European Union provide a useful paradigm. The Mastrich Treaty of 1993 establishes the EU's Committee of the Regions in order to give local and regional interests influence in EU decision-making. Regional identities that were seen as threats by European nation-states during their hey-day are flourishing inside the EU. They are not unlike the identities that animate the militias of Northeast India that make India's counter-insurgency officials and nation-builders so jittery. The European political landscape today is dotted by paradiplomacy—international activities on the part of regions and stateless nations. Thus there are more than 200 regional 'embassies' in Brussels that lobby the European Commission and network with each other. For national groups that straddle inter-state boundaries such as the Basque Country, Catalonia, Ireland or the Tyrol, the EU affords the opportunity to pool resources and pursue a transnational politics of recognition that has been able to compensate for their marginalization within nation states.

The model of industrialization characterized by capital and job concentration that had encouraged the internal social and cultural standardization as well as the depopulation of peripheral area at the height of the nation-state, has in Europe given way to economic models that put a premium on regions that often cross national borders. Can Northeast Indian and its transnational neighbours forge such a cross-border territorial system of action?

In the epilogue 'Beyond Durable Disorder' I explore what India's Look East policy, i.e. the overtures since the 1990s toward Southeast Asian countries, could do for Northeast India. I argue that the policy holds promises of historic proportions: there are opportunities for the region to acquire access to global markets and technology and to overcome the handicaps of its landlocked condition. At the same it could also create a transnational space for a less territorialized version of the politics of recognition that animate the ethno-national conflicts of Northeast India.

The rest of the chapters of the book are organized into five sections. Section 2 on 'Structures of Governance' has two chapters outlining the origins of today's cosmetic federal regional order and the region's parallel political systems. Section 3, 'Past and Present' includes two articles tracing the historical roots of Northeast India's current predicament to the economic incorporation of the region into the global capitalist economy in the nineteenth century. Of the two chapters in the section, one focuses on the tensions between global and local resource use regimes, a theme that gets lost in the colonial discourse of civilization and in the post-colonial discourse of development. Another chapter analyses the historical roots of the Naga conflict and traces Northeast India's contemporary ethnoscape to the region's ecology and the history of state formation. Section 4 includes three chapters on the United Liberation Front of Assam written during different phases of its power and influence. The chapter 'Citizens and Denizens' that constitutes Section 5 outlines an unfolding crisis of citizenship resulting from the tension between the politics of ethnic homelands and the logic of the region's actually existing political economy. The epilogue 'Beyond Durable Disorder' includes the chapter on the promises of the Look East policy.

Notes

[1] Parts of this chapter were published earlier in the *Economic and Political Weekly*. Reprinted with the permission of Sameeksha Trust from Sanjib Baruah, 'Gulliver's Troubles: The State and Militants in Northeast India,' *Economic and Political Weekly* 37 (41), 4178–82, October 12, 2002 and Sanjib Baruah, 'Protective Discrimination and the Crisis of Citizenship in Northeast India' *Economic and Political Weekly* 38 (17), April 26, 2003, 1624–6.

[2] The book was reviewed and discussed widely in India and abroad in academic journals as well as in newspapers and magazines. It is tempting to respond in details to the points raised in those reviews. However, I have decided not to do so. I have learnt from those comments and my own position on many issues have changed. An engagement with the reviews will be of limited interest to readers of this book. Yet on a couple of points in this chapter I do briefly engage two of my critics.

[3] The notion of a place-making strategy is from Amy Muehlebach (2001).

[4] There are women cadres in most militias, but not leaders.

[5] For an elaboration of the term ethnoscape see Arjun Appadurai (1990). Appadurai coined the term to deal with the flows of people across international borders and the emergence of multiple forms of diasporic identities. For Appadurai the suffix 'scape' serves to draw attention to the fact that these are not objectively given relations but 'deeply perspectival constructs.' Ethnic identities in Northeast India too are perspectival constructs. This is evident in the case of the contest over the phrase 'Naga-inhabited areas' discussed in Chapter 6.

[6] Thus Samir Kumar Das finds my notion of community-specific civil societies outlined in Chapter 6 a 'romantic projection.' He wants the conduct of inter-community relations to be a part of any definition of civil society less this area becomes the 'exclusive preserve of the state.' See S.K. Das 2002: 43–4. One can be sympathetic to the underlying vision of a 'modern' society that impels Das to refuse by definitional fiat to extend the term civil society to community-specific social spaces. But my goal is to understand the ideas and values nurtured in actually existing social spaces that animate the relationship between Northeast India's militias and their constituencies. As I show in this chapter, many commentators have been at a complete loss to explain the sympathy for ULFA especially when it had past its peak of visible political influence. In principle, my notion of actually existing civil societies is better able to grapple analytically with the emotionally layered relationships between militias and their constituencies. The kind of civil society that Das would like to see in Assam would involve the destruction or at least the marginalization of these actually existing civil societies. This imperative makes his definition somewhat complicit with the modernization project. As the case of Northeast India's durable disorder makes it apparent, the project of bringing about such a modern liberal civil society, whether it eventually succeeds or not, makes one complicit with significant state violence. While some may see this as necessary and creative destruction, the moral implications of such political analysis are problematical.

[7] The category 'tribal' and its definition are problematical in scholarly circles. In India, however, the term is part of a policy discourse because of an elaborate system of protective discrimination that exists in favour of groups of people listed as tribals. Article 342 of Indian Constitution provides for the President of India by public notification to specify the 'tribes or tribal communities or parts of or groups within tribes or tribal communities which shall for the purposes of the Constitution be deemed to be 'Scheduled Tribes'. In my use, by tribal, I simply mean a group included in that list—hence Scheduled Tribe (ST). A scholar who has examined how the Indian government has arrived at the list, notes that the tribes were 'defined partly by habitat and geographic isolation, but even more on the basis of social, religious, linguistic and cultural distinctiveness—their 'tribal characteristics'. Just where the line between 'tribals' and 'non-tribals' should be drawn has not always been free from doubt' (Galanter 1984: 150).

[8] This formulation is inspired by the theoretical discussion of linguistic transformation in Friedman 2003: 744.

[9] I borrow the phrase 'durable disorder' from Cerny, 1998.

[10] Dutta's essay includes an incisive critique of *India Against Itself.* She has read my book as a 'global citizen trying to localize himself' and charges that some of the comments printed on the book cover 'do not necessarily recognize the context he speaks from, to and about' (Dutta 2003: 148–9). Despite the importance of this critique, for reasons that I have explained in note 2 above, I will resist the temptation of responding to it.

[11] See endnote 6 above.

[12] It is hard to say whether these reports are true or the product of official disinformation campaigns—the product of what General Sinha describes as the psychological front of counter-insurgency operations.

[13] I owe this phrase to Zilkia Janer (2003).

SECTION II

*Governance Structure:
Formal and Informal*

2

Nationalizing Space

Cosmetic Federalism and the Politics of Development[1]

Arunachal Pradesh, a part of the eastern Himalayas with its breath-taking natural beauty and a sparse population, was until recently relatively insulated from processes associated with development. In no other part of the Himalayas, as Elizabeth M. Taylor (1996) points out, is there so much 'pristine forest and intact mega-biodiversity'. Many pre-industrial forms of production and exchange are still prevalent in Arunachal Pradesh (hereafter referred to as Arunachal). Many Arunachalis continue to practice 'semi-nomadic swidden horticulture, terraced wet agriculture, high montane pastoralism and traditional trade and barter'. The area is home to many endangered species including ten distinct species of pheasants, the great cats—tigers, leopards as well as clouded and snow leopards—and all three of the goat antelopes. It has 500 species of orchids, 52 species of rhododendron and 105 species of bamboo (Taylor 1996).

Arunachal is a part of one of the global 'hotspots' of biodiversity and its mountain eco-system is fragile. Indeed a case could be made for putting the area under a legal regime that would give priority to policies for protecting the interests of its indigenous peoples and to nature conservation. Even short of that, it is possible to outline a road to sustainable development that takes into account Arunachal's exceptional environmental wealth and its importance.

The late Indian environmentalist, Anil Agarwal once spoke of some of the ways in which Arunachal could have sustainable development 'even with a modern economic paradigm'. With relatively modest investments, he argued, there exists in Arunachal the resource base for creating industries such as herbal products, high value bamboo products and eco-tourism that could reach external markets even with a limited transportation infrastructure, and at the same time significantly raise the per capita income of Arunachal's population of less than a million. On the other hand, the rapid building of roads, often seen as a prerequisite to development in order to connect Arunachal to national and international markets, carries enormous risks. If industry is slow to take off because of the lack of a local market, roads could become, in Agarwal's words, 'excellent corridors to siphon off the existing natural resource of the region, its forests'. Moreover, building roads on this mountain terrain is no minor engineering challenge: unless built very carefully, construction could be the cause of major landslides (Agarwal 1999).

Development Discourse Comes to Arunachal

However, neither the language in which Indian officials (including Arunachali politicians) now speak of Arunachal's future, nor the changes taking place on the ground, leave much room for optimism that Arunachal will be following anything other than a conventional developmentalist[2] trajectory—albeit with some concession to qualifiers such as 'sustainable' and, perhaps, a few nature conservation parks. Arunachal's former Chief Minister Mukut Mithi, for instance, described his main challenge as 'the overall development of the state, which has hardly any industrial infrastructure'. Mithi told journalists that the state's primary problem is communications and that his goal is to achieve 'a peaceful and prosperous Arunachal with equal opportunities and gainful employment for all' (cited in Chaudhuri 1999a). It may be difficult to quarrel with a democratically elected politician who proclaims such aspirations for his state, but the route by which Arunachali politicians have come to articulate such a vision of the future has a political history that deserves attention.

This chapter will explore the ways in which the discourse of development has made its way to Arunachal. The goal of nationalizing a frontier space, I will argue, has been the major thrust of Indian policy vis-à-vis Arunachal and Northeast India as a whole. Subsequent sections of the essay will explore the way in which this national security driven process has led to creating a special regional dispensation of small and financially dependent states that in a forml sense are autonomous units of India's federal polity; in terms of power vis-à-vis the central government, however, the form of federalism is little more than cosmetic. The logic of developmentalism is embedded in the institutions of the Indian state that have been put in place in pursuit of the goal of nationalizing space. Through demographic and other changes in the region the process has made India's everyday control over this frontier space more effective, but at significant social, environmental and political costs.

Former Chief Minister Mithi enthusiastically supported the construction of power generation projects, especially two mega hydroelectric projects on the Siang and Subansiri rivers, and several road-building projects including three Assam-Arunachal Pradesh inter-state roads. He also advocated the construction of a National Highway along the middle belt of Arunachal Pradesh with extensions covering large parts of the state (*Assam Tribune* 2000a).[3] It may be tempting to assume that the prime mover of these projects is the desire of Arunachalis,[4] expressed through their elected representatives. However, this way of imagining Arunachal's future has been built upon the groundwork of a complex political process. 'Underdevelopment' is not simply a self-evident ground reality about a place or a people. It is, as post-structuralists would argue, discursively constituted (see, for instance, Escobar 1995; Ferguson 1990; W. Sachs 1992). In the words of Sachs: 'Development is much more than just a socioeconomic endeavor: it is a perception, which models reality; a myth, which comforts societies; and a fantasy, which unleashes passions' (W. Sachs 1992: 1). The privileging of discourse by post-structuralists is, of course open to criticism by those who emphasize the materiality of poverty and underdevelopment (see for instance, Kiely 1999; Little and Painter 1995). That debate lies beyond the scope of this article; this essay takes as its point of departure the post-structuralist insight that development discourse is not merely reflective, but it is also constitutive of the condition of underdevelopment.

The discourse generated by developmentalist institutions constructs places and peoples as under-developed, creating a structure of knowledge around that object that makes the case for development seem self-evident (Ferguson 1990). In Arunachal, I would argue, development discourse is the product of the Indian state's push to nationalize the space of this frontier region. The developmentalist path that Arunachal has embarked upon is neither the result of a choice made by policy makers about what is best for the well-being of the people of Arunachal, nor is it evidence of the inevitability of 'progress' and 'civilization'. Rather, it is the intended and unintended consequence of the Indian state's efforts to assert control over this frontier space and to make it a 'normal' part of India's national space.

The Changing Face of Northeast India

At the time of India's independence in 1947, the area that is now called Arunachal Pradesh was known as the North East Frontier Area, or NEFA. NEFA was a part of the province of Assam in the colonial era, but at the time of independence while it remained a part of Assam, it was separated from the control of the elected state government. The Governor of Assam headed the administration of NEFA operating as the Agent of the Indian President. Until the 1960s, when the process of dividing Assam into smaller states began, five of the seven states of Northeast India—Arunachal Pradesh, Assam, Meghalaya, Nagaland and Mizoram—were part of the state of Assam.[5] The two other states that are now part of official Northeast India— Manipur and Tripura—were princely states under British colonial rule. They became 'Part C states' soon after independence and subsequently, Union Territories. In 1955, the States Reorganization Commission recommended not only that Assam's boundaries be maintained, but also that Manipur and Tripura be eventually merged with Assam. It was expected that NEFA would become fully a part of Assam.

Tribal areas make up the bulk of the territory of Northeast India. The Sixth Schedule of the Indian Constitution makes special provisions for the administration of what were then 'the Tribal Areas in Assam'. In the colonial period those tribal areas were mostly protected enclaves, where tribal peoples could supposedly pursue their 'customary practices' including kinship and clan-based rules of land allocation. They were called 'backward tracts', later replaced by the term 'excluded areas'—so called because they were excluded from the operation of laws applicable in the rest of British-controlled India.

The Sixth Schedule provides for autonomous districts and autonomous regions within those districts with elected councils with powers to regulate customary law, to administer justice in limited cases and to determine the occupation or use of land and the regulation of shifting cultivation. At the time of the inauguration of the Constitution in 1950 some tribal areas were to have elected councils immediately, but other tribal areas that were largely un-administered during colonial times, or where state institutions were least present—mostly today's Arunachal and a part of Nagaland—were considered to be not quite ready for those institutions. The administration of these areas was to be temporarily carried out directly from Delhi with the Governor of Assam acting as the agent of the Indian President. In addition, the nineteenth century institution known as the Inner Line restricted the entry of outsiders (Indian citizens as well as foreigners) into what are now the states of Arunachal Pradesh, Mizoram, and Nagaland.

When India gained independence in 1947, Naga leaders rejected the idea that their land could simply pass on to Indian and Burmese hands at the end of British colonial rule. The Naga movement thus began immediately after independence, and in the 1950s, the situation escalated into armed confrontation between rebels and India's armed forces (see Chapter 5). Efforts to constitute a distinct Naga administrative unit in response to the Naga rebellion began in 1957, although it was only in the early 1960s that the process of restructuring the region began in earnest. The state of Nagaland itself came into being in 1963, with India hoping to end the Naga war by creating stakeholders in the pan-Indian dispensation. With the formation of Nagaland, statehood in Northeast India became de-linked from the questions of either fiscal viability or of compatibility with the constitutional architecture of the pan-Indian polity. This could thus be seen as the first step in the cosmetic federal regional order that came into being over the next few years.

The War with China and the Question of National Security

In 1962, NEFA was at the centre of a border war between India and China. The Chinese army made deep incursions into Indian territory before withdrawing. After India's humiliating defeat, Prime Minister Jawaharlal Nehru's policy of indulging Arunachal's isolation—a legacy of British colonial policy of an Inner Line in certain tribal areas beyond which the state did not extend its standard set of governmental institutions—was completely discredited. One opposition Indian politician even proposed that 100,000 farmers from Punjab be settled in NEFA in order to assimilate the area into India (R. Guha 2001: 295).

The war with China exposed India's vulnerabilities not only in NEFA but also in Assam as a whole. Not only was the Naga movement still active, there were stirrings of unrest in other parts of the region too, and some rebel groups were known to be in contact with India's external enemies. The cultural distance from the mainland and the threat of pro-independence rebellions in the region had already begun to make Indian officials anxious.

Nor is China the only foreign country bordering the region. In the post-colonial dispensation that emerged after the partition of British India in 1947, Northeast India also had borders with Burma, East Pakistan (Bangladesh since 1971) and Bhutan. Today the region is linked to the rest of India only by a narrow strip of land some 20 km wide. While Bhutan— whose foreign policy is governed by a special treaty relationship with India— and Burma present no direct threat, the weak presence of state institutions in those cross-border frontier lands has been a cause of Indian concern. Prior to the break-up of Pakistan and the formation of Bangladesh in 1971, India had experienced Pakistani hostility on this front. Nor—contrary to Indian expectations—did the creation of Bangladesh bring an end to the unfriendly international environment in the region. Bangladesh remains a haven for Northeastern rebels and India now accuses the Pakistani intelligence services of fomenting trouble in the Northeast. After the war with China, the managers of the Indian state began to fear the prospect of the external and internal 'enemies' in this region coming together and constituting a looming threat to India's national security.

The State-building Imperative

It was against this backdrop that a new Indian policy emerged, to extend the institutions of the state all the way into the international border zones, thus nationalizing this frontier space. The developmentalist path on which Arunachal has embarked can only be understood in the context of a Northeast policy that has been shaped by this concern for national security.[6] The governmental infrastructure of the region has been fundamentally redesigned to create a number of mini states, all endowed with the formal institutional apparatus of Indian state governments. However, the new regional order is federal only in a cosmetic sense: the central government has powers over important areas and the national security establishment in New Delhi even has the capacity to monitor and control political developments. This new arrangement has, in effect, enabled the penetration of the Indian state and has put some of the remote parts of this frontier region on a developmentalist track. The standard vision of development contained in the routine practices of the bureaucracy of India's developmentalist state has shaped the course of change through the allocation of funds to departments such as Public Works, Rural Development and Industries. That vision has only been bolstered by the patronage politics of an electoral democracy.

New Delhi's central role in shaping the development trajectory of the region is quite apparent. Most development projects are financed by the central government, and the planning and design of major projects all take place in New Delhi or in central government organizations located in the region. Projects such as building roads close to the international border are undertaken entirely by the Border Roads Organization—a central government organization—with little role for the state governments. Since 2001, India's central government even includes a Ministry for the Development of North-Eastern Region [DONER]: no other region of the country has such a presence in New Delhi.

Why has nationalizing space become such an imperative for the Indian state? In uncontested national spaces, the routine practices that reproduce the consent of the governed in a modern democracy—for example, the payment of taxes, voting, or provision of key services such as guaranteed public order by the state—are taken for granted. Such routines were either absent or barely present in many parts of Northeast India, especially, Arunachal and the Naga and Mizo areas that were either un-administered or lightly administered during the colonial period. The war with China and the pro-independence rebellions emphasized the dangers of this absence in the post-colonial era. The familiar transition from frontiers to borders in modern times underscores a distinctive spatial logic of the global political order of independent and sovereign nation-states. The war of 1962 brought home to Indian policy-makers the lesson that an infrastructure of state institutions is necessary to reinforce among the people of the region the sense that they are part of a pan-Indian national community.

Nation-building, observes political scientists Fearon and Laitin, is not a 'benign cousin' of state building. 'Filling lands within state boundaries by a population representing the nation-bearing population,' they write, 'has its gory character' (Fearon and Laitin 2001). They make this observation in the context of conflicts generated by states that sponsor migration into frontier regions as a tool of nation-building. India does not follow such an explicit nation-building strategy as, for instance, China does in some of its minority areas. Nor can one speak of a single nation-bearing population in the case of India. Nevertheless, the distinction between ethnic groups that are marked as indigenous to the region and those that are marked as immigrants from the rest of the subcontinent has remained quite significant in the politics of Northeast India. Extending state institutions with a developmentalist agenda therefore has had political functions not unlike those described by Fearon and Laitin. In a sparsely populated frontier region, a developmentalist trajectory invariably means changes in demography; this has made the political trends in the region increasingly more complex and contradictory, and has provided a significant political counterweight to actual and potential pro-independence rebellions.

The imperative to nationalize space dictated by the 'high politics' of national security has determined the choices made in every other policy area. The interests of the people of the area, or of the unique environment, the potential choices between alternative development strategies, the respect for the autonomy of sub-national governments enshrined in India's federal constitution, the rights of indigenous peoples, and even considerations of political stability—all have had to play second fiddle to the imperative of nationalizing space.

Reinventing the Northeast

The category Northeast India—now the standard term to refer to the region—originates in the creation of the post-China war cosmetic federal regional order. The designation of an official region, of course, does not mean that it corresponds with people's spatial imagination.[7]

It is interesting to note that despite the different political histories of India and Pakistan, there are now—in two corners of erstwhile British India—two entities whose culturally disembodied, directional nomenclature bear traces of the colonial past: Pakistan's North West Frontier Province and India's Northeast. Ironically, instead of the colonial use of the phrase 'Northeast' to refer to what is now Arunachal Pradesh (the erstwhile NEFA), in its postcolonial usage the term Northeast has been extended to include a wider region.

As indicated above, five of the seven states were part of Assam and two states—Manipur and Tripura—that were indirectly ruled princely states in colonial times were Union Territories during the 1950s and 1960s. A number of acts were passed by the Indian parliament, notably the North Eastern Areas (Reorganization) Act of 1971, to either create new units or to change the status of existing units. The territories all eventually became full-fledged states in terms of formal institutions.[8] Some of the states owe their boundaries to their prior status as autonomous districts with District Councils. While turning them into states, the preferences given to scheduled tribes [STs] were preserved. Thus in the Legislative Assemblies of Arunachal, Mizoram and Nagaland all but one seat are reserved for STs—in other words, only tribal candidates can contest elections. In Meghalaya, fifty-five of the sixty seats are reserved. The balance between reserved and unreserved seats in the legislative assemblies has been frozen by constitutional amendments in order to ensure that potential delimitation of constituencies as a result of demographic change does not alter the existing balance.[9]

A factor that is often cited as a cause of the break-up of Assam and the creation of the new regional order is the aggressive cultural policies of the ethnic Assamese political leadership of undivided Assam, such as their attempt to make Assamese the official language of Assam.[10] While this was a contributing factor, its significance as an explanation for the governmental re-structuring is often exaggerated. Assamese cultural policies undoubtedly offended some STs, but they cannot be an explanation for why an exceptional regional political order—anomalous in the constitutional architecture of the pan-Indian polity—was put in place. Compared to the sustained political mobilization that led to the reorganization of states in other parts of India, demands for redrawing boundaries in the Northeast, when they occurred at all, were rather tame affairs. In Arunachal there was no such demand from within at all; in parts of what is now Meghalaya there was a relatively mild political movement seeking the separation of the hill areas of Assam into a separate state; while Nagaland and Mizoram were created as a response to the Naga or Mizo rebellions that sought sovereign statehood. The apparently federal regional order of Northeast India was fundamentally a national security driven process that had its origins in New Delhi and not in erstwhile Assam (Baruah 1999: Chapter 5).

The seven units were all brought together into an institutional arrangement, the North Eastern Council (NEC). B.P. Singh was a senior Indian civil servant who held key positions both in the region and in the Indian Home Ministry. In his insider's account of the process, he referred to the 1971 law that created a number of the new units and the law that created the NEC as 'twins born out of a new vision for the Northeast' (Singh 1987a: 117). In his words, the 'Northeast emerged as a significant administrative concept ... replacing the hitherto more familiar unit of public imagination, Assam' (ibid.: 8).

Cosmetic Federalism and its Discontents

The Nigerian Nobel Laureate in literature, Wole Soyinka, once described the Nigerian military regime's view of federalism thus:

The understanding of some past dictators about the nature of federalism has been, very simplistically, the creation of more states. You increase the number of states within a nation, and you persuade yourself that you have thereby expanded the concept and practice of federalism, never mind if one state or two were created as a birthday present for your importuning spouse. Or as a bribe—the then going price of loyalty—to one constituency or another, and even—with diabolical calculation, to set one section of the nation against another through disputes over boundaries and assets. Non-viable state entities have been created which simply underline the contradictions inherent within a so-called federal system—they are kept alive only by sporadic blood infusions from the centre. Those states were never meant to be self-sufficient entities, and do not exist beyond the establishment of another bottomless pit of a parasitic bureaucracy (Soyinka 1999: 4).

The national security mind-set that led to the creation of the cosmetic federal regional order of Northeast India is not the same as the forces that had pushed Nigerian federalism, but some of the effects are similar. Most of the Northeastern states have very few revenue sources; they are 'Special Category States' that rely primarily on central government assistance, which they get on a concessional basis of 90 per cent grants and 10 per cent loans. As economist Gulshan Sachdeva puts it, most of the states 'were created mainly to fulfill the ethnic, political and cultural aspirations of the people', and when they were formed the issue of whether 'the territory in question must have revenue resources to meet its administrative and other non-developmental expenditure' was conveniently ignored (Sachdeva 2000: 60–1).

The problems of federalism under such conditions are entirely predictable. Without independent sources of tax revenue the autonomy of such units is compromised. This form of financing state budgets provides an incentive for local politicians to engage in rent seeking, and encourages fiscal irresponsibility. The overwhelming dependence on the central government for funds also means that most development projects are both funded and designed far away from the region, and with little likelihood of reflecting local visions of the future and these state governments have little power vis-à-vis New Delhi. At the same time, having states with state legislative assemblies and elected state governments comprised almost entirely of members of STs is a matter of no minor significance, considering the structural disempowerment of tribal peoples that typically accompany forces of economic change in India and elsewhere.[11] Yet the creation of mini states, completely dependent on New Delhi for their finances, and thus vulnerable to New Delhi's direct involvement in their affairs on a daily basis, fitted very well with India's national security goals in the region.

Making Cosmetic Federalism Acceptable

The tension between the promise of autonomy embedded in India's federal constitutional design, and the cosmetic federal regional order of Northeast India was apparent from the beginning. The North Eastern Council (NEC), envisaged as an institution to promote security and development (Singh 1987a: 20), initially did not even include the elected chief ministers of the states. It was made up of the governors, who represent the central government and who, elsewhere in India, are only the constitutional heads of state governments. It was only later that the elected chief ministers of states were brought in as members along with the governors. A military man, the inspector-general of the Assam Rifles, was the security adviser to the Council. However, the NEC could not be completely isolated from the democratic politics of the states indefinitely and as that isolation faltered, its security function became weaker. That security function did not devolve to the state governments, however; rather, it shifted directly to the Home Ministry in Delhi (see Chapter 3).

Singh writes of officials having to struggle with the challenge of making the NEC fit into the constitutional framework of federalism. The NEC was technically made an advisory body, so that 'it would not infringe upon the political autonomy of the constituent units' (Singh 1987a: 116), but this came into conflict with the desire for 'greater autonomy', which Singh saw as 'a vociferous demand in all the Northeastern states'. Some of the states chose to remain outside the NEC at first. From Singh's national security perspective, such tensions are inevitable when doing nation-building in a frontier region: 'In view of the distance from Delhi, and the legacy of all round non-development of the region, a regional planning authority, which the Council essentially is, must be accepted as a necessity'. The best the NEC could do, therefore, was to conduct itself in a way that would not 'hurt the sensitivities of member units and make them feel like second class states in India's federal structure' (Singh 1987a: 122–3).

The tensions between the new regional order and the principle of autonomy became serious enough that the NEC could not live up to its original design. It is 'in the very logic of things', Singh believes, that the NEC had to become a 'significant planning and security organ of India's territorial frontiers with Burma, Bangladesh, Bhutan, and Tibet' (Singh 1987a: 120). Indeed, the security imperative is so self-evident to Singh that the Indian Constitution's division of powers between states and the central government appears only as a minor irritant that needs managing. 'While insurgency is *technically* the responsibility of the law and order agency of the state,' he writes, 'over the years, the Union Home Ministry has been playing the role of the senior partner and coordinator' (ibid.). But because the NEC could not be sufficiently insulated from the democratic politics of the region, it was unable to become the security, development and intelligence powerhouse which Singh would have liked it to be. Instead, the Home Ministry in New Delhi had to step in directly.

Writing in the mid-1980s, Singh regretted that Indian intelligence agencies were not reporting to the NEC, nor looking upon it as the 'intelligence coordinator of the region'. In Singh's view, the NEC should have included an institute for 'defense, insurgency and ethnic studies' (ibid.: 121–2)—very similar to the mix of ethnographic expertise and intelligence that came together in colonial power centres.

Important Indian officials sometime inadvertently acknowledge that statehood in Northeast India is little more than an exercise in cosmetic federalism. Thus the former Governor of the state of Assam, Lt General S.K. Sinha, speaking to an elite New Delhi audience, spoke about the state of Nagaland as follows:

There were many efforts to pacify the Nagas, and through concessions in 1963, the State of Nagaland was created. This State was for a population of barely 500,000—less than the population of many of the colonies of New Delhi[12]—and yet all the trappings that go with full Statehood, a Legislature, Cabinet, Chief Minister, and later even Governor, went with this new status (Sinha 2002: 8).

As I argue in Chapter 3, by appointing retired military generals, such as Sinha, and former intelligence and police officials with close ties with the security establishment in New Delhi as governors, India's Home Ministry manages to oversee a parallel political structure in the Northeast, which is both directly controlled from New Delhi and autonomous from the formal democratically-elected governmental structure of the states.

Reforming the Regional Order?

There have been some recent changes to the regional order of Northeast India. In 2001, a new Ministry for the Development of North-Eastern Region (DONER) was added to India's national government, and in 2002 the NEC was expanded to include an eighth state, Sikkim. Indian and Northeastern public opinion has got so used to the cosmetic federal regional order that an editorial in the *Assam Tribune*, the oldest newspaper of the region, described Arun Shourie, the first Cabinet Minister to head DONER, as a 'patron of the Northeast'. The editorial expressed the hope that under Shourie's leadership the 'feeling of neglect nursed by the Northeasterners and the absence of a Northeast lobby in Delhi' would be rectified (*Assam Tribune* 2001b). B.G. Verghese, however, could see the incongruity of creating a new Ministry in New Delhi for the development of the Northeast at a time when the rest of the country (and the world) is going through devolution and liberalization, even though he calls the new cabinet department a 'welcome first step'. Verghese recommends that 'the locus of planning must shift from Delhi to Shillong [the present-day capital of Meghalaya, and significantly, the capital of undivided Assam], if the region is to assume ownership of the North East Plan'. He suggests that the minister should be the ex-officio chairman of the NEC and an ex-officio member of the Indian Planning Commission, and that he or she should be based in Shillong, travel in the region, and make periodic visits to New Delhi—rather than the other way round (Verghese 2001b). The notion of a member of the Indian cabinet having his or her office in Shillong, so that 'the region'—itself conceived as part of the national securitization of governance—can 'assume ownership' of the plans and policies conceived in New Delhi, gives new meaning to the idea of federalism, even to the cosmetic version practiced in India's Northeast for the last three decades.

The Developmentalist Road to Nationalizing Space

Apart from security, the other avowed purpose of the new cosmetic federal regional order was, of course, to promote development. The attractiveness of such an arrangement becomes apparent when one considers the dangers of an alternative approach to nationalizing space: filling lands with a 'population representing the nation-bearing population', to use Fearon and Laitin's evocative phrase (Fearon and Laitin 2001). As mentioned above, one of the proposals made after the China war was just such a strategy of nation-building through forced demographic change. That would have meant an explicit policy of marginalizing the tribal peoples in their own habitats and, in effect, dismantling the institutions of tribal autonomy established in colonial times and modified and reinforced by the Constitution's Sixth Schedule. This course would have obviously been politically unwise at a time of a full-blown pro-independence rebellion among the Nagas and signs of discontent among some of the other peoples of the region.

It was therefore necessary to find a middle ground that would enable the penetration of pan-Indian institutions and, at the same time, allay the fears of the people of this sparsely populated area about being swamped by immigrants from the rest of the country. Cosmetic federalism became this middle path. Building on the elementary apparatus of state institutions created by the Constitution's Sixth Schedule became a good way to ensure both the penetration of the state and the creation of local stakeholders in the pan-Indian dispensation. The strategy, however, is full of contradictions.

Indian official developmentalist texts about Arunachal are strikingly different from the texts about the area's bio-diversity and environmental wealth mentioned at the beginning of this chapter. The difference illustrates the post-structuralist argument on how underdevelopment gets constituted discursively. Typical of this the 'state profile' of Arunachal that appears in a report of the Indian Ministry of Small Scale Industry. Analysing official economic data—remarkable developmentalist texts in themselves—on Arunachal's economy, the report concluded,

Arunachal Pradesh is one of the most industrially backward states in the country although the state is endowed with vast natural resources. The reason for its perennial industrial backwardness appears to be more than one. Lack of transport and communication facilities, low capital formation, dearth of skilled technical hands, poor literacy among the people of the state and more so the absence of an industrial climate are some of the few reasons attributed for its industrial backwardness. This is evident from the fact that there are no large-scale industries in the state although there are 18 medium scale industries mostly plywood and sawmills, which are closed on account of [the] Supreme Court order [of 1996 banning the felling of trees in all forests] (Government of India 2001: 4).

Once the presence of industry is defined as progress, its absence, by definition, becomes a mark of 'backwardness', and a vision of the future which incorporates more industries and the displacement of the local resource use regime by national and global resource use regimes does not even have to be explicitly formulated, let alone defended. This image of Arunchali reality inevitably carries a rather different vision of its future than for instance, the description of Arunachal by Elizabeth Taylor with which the chapter began. It is these official texts that provide the basic script for the developmentalist course that Arunachal has now embarked on.

As state institutions have penetrated deeper into Arunachali life, developmentalism has increasingly been able to capture the imagination of local elites and development discourse has been able to bring the aspirations of Arunachal's new elites into line with New Delhi's national security-driven goals. Greater mobility of Arunachali elites within the country—through educational opportunities, most of them financed by the central government, visits to New Delhi by Arunachali officials, politicians and businessmen—have also contributed to this convergence of goals within the discursive space of developmentalism.

Since the funds for development come directly from New Delhi and since all projects are designed in Delhi, Arunachali officials have had to learn to make their case for funds to institutions such as the Planning Commission and various central government departments by tailoring poposals to fit central government plans and projects. For instance, at a meeting of the National Development Council, while making a case for more funds to build roads, then Chief Minister Mithi spoke of road density as if it were a universal value that applies to every inch of the earth's land surface. Whether an area is an industrial belt, a nature preserve, a highly settled plains area or a pristine mountain, he seemed to imply, to be considered 'developed' they all have to have the same road density. The average road density in Arunachal, Mithi complained, is 'is only 17 kilometres for every 100 square kilometres, while the national average is 73 kilometres per 100 square kilometres'. He argued that this disparity illustrates the seriousness of the 'problem of accessibility' in his state. Arunachal, he pointed out, has 'to bear the unique burden of air dropping food items in inaccessible areas'—which of course is extremely expensive. Thus 'surface connectivity' to those remote areas has to be established (Mithi 2001).

Mithi then proceeded to give an example of the difficulties that Arunachal faces since it does not qualify for many of India's countrywide road-building programmes. For instance, the national goal of connecting all habitations with a population of more than 1000 does not fit with Arunachal's conditions, where its mountain villages have far fewer people.

Even if the project goal was to connect all villages with a population of 500, he argued, 92 per cent of Arunchal's villages would 'automatically be deprived of the benefits of the scheme'. Mithi therefore appealed to the Indian Planning Commission to 'imaginatively' address such 'rigidities' and make funds available for road-building projects to connect the especially remote and the high altitude settlements of Arunachal (ibid.).

Pedagogy of Development: Bureaucrats in Command

Former Chief Minister Mithi was an articulate spokesman for Arunachal and he knew how to frame his demands for funds in a language that Indian planners and nation-builders in New Delhi felt comfortable with. However, this is not typical. Generally there is a pedagogical dimension to the implementation of the developmentalist vision: Arunachali elected officials have to learn the language of development and the virtues of development from bureaucrats—most of them sent from New Delhi—who are experts in bureaucratic procedures. The process of development in Arunachal now takes place at many levels, well below the level of the state government. India's three-tier rural local-government structure of *Panchayati Raj* has been introduced in Arunachal, and it too functions primarily as part of the expanding apparatus of developmentalism.

Tanya Dabi, an Arunachali scholar who studied the functioning of these local government institutions, has noted the difference between these institutions in Arunachal and in other parts of the country. Even though the structure of Panchayati Raj in Arunachal is similar to that of the rest of India, says Dabi, it has 'different aims and objectives'. While decentralization is the objective of Panchayati Raj in the rest of India, in Arunachal the goal is 'to bring uniform political practice' by introducing an 'integrated political system' to the region. Panchayati Raj in Arunachal seeks to bring about rural development and to 'forge a distinct political identity, thereby to develop a new political culture ... by integrating the different communities into the larger national life'. The uniformity of 'political practice' or what Dabi called a 'new political culture', is indeed the cultural practice of developmentalism and it is the prism through which, Dabi recognizes, Arunchalis are expected to imagine their shared future as citizens of India and to integrate into 'the larger national life' (Dabi 1997: 231).

One effect of this pedagogy of developmentalism in the context of Arunachal's Panchayati Raj institutions is that, for all practical purposes, the elected local politicians to these bodies have to play subordinate roles vis-à-vis appointed civil servants. The meetings of the intermediate level and the district level Panchayati Raj institutions—the *anchal samitis* and *zilla parishads*—Dabi notes, are virtually conferences of 'officers' (civil servants). These bureaucrats shape the agenda of these meetings, manage the proceedings and propose various initiatives. The elected members of Panchayats make requests regarding particular projects to the bureaucrats and 'it is up to the officers to accept or not to accept their requests'. This arrangement also means that the elected members are not accorded the respect and status due to them as democratically elected people's representatives. The bureaucrats look down on them as 'ignorant and uneducated'. Dabi contrasts the Panchayati Raj institutions with the *kebang*—the traditional institution of representative governance of the Adi people and similar institutions of other Arunachali peoples that provided real opportunities for self-governance. The Panchayati Raj institutions inculcate what Dabi calls 'political awareness' but they have also 'brought about the degeneration of traditional democratic institutions' (Dabi 1997: 232–5).

Politics of Demographic Change

Well before the developmentalism of the post-China war era, Northeast India had been a land frontier attracting large-scale immigration from the rest of the subcontinent. The Sixth Schedule, the Inner Line and other restrictions historically were mostly policy responses to try to set some limits on what appeared to be the unstoppable demographic transformation of this frontier region. Some of those instruments were designed under the very different political conditions of British colonial rule, but once in place it has proved difficult to reverse them, especially against the political backdrop of pro-independence rebellions. In spite of these rules of exclusion, however, the demographic transformation of the region continued—most noticeably, but not exclusively, in those parts of present-day Assam and Tripura that were not designated as tribal areas. While immigrants have come from all parts of South Asia, the largest numbers have come from East Bengal. The fact that after the partition of India in 1947, the area became a part of the foreign country—first Pakistan and then Bangladesh—made this immigration more visible and controversial.

While the large-scale immigration to the region has often been the subject of comment, much of the attention has been focused on what scholars of migration call 'push factors'. This has obscured the role of the development process itself as a 'pull factor'. Development projects, for instance, have actively sought to bring about a transition from shifting cultivation to settled agriculture and from the clan control of land to commodification of land, creating new opportunities for immigrants. The priority attached to infrastructure building in order to link the economy to national and international markets and development projects that aim at the transformation of pre-capitalist economies, also generate economic niches attracting new immigrants. Furthermore, in sparsely populated areas like Arunachal, the state bureaucracy itself is a substantial demographic presence in the new urban centres. The net result has been a consistently high rate of population growth rates in the Northeastern states (see Table 2.1).

TABLE 2.1   NORTHEASTERN STATES: POPULATION GROWTH RATES, 1961–2001

States	Population 2001	% Growth 1991–2001	% Growth 1981–91	% Growth 1971–81	% Growth 1961–71
Arunachal	1,091,117	26.21	36.83	35.15	38.91
Assam	26,638,407	18.85	24.24*	23.36*	34.95
Manipur	2,388,634	30.02	29.29	32.46	37.53
Meghalaya	2,306,069	29.94	32.86	32.04	31.50
Mizoram	891,058	29.18	39.70	48.55	24.93
Nagaland	1,988,636	64.41	56.08	50.05	39.88
Tripura	3,191,168	15.74	34.30	31.92	36.28
India	1,027,015,247	21.34	23.86	24.66	24.80

* There was no census in Assam in 1981. These figures are based on estimates of Assam's 1981 population made by India's Census Department.

Source: Census of India (various years).

In the period 1991–2001 most of the states show growth rates that are well above the national average (the exceptions are Assam and Tripura, where the growth rates were very high during earlier census periods). Nagaland's growth rate of 64.4 per cent for this period is the highest in India. In the states of Arunachal Pradesh, Meghalaya, Mizoram, and Nagaland as well as in Assam's two tribal districts (Karbi Anglong and North Cachar Hills), the size of the tribal population as a proportion of the total population is on the decline, although at the moment—except for the tribal district of Karbi Anglong in Assam—the majority status of tribal peoples is not immediately under threat (see *Census of India 2001*).

There are important political consequences of this demographic trend. In frontier situations when indigenous populations engage in rebellions, immigrant groups typically function as a conservative force (Fearon and Laitin 2001). Immigrant communities are unlikely to sympathize with pro-independence politics. They may even be targets of pro-independence militants, since their very presence embodies the project of nationalizing space that those seeking autonomy are trying to resist. In a political sense, New Delhi therefore can be seen as acquiring a large population base that can be mobilized as a political counter-weight to pro-independence rebellions for which the indigenous populations are the actual or potential support-base.[13]

The Future of Protective Discrimination

The rules of exclusion enforced by the Inner Line, and the restrictions on property ownership by non-tribals in the tribal states of Northeast India, effectively compromise the constitutional right to free movement of Indian citizens. A similar constitutional provision in Jammu and Kashmir has proved highly controversial. The absence of controversy over the exclusionary rules in Northeast India can be explained by either the lack of interest in the region on the part of India's political classes, or the perception that, in this case, these are necessary short-term costs of the project of nationalizing space. The institutions of exclusion, however, have come under increasing stress as a result of the demographic change through immigration into the region that is inherent in the logic of developmentalism.

Indian policy analysts not only acknowledge the tension between the protective discrimination regime and the logic of developmentalism, they even recommend that some form of loosening, if not outright dismantling of the regime, should take place in the not-too-distant future. According to Gulshan Sachdeva of the Centre for Policy Research in New Delhi, it is clear that 'rigid barriers—which aim at restricting outside penetration—are contrary to the move to integrate these economies with the dynamic

world economy' (Sachdeva 2000: 162). Elsewhere Sachdeva has argued for
fundamental changes in land and labour policies of the region in order to
attract private capital. While the tribal population constitutes only about a
fourth of the population of the region, he points out, about two-thirds of
its land is 'owned, controlled or managed by tribes, clans or village
communities' (Sachdeva 1999). The idea that population size of indigenous
peoples should exactly match the amount of land they control—typically a
legacy of modes of production other than settled cultivation—is a curious
way of looking at land rights.

Sachdeva, nevertheless, is quite clear on why these forms of land control
are hurdles on the road to development, arguing that: 'it is almost impossible
to transfer this land to non-tribals and outsiders'. He sees changes in the
land tenure system as essential, so that land can be made 'available to investors
for industry, plantation, horticulture, etc. either on lease or on ownership
in a transparent manner'. Except for Assam's Brahmaputra valley and Tripura,
he points out, Northeast India is a labour-scarce region and institutions
like the Inner Line restrict the movement of labour. He believes that the
region has to be open to outside labour, though given the sensitive nature
of the issue, he adds, 'some control mechanism could be worked out'
(Sachdeva 1999).

In 1980, anthropologist Christoph von Fürer-Haimendorf re-visited
the Apa Tanis of Arunachal Pradesh, whom he had studied in the 1940s.
He viewed the changes that were unfolding very positively. Referring to the
Inner Line, he wrote:

Apa Tanis of the present generation, both traditionalist and modern, fully support
this policy, and there are no indications that they would welcome the lifting of the
protective barrier which interferes in no way with the movement with Apa Tanis and
other tribesmen but keeps out potential exploiters. It is difficult to imagine that in
the foreseeable future [the] Legislative Assembly of Arunachal Pradesh composed
overwhelmingly by tribal representatives, would agree to open the territory to
uncontrolled influx of population from the plains (Fürer-Haimendorf 1980: 218).

So confident was Fürer-Haimendorf about the capacity of the Inner Line
and other institutions of protective discrimination to protect the best of
the traditional Apa Tani life-style and the local resource use regime against
the onslaught of developmentalism that he ventured to predict that, 'for a
long time to come, the Apa Tani Valley will remain a heaven for a self-
contained society unsurpassed in its skill to utilize the natural resources of

its environment and to invest life with a *joie de vivre* such as few Indian societies can rival' (Fürer-Haimendorf 1980: 217–8). While there is enough evidence that Arunachali politicians will staunchly defend the protective discrimination regime, they may not be able to hold back the logic of demographic change that developmentalism—determined by the goal of nationalizing space—entails. A time will inevitably come when Arunachali elites would have to confront the tension between that regime and the developmentalist vision of Arunachal's future that they themselves share.

It is unlikely that the protective discrimination regime of Northeast India will come down quietly any time soon, but the strains on the regime as a result of demographic change are quite apparent. In order to contain the potential political fall-out, the government of India, through constitutional amendments, has frozen the balance of seats reserved for STs in the State Assemblies of the region. This should not obscure the political significance of the demographic facts on the ground: whether intended or not, the trend towards the minoritization of the indigenous populations, despite the symbolically significant phenomenon of state legislatures and state governments made up of their representatives, appears to be one of the most predictable effects of developmentalism and cosmetic federalism in Northeast India.

Cultural Battlefronts

Nationalizing space also has an important cultural dimension. It is, for instance, not accidental that the post-1962 cosmetic federal order involved giving new Sanskritic names to Arunachal Pradesh (the land of the mountain sun) as well as Meghalaya (abode of clouds)—names that in a Hindu nationalist world-view proclaim the region's ties with the rest of India, unlike names like Nagaland (especially the English word 'land') and Mizoram, that highlight the cultural distance from the bulk of the country. Indeed, the naming of Nagaland and Mizoram bears testimony to the accommodation that the government of India has had to make to the voices of cultural self-assertion in the region.

Pre-empting similar rebellions and comparable cultural concessions was the goal of the new regional order. However, the evidence of the last thirty years suggests that the push for nationalizing space has only stirred up more discontent in the region. In 1994, a journalist with a long history of reporting on Northeast India wrote that what was (more than four decades ago) 'an obscure speck of discontent' among some of the Nagas of Assam, had 'grown into an insurgency which has spawned and inspired other insurgencies in every part of the region' (Prabhakara 1994). The situation is significantly worse today.[14]

The cultural politics behind the pro-independence movements of Northeast India have received little attention. For instance, in Assam and Manipur there has been a new revisionist historiography that privileges the region's historical and cultural links to Southeast Asia and de-emphasizes its connections to the rest of India.[15] Despite India's democratic institutions and cultural resources, the Indian state's response to this significant cultural challenge has been remarkably crude; the cultural battle appears to be waged mostly by military generals and intelligence bureaucrats as a complement to their counter-insurgency strategy, although there are now a few Hindu nationalist pamphleteers joining the battle.

Thus Assam's former Governor Lt General S.K. Sinha (retired) described the government's counter-insurgency operations against the United Liberation Front of Assam [ULFA] as three-pronged: 'the first prong was the containment of violence; the second involved psychological initiatives; and the third sought to catalyse economic development'. He tells of the success of the military dimension as follows: 'We were able to kill more than one thousand militants in encounters,[16] we recovered three thousand weapons and a large amount of cash; and over three hundred militants surrendered in batches. These were backbreaking statistics for any militant organization, but still the ULFA has survived' (Sinha 2002:18).

While this account of military aspect of counter-insurgency is chilling, his account of the battle on the 'psychological' front highlights a conflict over history and memory that has accompanied the Indian project of nationalizing space. Within a few weeks of his taking over as Governor, he claims to have seen an opportunity to check out his 'psychological' weapon. Sinha was invited to inaugurate a meeting of historians and in his address he talked about the neglect of Assam by Indian historians. While Indian historians speak of the Indus Valley Civilization and the Ganges Valley Civilization, said the General-turned-historian, they never speak about Assam's Brahmaputra Valley Civilization. While military heroes of other regions of India such as Rana Pratap and Shivaji are known and admired nationally, 'an Assamese military hero of the same mould, Lachit Barphukan's name was not known outside Assam' (Sinha 2002: 18–19).

Lachit Barphukan was a General of the Tai-Ahom state of pre-colonial Assam, celebrated in Assamese pro-independence narratives for his successful resistance to Mughal invasions. Clearly, Sinha's goal is to appropriate a secular Assamese pro-independence symbol for a Hindu nationalist project of historical revisionism. The thrust of the psychological offensive, said Sinha, was to make the people of Assam feel proud of their past, and for the rest of India to feel proud of Assam. He would use history, he said, as 'a weapon to fight militancy'. Since 'they' (i.e. Assamese pro-independence intellectuals) speak in terms of Assam never being a part of India, his goal is to 'prove how wrong they were' (Sinha 2002: 19).

In order to do that Lt General Sinha selected 'three individuals whose contribution was great but was not known outside Assam'. Besides Lachit Barphukan, the other two were Shri Sankar Dev, the fifteenth founder of Assamese Vaishnavism and Gopi Nath Bordoloi, a major Assamese political leader during the transition to post-colonial rule. On Sinha's initiative, a statue of Lachit Barphukan was installed in the National Defence Academy—the college for training Indian army officers—and a gold medal for the best cadet named after him. Even though Gopi Nath Bordoloi died half a century ago, Sinha successfully secured for him a number of awards, including his image on an Indian postage stamp and the naming of the Guwahati International Airport after him.

Whatever the success of counter-insurgency in Assam and in other parts of Northeast India on the military front, the jury is still out on whether the 'psychological' strategy of a General-Governor could win the battle of memory and forgetting against the passionately engaged historiography of pro-independence local intellectuals. Sinha himself believes that his three-pronged offensive had been demonstrably successful (Sinha 2002: 19).

Conclusion

In 2000, a news report from a small town in Arunachal appeared in the *Assam Tribune*, with the intriguing headline, 'Dindu Miri: The man who came in from China'. According to the report, Miri was an Idu tribesman who was born in 1946 in a village in Arunachal. In 1955, as a young boy, Miri and a number of his friends went to Beijing to study. In his words, China (i.e. the Tibet region) was nearer to his village than any part of India. It was a four day walk from Agula Pass in the Dri Valley to Bapa village in Tibet, Miri explained, where there was a community of fellow Idu tribesman.

From Bapa 'he had to cross Rohlipo, a day's walk, Alepo a three hours' walk and then a day's walk to reach Beijing'—presumably referring to the place from where he could find transportation to Beijing.

After completing his education Miri held a Chinese government job as 'political interpreter'. He worked on that job during the Sino-Indian war. 'Our brigadier', he said, 'asked me to lead the Chinese troops towards Indian posts because I knew the routes to India'. He returned to Arunachal in 1963—a year after the China war. In 2000, Miri was still working as a 'political interpreter', but this time for the government of India. Miri recalled the days when he and other Idus of Arunachal could meet their kinsmen across the international border. But now they stay in touch with them only through 'secret messengers' (Tara 2000).

The story evokes a bygone era, rather dissonant with our era of policed national borders. The political geography of a historical frontier region and India's policy of tolerating its isolation in the years immediately following independence, made it possible for Miri to have, for all practical purposes, both Indian and Chinese nationality. But as vague frontier regions make room for precise borders, such ambivalence is no longer tolerated. Indeed the fact that Miri's story was published as a news item reflects the transition from a frontier to a border that had already taken place.

Until the outbreak of the China war, a British-born anthropologist Verrier Elwin was the major architect of India's policy in NEFA. Commenting on the path of development on which Arunachal has since embarked, Elwin's biographer writes: 'In his darker moments, Elwin would have admitted his work was mainly to delay the inevitable, to help the Arunachalis hold out and hold their own for a few decades. Civilization would catch up with them or crush them .... [H]ere it has come chiefly in the shape of a chain saw .... Aided by corrupt politicians the plywood industry has deforested large parts of Arunachal in the last decade' (Guha 2001: 323). But reading the inevitability of 'civilization' into Arunachal's developmentalist trajectory is misleading. In theory, other models of nature conservation and sustainable development—with very different consequences for the people of Arunachal—are still possible, but they presume the conditions of a politically uncontested space. In the spatial order of bounded nation states the ambiguities of frontier spaces have become suspect. To the guardians of India's national security, the political dangers of such ambiguity became painfully apparent in the 1960s. The policy to nationalize space by constructing a cosmetic federal regional order with its built-in developmentalist logic was a response to those dangers.

The costs of developmentalism for Northeast India—to the environment, to the sources of livelihood of peoples, to their sense of ontological security,[17] to the quality of Indian democracy and even to the region's political stability—are relatively well established by now. It is hardly surprising that the push for the nationalization of space has generated significant political and cultural resistance in the region. Lt General Sinha's chilling account of India's counter-insurgency strategy and the gradual militarization of the region suggest that the project could remain conflictual and even bloody for the foreseeable future. But the gains for India are no less evident: developmentalism and cosmetic federalism create stakeholders in the pan-Indian dispensation and the changed demographic reality can be a political counter-weight to pro-independence rebellions. To the average citizen of Northeast India security will probably remain elusive for a long time to come. Yet the narrative of development appears poised to succeed not only as an instrument in the project of nationalizing space; for the region's emerging modern elites—the beneficiaries of developmentalism and cosmetic federalism—it also provides a mental map to navigate the increasingly problematic social reality around them.

Notes

[1] The chapter first appeared in *Development and Change*. Reprinted by permission of Blackwell Publishing from Sanjib Baruah, 'Nationalizing Space: Cosmetic Federalism and the Politics of Development in Northeast India,' *Development and Change* 34 (5): 915–39. © Institute of Social Studies 2003.

[2] In this paper I use the term developmentalist to describe the notion of development as *nirvana*, implicit in the early models of development and modernization proposed mostly in the1950s and 1960s. Developmentalism is oblivious of critiques of development, especially the post-structuralist critiques of the 1990s.

[3] These projects are unlikely to come to fruition immediately, however, since they would require substantial resource commitments, all of which would have to come from the central government.

[4] The term 'Arunachali' of course ignores important divides between ethnic groups such as Adis, Nishis and Apatanis that loom large in the politics of Arunachal Pradesh.

[5] In 2001 an eighth state, Sikkim was added to the North Eastern Council, a key institution of the new regional order. In this book, however, Sikkim is not included in the term Northeast India.

[6] It should be stated that intellectuals from Northeast India have misgivings about the idea of India having a Northeast policy. Mrinal Miri, a distinguished academic from the region, puts it this way: 'to whom, or for whom, do you have a policy? ... The Northeast is a part of this country and at the same time we think that the people of the Northeast should be made the object of a policy'. Human beings do not have a policy towards family members or friends. To be made an object of policy, he says, implies that the peoples of the region are not in a relationship of 'human concerns such as love, friendship, understanding of the other', but in a relationship of manager and the managed (Miri 2002).

[7] As illustrated, for instance, by an incident at the 1996 International Film Festival of India, held in New Delhi. Most of the film-makers—Indians and others—were given the opportunity to meet the press individually. For Assamese, Bodo and Manipuri film-makers, however, the bureaucrats at the Indian Press Information Bureau (a government entity) organized a single session for film-makers from Northeast India. The Assamese filmmaker, Bhabendranath Saikia chose to stay away: as he said late, 'We often use the term South India, but does it mean that we club together Kerala and Tamilnadu or Adoor Gopalakrishnan and Mani Ratnam?' (cited in Misra 2000: 2–3).

[8] Meghalaya was an autonomous state within Assam for a brief period, and the other new states were Union Territories for some time.

[9] For a discussion of the tensions between the logic of the political economy of the region and the protective discrimination regime that has generated significant ethnic conflicts and displacements in Northeast India, see Chapter 9.

[10] Thus in a recent article Gurudas Das argues 'the relentless efforts made towards homogenization and realization of the goal of making Assam a nation-province during the 1950s and 1960s had resulted in an unmanageable discontent among various groups, which ultimately led to the reorganization of Assam in 1972 along ethnic lines' (Das 2002).

[11] See endnote 7, Chapter 1.

[12] Colony in this context refers to residential neighbourhoods. General Sinha's figure on Nagaland's population is not quite accurate. It perhaps refers to the time when Nagaland was created. The population of Nagaland, according to the 2001 census was nearly 2 million.

[13] An interesting contradiction, however, has developed in Northeast India. Since a significant part of the immigration is from Bangladesh, one of the political consequences in recent years has been the rise of some level of Islamic militancy that makes Indian security officials quite nervous.

[14] For an analysis of the politics of militancy in the region see Chapter 1.

[15] In the case of Manipur see the excellent article by Sohini Ray (Ray 2003).

[16] Human rights organizations believe most of these encounters are fake.

[17] By ontological security I mean a sense of confidence in what Giddens calls 'the continuity of ... self-identity and in the constancy of the surrounding social and material environments of action' (Giddens 1991: 92).

3

Generals as Governors[1]

'Isn't there a brigadier in Shillong?' This was how Sardar Vallabhbhai Patel, India's Deputy Prime Minister responded in 1949 to reports that the 'native state' of Manipur might be reluctant to merge fully with the Indian Union (Rustomji 1973: 109). In September of that year, the governor of Assam, Sri Prakasa, accompanied by his advisor for Tribal Areas, Nari Rustomji, flew to Bombay to apprise Patel of the situation. When British rule of India ended in 1947, the fate of Manipur and other indirectly ruled 'native states' presented a significant constitutional problem. Indeed, the historical origins of the Kashmir conflict between India and Pakistan are traced to the decision of the Kashmiri Maharaja to accede to India.

Patel and other senior Indian officials might perhaps have pondered more on the potential difficulties that could arise from decisions by major 'native states' like Kashmir and Hyderabad on the post-colonial dispensation in the subcontinent. But the thought that tiny and remote Manipur on India's border with Burma, might hesitate about fully joining India had probably never crossed their minds. The meeting of Sri Prakasa, Rustomji and Patel was brief. As Rustomji recalls in his memoir, apart from asking whether there was a brigadier stationed in the region, Patel said little else. It was clear from his voice what he meant, wrote Rustomji, and the conversation did not go any further (Rustomji 1973: 109).

Within days the Maharaja of Manipur, on a visit to Shillong, found himself virtually imprisoned in his residence. The house was surrounded by soldiers and under the pressure of considerable misinformation, the Maharaja—isolated from his advisors, council of ministers and Manipuri public opinion—signed an agreement fully merging his state with India. When the ceremony to mark the transfer of power and the end of this ancient kingdom took place in Imphal on 15 October 1949, a battalion of the Indian army was in place to guard against possible trouble (Rustomji 1973: 109).

The circumstances attending Manipur's merger with India haunts the politics of the state to this day. Like in the case of other 'native states,' Manipuri politics at that time did not present a single uniform position on the merger. Pan-Indian anti-colonial political ideas had entered Manipur. While there was support for the Maharaja, republican opposition to him was building up as well. There was thus support for the merger along with signs of opposition. However, in Manipuri public life today there is bitterness about the merger, especially about the circumstances under which the agreement was signed. A number of militias today regard the merger as illegal and unconstitutional. While Manipur has an elected chief minister and an elected state legislature—like other states in the Indian Union—there is also, what I would argue in this chapter, a de facto parallel structure of governance directly controlled from Delhi that manages counter-insurgency operations. Visitors to Manipur cannot but notice the strong military presence. Indian security forces occupy even historic monuments such as the Kangla Fort of the old Manipuri kings, and parts of the complex in Moirang that commemorates the planting of the Indian flag on Indian soil by soldiers of Subhash Bose's Indian National Army.

It is not hard to see why there is such a massive security presence in the state. Manipur tops the list of Northeast Indian states in the number of ethnic militias (ICM 2002). Apart from major groups such as Meities, Nagas, and Kukis, smaller ethnic groups such as Paites, Vaipheis, and Hmars also have their own militias. In recent years the official count of lives annually lost in insurgency-related incidents in Manipur has been in the hundreds. In addition the role of ethnic militias in inter-ethnic conflicts, such as that between Nagas and Kukis and, more recently between Kukis and Paites, have made those conflicts extremely violent.

Many of these conflicts appear intractable and some of them have their roots in the profound social transformation that these societies are undergoing. Yet unless one believes that a coercive state is a necessary instrument to manage change, it is hard to avoid the question: were the symbols and practices of the traditional Manipuri state—despite the significant erosion of its authority and power under British colonial rule—better-equipped to achieve social cohesion? Was Patel's readiness to use force just as the rest of India was setting off on a path of democratic rights and liberties, an early acknowledgement that Indian democracy in the Northeast would necessarily have an authoritarian accent?

Manipur is not unique. Except for Arunachal Pradesh and Mizoram, five of the seven states of Northeast India today—Assam, Manipur, Meghalaya, Nagaland, and Tripura—have militias of varying levels of activity and intensity.[2] Some of them, such as the United Liberation Front of Assam (ULFA), Nagaland's National Socialist Council of Nagalim (NSCN), now divided into two factions, and the Manipur People's Liberation Front (MPLF), which consists of the United National Liberation Front (UNLF), the People's Liberation Army (PLA) and the People's Revolutionary Party of Kanglaipak (PREPAK), have independentist agendas. Other ethnically based groups are typically dressed up as national fronts defending this or that ethnic group.

As a response to those insurgencies there are many more brigadiers in Northeast India today than Sardar Patel could have imagined. Military formations much larger than brigades—corps headed by lieutenant generals and divisions headed by major generals—are now stationed in Northeast India. In Vairengte, a Mizoram village, there is even a Counter-Insurgency and Jungle Warfare School for training officers to fight the militants. And the Indian Army is only one of the security forces deployed in the region. Other paramilitary units controlled by the central government, such as the Central Reserve Police Force (CRPF), the Border Security Force (BSF), the Assam Rifles, various intelligence bureaus and the police forces of each state, are also involved in counter-insurgency operations. And, as I would argue in this chapter, overseeing these operations is a parallel political structure that works outside the rules and norms that govern India's democratic political institutions.

Political violence—murders, bombings, kidnappings, extortion by militants, and killing of militants by security forces in actual or staged encounters—has become a routine part of news from the Northeast. True, there is also news of elections, cease-fires and talks—or prospects of talks—with militias. But the two kinds of news and images co-exist with disturbing ease. No one finds the image of democratic elections being conducted under massive military presence anomalous. Nor does anyone expect talks with insurgents to bring about sustained peace. Indeed in some ways, insurgencies themselves have become incorporated into the democratic political process. Good political reporters of the Northeast know the precise role that insurgent factions play in elections or the ties that these factions have with particular mainstream politicians.

For politicians, the use of the army to fight insurgencies has now become something of a habit. For instance in 1999, after attacks on Bengalis by tribal militants in Tripura, political parties belonging to the state's Left Front government observed a 12-hour *bandh* to put pressure on the central government to send in the army to deal with the situation. Chief Minister Manik Sarkar complained that even though 27 police station areas in the state had been declared disturbed, 'the Centre is silent over the state's demand for additional forces' (cited in Chaudhuri 1999b: 62). One would hardly guess from such statements that the law that these democratic politicians were relying on—the law that permits army deployment in 'disturbed' area— is a law that contravenes all conceivable human rights standards.

According to the Armed Forces Special Powers Act (AFSPA), in an area that is proclaimed as 'disturbed', an officer of the armed forces has powers to: (a) fire upon or use other kinds of force even if it causes death; (b) to arrest without a warrant and with the use of 'necessary' force anyone who has committed certain offences or is suspected of having done so; and (c) to enter and search any premise in order to make such arrests. Army officers have legal immunity for their actions. There can be no prosecution, suit or any other legal proceeding against anyone acting under that law. Nor is the government's judgment on an area being 'disturbed' subject to judicial review (Government of India, 1972).

As Ravi Nair of the South Asia Human Rights Documentation Centre in New Delhi has pointed out, the AFSPA violates the Indian Constitution's right to life, the right against arbitrary arrest and detention, the rules of the Indian Criminal Procedure Code relating to arrests, searches, and seizures, and almost all relevant international human rights principles (SAHRDC 1995). There was a time when reports of human rights violations in the Northeast were taken seriously. But many Indians now regard human rights organizations as being at best naïve, or at worst, sympathizers of insurgents masquerading under the flag of human rights. The violation of human rights in the Northeast is seen as the necessary cost of keeping the nation safe from its enemies inside and outside.

Thus in 1991, when the United Nations Human Rights Committee asked the Attorney General of India to explain the constitutionality of the AFSPA in terms of Indian law and to justify it in terms of international human rights law, he defended it on the sole ground that it was necessary in order to prevent the secession of the Northeastern states. The Indian government, he argued, had a duty to protect the states from internal disturbances and that there was no duty under international law to allow secession (cited in SAHRDC, 1995).

State within a State

In the insurgency-hardened Northeast, democratic India has developed a de facto parallel political system, somewhat autonomous of the formal democratically elected governmental structure. This parallel system is an intricate, multi-tiered reticulate, with crucial decision-making, facilitating and operational nodes that span the region and connects New Delhi with the theatre of action.

The apex decision-making node is the Home Ministry in New Delhi housed in North Block on Raisina Hill. The operational node which implements the decisions consists of the Indian Army, and other military, police, and intelligence units controlled by the central and state governments and involves complex coordination. This apparatus also involves the limited participation of the political functionaries of the insurgency-affected states. Elected state governments, under India's weak federal structure, can always be constitutionally dismissed in certain situations of instability. But New Delhi has generally preferred to have them in place while conducting counter-insurgency operations. Since the insurgencies have some popular sympathy—albeit not stable or stubborn—the perception that the operations have the tacit support of elected state governments is useful for their legitimacy.

Consequently, the command structure may include some state-level politicians and senior civil servants. This is perceived to be the weakest link in the chain because of the fear that the presence of these 'locals' might potentially subvert the counter-insurgency operations. Consider the following news reports:

1. In December 2000, the central government asked the Manipur government to investigate links between at least five ministers and insurgent groups. The Home Ministry forwarded a report to the state authorities that included evidence of such a nexus between the ministers and insurgents. Manipur's then caretaker Chief Minister Radhabinod Koijam, just before the fall of his government dropped six ministers from his cabinet. Koijam was

in the middle of a political battle for survival, and there were other reasons for their removal. But he defended his action saying that their names appeared in the Home Ministry's list of 'tainted' politicians.

2. In January 2001, the Union Home Ministry proposed the setting up of a judicial enquiry commission to probe into the allegations and counter-allegations of the insurgent-politician nexus in the Northeastern states.

3. In the May 2001 elections in Assam, former Chief Minister Prafulla Kumar Mahanta repeatedly accused the Congress party of having a nexus with ULFA. The Congress party dismissed the charge as election propaganda and claimed that its victory proved that the electorate did not believe the accusation. In the elections of 1996, the roles were reversed: the Congress had made similar charges against Mahanta's party, the Asom Gana Parishad (AGP).

There are, of course, many reasons why democratically-elected politicians of a region, where ethnic militias and mainstream political parties may share the same social, political, and cultural space, would sometimes know and have ties with each other. Pervasive corruption also leads politicians to cultivate ties with insurgent groups. They, like others with a reputation for making illegal money, consider it prudent to try to keep the insurgent groups happy by sharing parts of their illicit income with them. Rather than a hard boundary separating militants and mainstream politicians, in these circumstances, a nexus between some of them becomes inevitable, despite the fact that such ties may cost these politicians in terms of their credibility as far as New Delhi is concerned.

A former Home Minister of Nagaland, Dalle Namo, who had been part of the Naga 'underground', once movingly acknowledged his debt to the pioneers of the movement for Naga independence. He told journalist Nirmal Nibedon that he is conscious of the fact that he lives,

'in this big bungalow because men like Phizo and Imkongmeren and many others once lived in caves. All these chandeliers and lights [are there] because for them the stars were their only light; [I have] these expensive wall-to-wall carpets because they walked on moss and grass' (cited in Nibedon 1987: 7).

Of course, such sentiments connecting insurgents with mainstream politicians are far from universal. It is unlikely, for instance, that Prafulla Kumar Mahanta, former Chief Minister of Assam or Nagaland's former

Chief Minister, S.C. Jamir, whom militants have tried to kill more than once, would share similar idealized views about leaders of the Assamese or the Naga 'underground'. However, even these leaders have not always been free of ties with militants. The Khaplang-led faction of the National Socialist Council of Nagalim, for instance, is reputed to have enjoyed the patronage of Jamir.

This is the paradox of counter-insurgency. On the one hand, it must draw on the legitimacy of the elected establishment. On the other, it must protect itself from this establishment's susceptibilities. Namo's account and the repeated charges of a link between politicians and insurgents underscore why India's security establishment would want a parallel structure of governance that is as autonomous as possible from the democratic politics of the state in question. For instance, in the case of the Indian government's allegation of a nexus between the five Manipuri politicians and insurgents, if the Home Ministry had provided evidence of such a nexus to the 'authorities' in Manipur, it is unlikely, that this report would go to the elected members of the state government—some of whom were themselves the object of suspicion. The most likely person to have received that report from New Delhi, one can reasonably speculate, was the Governor of Manipur.

Bending the rules of constitutional democracy, and building and maintaining a parallel structure however, is not always easy. Not all elected state governments have been willing to give up their constitutional prerogatives. For instance, in Assam, because of the complicity of the then Chief Minister Mahanta, after 1997, counter-insurgency operations were conducted by a Unified Command, under which all forces including the state police came under the operational command of the Indian Army. But his successor Tarun Gogoi, following the Congress' election victory in May 2001, in one of his first statements as Assam's Chief Minister said that he would like to see the Assam police play more of a role in the Unified Command because of its superior knowledge of local conditions. Gogoi did not seek to end the use of Unified Command structure in Assam. In Manipur elected politicians have so far resisted pressures from the Indian Home Ministry and the Indian Army to have a Unified Command structure. Former Chief Minister of Manipur, W. Nipamacha, for instance, maintained that since legally speaking, the army was deployed in the state only to assist the civil administration it should remain under the command of the state government.

Such potential conflicts between the compulsions of the democratically elected state governments and the concerns of the security establishment make the governors of these states crucial nodes in the counter-insurgency network. The management of this difficult equation, in fact, confers on the governor's office a role that far exceeds the more ceremonial functions it is constitutionally restricted to elsewhere and in normal circumstances. The career profiles of the incumbents in the Northeast provide an index of the importance of the gubernatorial office to the parallel political system. Tables 3.1 and 3.2 listing the governors of Northeastern states in 2001—when this article was first written—and in April 2004 are illustrative.

TABLE 3.1   GOVERNORS OF NORTHEAST INDIAN STATES: 2001

Arunachal Pradesh:	Arvind Dave, former Director, Research and Analysis Wing (RAW)
Assam:	Lieutenant General (retired) S.K. Sinha
Manipur:	Ved Prakash Marwah, Indian Police Service officer and former chief of Delhi Police
Meghalaya:	M.M. Jacob, former minister, Government of India, and former Deputy Chairman of the Rajya Sabha
Mizoram:	A.R. Kohli, businessman with political ties
Nagaland:	O.P. Sharma, former officer of the Indian Police Service and former Director General of Police (Intelligence), Punjab
Tripura:	Lieutenant General (retired) K.M. Seth

Since a few individuals have continued as governors either of the same state or of another Northeastern state, the two lists have only eleven and not fourteen names. Nearly all of them have either occupied high and sensitive positions in India's security establishment or have had close ties to it. Three of them are retired military men, four are retired police officers, and one is the former head of Research and Analysis Wing, the intelligence agency engaged in operations abroad and at home. Another retired police officer, Shyamal Dutta, Governor of Nagaland, headed the Intelligence Bureau. His predecessor O.P Sharma also was a retired police officer who headed the intelligence wing of the Punjab police during counter-insurgency operations when many disappearances had taken place. Of the three without any ostensible ties with the security establishment, M.M. Jacob, Governor of Meghalaya, was once Minister of State for Home Affairs in New Delhi; and A.R. Kohli, Governor of relatively peaceful Mizoram, who had a career in business, has strong ties with the RSS, suggesting proximity to former Home Minister L.K. Advani, and Vinod Chandra Pandey, present Governor of peaceful Arunachal was former Cabinet Secretary of the Government of India.

TABLE 3.2   GOVERNORS OF NORTHEAST INDIAN STATES: APRIL 2004

Arunachal Pradesh:	Vinod Chandra Pandey, former Cabinet Secretary, Government of India.
Assam:	Lieutenant General (retired) Ajai Singh
Manipur:	Arvind Dave, former Director, Research and Analysis Wing (RAW)
Meghalaya:	M.M. Jacob, former minister, Government of India, and former Deputy Chairman of the Rajya Sabha.
Mizoram:	A.R. Kohli, businessman with political ties
Nagaland:	Shyamal Dutta, former officer of the Indian Police Service and former Director, Intelligence Bureau.
Tripura:	D.N. Sahay, former officer of the Indian Police Service, and former Director General of Police, Bihar.

The Northeast Study Group constituted by the Home Ministry recommended the end of the practice of appointing men in uniform (or rather men who have just shed their uniform) as governors since they send the 'wrong signals' (rediff.com, 2003). The appointment of retired security officials as governors of Northeastern states has become somewhat of a sensitive subject since this article had first appeared. This probably accounts for the decrease of men with such credentials by one in the list of governors in 2004. But whatever the 'signals,' the Indian Government clearly has not found practicable to end this practice. When Lt General S.K. Sinha's term as Governor of Assam ended in 2003, he was moved to Jammu and Kashmir (as Governor), another state in which the Northeastern experience is considered relevant. The first name considered as Lt General Sinha's replacement was K.P.S. Gill, the former police chief of Punjab credited with the ruthless and violent counter-insurgency campaign against militants in that state. When the Assam Chief Minister Tarun Gogoi objected to that choice (rediff.com 2003) the person chosen was another retired military man, Lt General Ajai Singh. Among his credentials presumably considered pertinent to this appointment was the fact he commanded the Indian army's Fourth corps, based in Assam, during its counter-insurgency operations against ULFA in the 1990s. Only in relatively peaceful, Arunachal Pradesh, it has been considered practicable to break away, at least for the moment, from the practice of appointing retired security officials as governor; there a civilian has replaced a former spy as governor.

The fact that so many of the appointees are men who have just shed their uniform and all the appointees have had fairly intimate connections with the security establishment cannot be mere coincidence. As appointees of the central government and as facilitating agents in the counter-insurgency regime, such antecedents serve very practical ends, particularly in ensuring that the demands of security override the rules of democracy in the event of a conflict between the two.

Counter-insurgent Constitutionalism: Governor as Judge

Instances of gubernatorial interventions point to the role they play in insulating counter-insurgency operations from democratic processes and scrutiny. Governors often act in ways that not only stretch constitutional propriety but also sacrifice democratic procedures at that altar of security expediencies. A case of what can be called counter-insurgent constitutionalism took place in Assam in 1998 when the Governor, Lt General Sinha, intervened to stop the Central Bureau of Investigation (CBI) from prosecuting then Chief Minister Mahanta on a serious corruption charge. Mahanta's acquiescence in the Unified Command structure was clearly important to the security establishment. At the same time, the legal pursuit of a credible corruption charge against an elected chief minister could have significantly raised the legitimacy of India's democratic governmental institutions in the public eye. There was a choice between two sets of values: the perceived political requirements of counter-insurgency versus an opportunity to raise the public esteem of India's democratic institutions in a region where those institutions lack legitimacy.

The corruption charge against Mahanta, went back to what is commonly referred to as the 'Letters of Credit scam', involving at least Rupees 200 crores between 1986 and 1993. During a part of this period Mahanta was Chief Minister of the state [between 1991 and 1996 Assam had a Congress ministry under Hiteswar Saikia]. The state's animal husbandry and veterinary departments issued fake letters of credit to draw money from the treasury, and a number of politicians of both the then ruling Congress and the opposition AGP, were implicated. It was also suspected that a part of the money found its way to the ULFA.

The CBI investigated a number of politicians. The case against Mahanta was that the kingpin of the scam, Rajendra Prasad Borah, had paid him Rupees 40 lakhs during the 1991 elections, and that Mahanta's air travels during the campaign had been financed by Borah. According to the CBI, in that election, Borah had distributed house-building material to purchase votes in Mahanta's electoral constituency. Borah, it was alleged, had also paid for bank drafts distributed by Mahanta, in his electoral district (Kashyap 1999).

For a Governor—a former military general—to make a legal judgment on whether a chief minister should be prosecuted pushes the limits of constitutional propriety. To be sure, this power of Indian governors is not limited to the Northeast and as the Delhi-based magazine *India Today* pointed out in an editorial, 'there is something profoundly undemocratic about a mechanism which requires the governor's permission to even begin legal proceeding against a chief minister seen as corrupt.' Asking the Governor to veto the CBI's charge-sheet against a chief minister, said the editorial, is 'anachronistic' and warned of the dangers of 'a cozy governor-chief minister nexus' turning into 'a protection racket' (*India Today* 1998: 6). In the Northeast, given the parallel power structure in place, the potential for abuse of that power—or, perhaps its use—as a means of securing support for the security regime from a corrupt chief minister is enormous. From the perspective of constitutional law, a Governor—a former military general—making a legal judgment on whether a chief minister should be prosecuted would seem remarkable.

The Governor's reasons for disallowing the CBI's prosecution of Mahanta, involved a number of legal rationalizations. Sinha pointed to the lack of evidence, and questioned the reliability of the witnesses who formed the basis of the CBI's case. The CBI, according to the Governor, had not established Mahanta's culpability. The Governor found that there was no evidence in the case presented by CBI of Mahanta entering into a criminal conspiracy with Borah to defraud the state.

Obviously, governors enjoy extraordinary powers to get chief ministers support the parallel regime. In this particular case, it is difficult to avoid speculating on a very obvious connection. In Assam after 1997, the Unified Command structure became possible because of Mahanta's consent and it was highly controversial. That was a year before the Governor was called upon to make this crucial judgment in the corruption case. Was there a quid pro quo in the governor's decision to protect Mahanta from legal prosecution so as to ensure his continued support for the Unified Command structure? Did the perceived needs of counter-insurgency trump the value of achieving greater transparency in government? More importantly, what has this entire edifice and its strategies achieved by way of ending insurgency and restoring peace?

Why is Peace so Elusive?

This counter-insurgency apparatus and its modus operandi are geared fundamentally, and more or less exclusively, to containment. So long as insurgencies are only contained, and no sustainable peace processes are in place, democracy in the Northeast is likely to continue to co-exist with the use of authoritarian modes of governance. With the significant exception of the Mizo movement, most insurgencies in the Northeast have been transformed, or are currently transforming, into long-term, low-intensity conflicts. The perceived need for counter-insurgency operations never seems to go away. Even in Mizoram, at least if one goes by military presence in that state, the end of the insurgency has not meant that the state within the state has been dismantled.

There are three reasons why most Northeastern insurgencies turn into protracted conflicts of attrition: (a) the goal of counter-insurgency is limited to creating conditions under which particular insurgent groups or factions surrender weapons, come to the negotiation table on the government's terms and make compromises in exchange for personal gain; (b) counter-insurgency operations do not dramatically change the conditions on the ground that breed and sustain the insurgent political culture and lifestyle; and (c) the political initiative that accompany and supplement counter-insurgency operations try to utilize former militants in the war against insurgents, thus creating a climate of mistrust and a cycle of violence and counter-violence between anti-government and pro-government insurgents.

The need for a powerful military presence can hardly disappear under these conditions. Assam's growing violence—which at one time included secret killings by death squads—exemplifies the results of a counter-insurgency strategy that in fact transformed an insurgency into a wider and long drawn-out conflict. The bloody elections of May 2001 in which scores of people were killed are at odds with Lt General Sinha's euphoric claim of the 'ballot having won against the bullet'.

The Mizoram exception, of course, is important.[3] In 1986, Laldenga, the leader of the Mizo National Front, signed an accord, with Prime Minister Rajiv Gandhi and this remains the only instance of an accord successfully ending an insurgency in Northeast India. Laldenga became the Chief Minister of Mizoram and when he lost elections two years later, there was no call for a return to insurgency. Among the factors that accounts for the successful end of the Mizo insurgency were the undisputed leadership of the insurgency in the hands of a single individual who was willing to compromise and who could deliver his part of the deal; the feasibility of offering Laldenga the post of Chief Minister of Mizoram in exchange for ending the insurgency; the existence of large and organized church-related institutions that were actively involved in creating and supporting the consensus for peace; and a political climate in New Delhi during the Rajiv Gandhi years that was relatively open to making political compromises with insurgents. However, as I have argued in Chapter 1, the success of the Mizo Accord needs to be qualified in light of two factors: (a) the persistence of ethnic conflicts and violence in neighbouring states where there are communities with whom Mizos share ethnic affinity and whom the Mizo movement once sought to bring under a single political umbrella, and (b) the homeland model on which the Mizo Accord is premised establishes a regime of ethnic entitlements that has significant negative consequences for the citizenship rights of non-privileged groups.

In any case, keeping in mind these qualifications, to date, the Mizo case has been the only exception, and the other insurgencies refuse to die down despite the sophistication and resources of the counter-insurgency establishment. In seeking to understand why peace continues to elude Northeast India, it is important to look at how insurgencies are able to sustain themselves in the face of such enormous military action. One perspective on the longevity of armed civil conflicts focuses attention not so much on the grievances that are articulated by insurgent groups but to the ability of these groups to finance their activities. For example, economist Paul Collier, looking at the global patterns of armed civil conflicts, argues that the most significant factor of civil conflicts is the ability of rebel organizations to be financially viable. He also found a strong correlation with a specific set of economic conditions such as a region's dependence on exports of primary commodity and low national income (Collier 2001).

It is not that poverty breeds armed civil conflicts Collier surmises, but that certain economic conditions are conducive to the mobilization of revenue by armed insurgent groups. Primary commodities are highly lootable, primary production centres located in conflict-zones, are easily accessible, and production cannot be moved elsewhere. Unlike a manufacturing unit, which is not worth much once production ceases, owners and managers of such centres continue to be dependent on existing production sites, making them vulnerable to extortion. Low national income, Collier argues, is co-related with armed civil conflicts not because the objective condition of poverty sustains rebellion, but because in a context of poverty and unemployment, an insurgent group that is able to raise enough money, can recruit new members quite inexpensively (Collier 2001).

The Collier thesis is useful to explain the resilience of the Northeast insurgencies. It draws attention to the conditions that permit illegal tax collection. For instance, in those areas of large countries where the state's presence is weak, it is easier for rebel organizations to establish illegal taxation structures. The availability of foreign material support also becomes an important factor in explaining the persistence of armed civil conflicts. The civil war in Sierra Leone perhaps most dramatically supports the Collier thesis: the control over diamond mining and international diamond smuggling was clearly what had allowed the armed rebels to continue the fight.

While Northeastern India is no Sierra Leone, it is nevertheless striking that the region is both poor and a primary commodity-producing region—factors that, according to Collier, make an area conducive to illegal tax-collection and to the persistence of armed civil conflicts. Indeed, the production and transportation of primary commodities that Northeast India produces and exports—tea, timber, coal and so on—have been a major source of legal taxation by governments, a source of extortion by officials, and the favourite source of illegal taxation by insurgent groups, and increasingly by pro-government insurgent groups that collaborate in counter-insurgency operations, like Assam's SULFA (former members of ULFA who have 'surrendered', and hence the 'S').

Indian *Toka*, Naga *Toka*

During 1994–5, Sanjoy Ghose, a social activist who was kidnapped and killed by ULFA in 1997, travelled extensively in the Northeast. His travel diaries were published posthumously (Ghose 1998). In his travels through Nagaland, Ghose found a formalized system of tax-collection imposed by the NSCN. 'Every-body' paid, and in the case of the state government's Public Works Department (PWD)—perceived as being highly corrupt—Ghose found that there was a progressive system of illegal taxation in place. Those of the rank of executive engineers and above paid one-third of their net salary. This percentage may seem high to someone unfamiliar with the culture of corruption in the region, but the fact is that the formal, official salary is only a small part of the actual income of a government engineer. A senior police officer of Nagaland confided to Ghose that though he himself was not paying, most of his colleagues did 'contribute' (Ghose 1998: 175–6). Such stories about systems of illegal taxation—perhaps not equally formalized everywhere—are heard all through the Northeast. Indeed it is not merely insurgent organizations, but mainstream political parties, student organizations, corrupt officials, all resort to coercive and illegal modes of 'tax collection' from businesses—big and small.

Pervasive corruption and the preponderance of those who are seen as 'outsiders' in the economy of the region make the climate especially conducive to illegal taxation. Indeed, as Sanjoy Ghose found in the case of PWD engineers in Nagaland, unlike government tax collectors who could target only what is officially declared as income, insurgents—drawing on popular perceptions and credible rumour—can impose higher taxes based on a better information base that allows them to assess income more realistically. It is in not in the interest of those who give in to extortion demands and make payments that involve mostly illegal income to report to law enforcement agencies.

Krishnan Saigal, a former Indian civil servant who was Assam's Planning and Development Commissioner and who is familiar with the process of development finance in the Northeast, has written about the way development funds allocated to the region are a bonanza for a group of contractors and license holders—mostly from outside the region—whose 'main ambition is to make a fast buck and get out of the area as quickly as possible'. As the Indian state has increased development expenditures in response to the voices of discontent in the Northeast, he writes, there has been an even 'quicker siphoning off of funds to the heartland with the few benefits accruing to those in power through the usual corrupt forces.' Saigal believes this has led to increasingly corrupt regimes in the Northeastern states. And the people of the region, he believes, even see them as representing central power in order to keep their state underdeveloped (Saigal 1992: 215–16).

The perception that New Delhi is throwing money away in order to buy peace gives an aura of legitimacy to tax collection by insurgents. The manifesto of the NSCN is a case in point: 'The pouring in of Indian capital in our country for political reasons has shattered the Naga people into a society of wild money,' creating a parasitic, exploiting class of 'reactionary traitors, bureaucrats, a handful of rich men and the Indian vermin' (cited in Verghese 1996: 97–8). Such a view of the politics underlying New Delhi's development expenditures allows Naga insurgents to take the moral high ground: it is only fair that such ill-gotten wealth be shared with an organization that works for the greater good of the Nagas. To give another example of the consequence of this perception, in Nagaland it is said that during elections when political parties distribute money to buy votes, acceptance of that money is seen as legitimate since it involves only 'Indian *Toka*' [Indian money], not 'Naga *Toka*' [Naga money].

In order to discredit militants in the eyes of their supporters, military and intelligence officials have in recent years started speaking about the luxurious lifestyles of insurgent leaders or of the insurgents being nothing more than bandits seeking 'easy money'. While all this is not news to anyone living in the Northeast, whether such statements from security officials involved in counter-insurgency operations increases the legitimacy of governmental institutions vis-à-vis the rebels, is a different matter. Despite some highly publicized successes such as unearthing evidence that one of India's major business houses—the Tatas—were providing support to Assamese rebels, it is doubtful that the focus on the expropriative aspect of insurgencies has so far led to any systematic change affecting the illegal tax-collection capacity of insurgent groups.

Here are two recent newspaper reports that illustrate how routine the taxation systems of insurgent organizations are and how impervious they have been to decades of counter-insurgency operations:

1. In February 2001, the NSCN (Issac-Muivah) announced, and Indian newspapers routinely published the news of, a 'tax break' for industries. According to the *Times of India*, the NSCN (I-M) announced an exemption of 'loyalty taxes' for two years on certain categories of businesses—some of them even state-owned businesses. Quoting the organization's Information and Publication

Secretary, V. Horam, the news report said that the tax break was given in order to boost economic activities in the Naga areas of the Northeast. The 'tax exemption', said the notification, applied to enterprises that were less than two years old. However, the taxes on other businesses and the income tax on salaried people would continue (*Times of India* 2001a).

2. In March 2001, militant groups demanded Rupees 40 lakhs from eight Christian missionary schools in Manipur's capital city, Imphal. When the schools expressed their inability to pay, the militants imposed a fine of Rupees 2 crores and ordered them to close down. The matter was raised in the Manipur State Assembly. The press reported that security in and around the missionary schools was increased. The Chief Minister of Manipur told the state legislature that cases were registered with the police in connec-tion with the extortion demands and were being investigated. But no one expected such investigations to go very far. In May 2001, militants murdered three Christian missionaries apparently because of non-payment of those levies.

There seems to be little evidence that in these two states, years of counter-insurgency has had any significant impact on the conditions that have bred and sustained insurgency, i.e. the relative incapacity of civil administration to provide protection (despite its strong military presence) and the continued ability of insurgent organizations to collect illegal taxes. It appears that insurgent groups can guarantee security and collect tax better than the state can. It is hardly surprising then that many people—politicians, traders, government officials, and even major corporations—make their uneasy peace with insurgent groups, just as they learn to live with counter-insurgency operations without high expectations of an end to the fighting.

What then accounts for this fundamental failure? It must be that New Delhi's Northeast policy has yet to come to grips with the dense social networks of Northeastern societies and the ideas and values that animate the insurgencies.

People Without Histories?

How has liberal democratic India countenanced the informal Northeastern political system that has paralleled the formal democratic political institutions in the Northeast? To answer this question future historians will probably turn to the realm of ideas. How do Indians from the mainland think about the Northeast—especially its 'tribal' peoples?

B.P. Singh, a senior Indian civil servant has had a distinguished career that includes appointments to important policy-making positions in the Northeast and the position of Home Secretary of India. In an article about Northeast India published in 1987, he concluded:

'There is no tangible threat to the national integration ethos in the region despite the operation of certain disgruntled elements within the region and outside the country. But in the context of a history of limited socialization and ethnic conflicts, and rapid modernization after 1947, the unruly class-room scenario is likely to continue in the region for years to come' (Singh 1987b: 281–2).

Singh's prediction of a continually troubled but manageable Northeast has been proven correct. He writes with sympathy for the peoples of the Northeast; he does not believe that they are out to break up India. But he believes that there are those troublemakers: the 'disgruntled elements'. And given 'limited socialization'—presumably to pan-Indian values—and the opportunities provided by the destabilizing effects of social change, the troublemakers will continue to make trouble. 'Unruly class-room' is a telling metaphor: a reminder of a past when certain subordinated peoples— colonized 'natives,' slaves, servants or 'primitive tribals'—were seen as children by dominant groups. What is needed, Singh implies, is a paternalistic and disciplinarian teacher who knows what is good for the children and, occasionally uses the stick for their own good—the role that he apparently sees the state within the state playing in the region.

Indian officials are not shy of openly using the metaphor of children to describe Northeast India. For instance, in February 2004 the Mizoram Governor A.R. Kohli described the region as a spoilt child. Contrary to the charge that the Northeast is 'the most neglected region,' he said it is 'in fact, the most spoilt child in the country.' The central government, he said, 'showers funds and other goodies' liberally on the region. But the funds are not properly utilized or they do not reach the intended beneficiaries. A news report paraphrased the Governor as comparing the region 'to a petulant child who is showered with goodies but does not know what to do with them' (Telegraph 2004a).

Given the prevalence of such ideas it is hardly surprising that 'conventional historiography,' according to Sanjay Barbora, has silenced the 'tribal question' in Northeast India. There is no coherent historiography;

there are only narratives about tribal communities that show 'the overwhelming influence of an ethnological tradition' obsessed with things like their myths of origin. Barbora points at an interesting paradox in the cultural politics of Northeast India. Traditional historians had proclaimed that old kingdoms associated with tribal communities 'including vassal chiefs of Beltola, Rani, Dimoria, Gobha, etc.' had 'vanished without a trace' in the nineteenth century (Saikia 2000: 40, cited in Barbora 2004). Yet in the context of today's vibrant politics of ethnic assertion these kingdoms have reappeared with 'great pomp and vigour' (Barbora 2004). The Dutch scholar Willem van Schendel (writing mainly with Bangladesh and the Chittagong Hill Tracts in mind) has commented on the 'remarkably stagnant view of the hill people' that has prevailed in South Asia. The classic nineteenth century Western assumptions about social evolution from a state of savagery to civilization got superimposed on an ancient South Asian distinction between civilized society and nature. The later distinction, indicated in the categories *grama* (village) and *aranya* (forest), implies a relationship that is complementary but always unequal. These two traditions, writes van Schendel, combined to generate a dominant view that considers the tribal peoples as remnants of some 'hoary past who have preserved their culture unchanged from time immemorial. Backward and childlike, they need to be protected, educated and disciplined by those who are more advanced socially' (van Schendel 1995: 128). The comments of the Indian officials, cited above support van Schendel's observation.

Past and Present

How can the Northeast ever hope to get out of this quagmire, in which a democracy lives comfortably with the most arbitrary of powers in 'disturbed' areas? There might be occasional doubts in India about what counter-insurgency can achieve. But one idea that enjoys widespread acceptance is that once the problem of the region's economic backwardness is taken care of, the main source of political turmoil will go away. Indeed it would probably be hard to find a more diehard group of economic determinists than Indian bureaucrats and politicians engaged with the Northeast.

This faith in economic development contrasts sharply with the vision of insurgent groups in the Northeast. While those who try to solve the 'insurgency problem' mainly talk about economic development and modernization, the insurgents hark back to history. Thus ULFA speaks of

Assam's lost independence when the Yandaboo Treaty was signed between the British and the Burmese kings in 1826, Manipuri rebels raise questions about the constitutionality of the merger agreement of 1949, and Naga rebels query 'how these long stretches of frontiers which were neither Burmese nor Indian territories could simply disappear into India and Burma after 1947' (Iralu 2000: 6)?

True, militant groups, political parties and public opinion in North-eastern states do complain about the region's economic underdevelopment but their primary grouse appears to be perceived injustices grounded in the history of how the Indian post-colonial constitutional order came into being. But what is striking is that the bureaucrats, politicians, and military officers who make Northeast policy are either oblivious of the historical issues that insurgencies raise, or consider them too trivial to merit substantive engagement. Thus, exploring different ways of granting greater constitutional autonomy as a response to these historical claims, is not at all part of the Indian policy-maker's basket of solutions.

In the history of ideas there are numerous examples of the authoritarian consequences of dealing with places and people only in terms of their supposed future—framed in terms of ideas about backwardness and progress—without taking into account their past. After all, that is how an entire generation of liberal and progressive British thinkers, e.g. Jeremy Bentham, James Mill, John Stuart Mill, and Thomas B. Macaulay, managed to endorse empire as a legitimate form of government, and even justify its undemocratic and unrepresentative structure. The key to understanding this paradox of the liberal defence of empire, writes political theorist Uday Singh Mehta lies in the reforms proposed by the liberals. Developmentalism, Mehta suggests, is an integral feature of liberalism. Liberal thought identified India's backwardness so imperial rule could be justified by the initiation of endless projects for economic development, social reforms, etc. (Mehta 1999).

By contrast, the conservative Edmund Burke had a harder time accepting British rule of India. Of course Burke did not oppose empire; he argued for good government, not Indian self-government. Yet his was a sharper critique of empire because he saw India in terms of its existing established communities, and he did not want to see them threatened. And unlike liberals who worried about whether India was to be regarded as a nation or just a conglomeration of innumerable castes and tribes, Burke assumed that peoples living in one place for generations had to be regarded as political communities. Most importantly, unlike liberals, Burke never presumed the 'transparency of the unfamiliar' or 'the foreknowledge of other people's destiny' (Mehta 1999: 192). He did not 'rely on the strategy of aligning societies that are in fact contemporaneous ... along a temporal grid that moves them 'backward' on account of their difference, so as to give lineal coherence to the idea of progress' (Mehta 1999: 41). Indian bureaucrats will do well to take more seriously the histories of the peoples of the Northeast, and give up the assumption of foreknowledge of their destinies that is implied in the talk about bringing development and modernization to remote tribal peoples.

Recognizing the Northeast as a region where the people have histories, of course, does not mean that the region's history will have ready answers to its contemporary problems. But taking history seriously can have important implications. There is the example of the negotiations between Naga leaders and the Government of India where both sides have failed to arrive at a common ground—the Naga idea of a Nagalim or greater Nagaland, is a source of anxiety to a number of neighbouring Northeastern states, especially Manipur.

It may be tempting to think of the issue entirely in terms of ethnic anxieties. But as I will elaborate in Chapter 5, the region has more interconnections and continuities than today's obsession with ethnic identities might suggest. In the nineteenth century, James Johnstone, a colonial official, described political rituals of the Manipuri kings that were remarkably inclusive. The investiture ceremony of the Manipuri kings required the queen to appear in Naga costume; the royal palace always had a house built in Naga style; and when the king travelled he was attended on by two or three Manipuris with Naga arms, dress and ornaments (Johnstone, 1971: 83). The interconnections between Nagas and Manipuris suggested by these practices and rituals may not provide ready answers to resolve the Nagalim issue today. But one thing is clear: rather than secretive deals between Indian bureaucrats and leaders of one or the other insurgent organizations, these questions are best addressed by creating a space in which all the stakeholders in these conflicts can express their views and aspirations—discussions that first and foremost, take into confidence the peoples of the region.

Rather than trying to contain insurgencies, India needs to raise its expectations of what is possible. Even the most protracted of armed civil conflicts in the world—Northern Ireland—is today closer to resolution than ever before. Establishing a blue-ribbon committee to examine the accomplishments and failures of the last five decades of India's strategy and tactics of counter-insurgency in the Northeast may be a good place to start from. The Armed Forces Special Powers Act is almost as old as the Indian Constitution. It was introduced to deal with the Naga insurgency. Four-and-a-half decades later, not only has peace remained elusive in Nagaland, insurgencies enveloped formerly peaceful parts of the Northeast. The extension of this law to the entire region has compromised Indian democracy in the Northeast in unacceptable ways.

Surely half-a-century is a long enough period for honest stocktaking and reassessment of goals and achievements. Until such rethinking takes place, withdrawing the AFSPA, appointing as governors those whose accomplishments are in fields other than national security, and removing the military presence from historical monuments such as the Kangla Fort and the INA memorial, will be powerful symbols to indicate the desire for a new beginning that would shape a fully democratic Northeast in the 21st century.

But these are civil measures substantially at variance with the 'military-economic' solution that currently finds favour. The question that remains is whether an honest review of options is at all possible given the extra-ordinary influence of the security establishment and the interests it has acquired in the 'disturbed' Northeast. The appointment of retired military governors and security officials to oversee the dilution of civil political authority seems to suggest that democratic alternatives will not merit even passing consideration. After all, if a lasting peace is restored in the region, generals will no longer be governors. And there will be no need for so many brigadiers.

Notes

[1] The original version of this chapter was published as the cover essay of an issue of *Himal* (Kathmandu). Reprinted with the permission of Himal Media from Sanjib Baruah, 'Generals as Governors: The Parallel Political Systems of Northeast India', *Himal South Asian* 14 (6), June 2001: 10–20. This version has been slightly expanded and revised.

[2] Even Arunachal Pradesh and Mizoram, as I have explained in Chapter 1, are not free from insurgencies with roots outside the state.

[3] But see the discussion under the section 'Durable Disorder' in Chapter 1.

SECTION III

Past and Present

4

Clash of Resource Use Regimes
in Colonial Assam
A Nineteenth Century Puzzle Revisited[1]

In the latter part of the nineteenth century, the British colonial government in Assam tried to change the land titles of Assamese peasants from annual leases to decennial leases.[2] The colonial government's efforts at regularizing the land rights of peasants to their land were also the time when the foundation of the tea industry in Assam was laid. Assam today is one of the world's leading tea-producing regions—and tea occupies much of Assam's best agricultural lands. In 1868, the Land Revenue Regulation sought to make it compulsory for government *ryots*—i.e. owner cultivators—to take ten-year renewable leases on their land. Annual titles were to be given only in the *firingoti* or *chapori mahals* (land revenue belts on the flood plains demarcated for seasonal cultivation) or on land cultivated by tribal peasants on the northern edges of the valley. The goal was to get the Assamese peasantry 'accustomed' to the virtues of exclusively settled agriculture and to relieve officers from the 'useless labour' of writing hundreds and thousands of land titles every year (Government of Assam 1882: 6).

But the colonial authorities faced an unexpected hurdle. The Assamese peasants were not interested in long-term titles. They mostly abandoned their claim to their land after a single harvest. The process of converting annual land titles to decennial titles therefore was painfully slow. The process began in 1868; but by 1875–6 only 8,000 acres were under decennial titles, while 1.3 million acres of land remained under annual titles. The next year the area under decennial titles went up slightly to 10,000 acres, but land under annual title also went up (Government of Assam 1878: 19). The report of 1889–90 noted that even after ten years the Assamese peasant was yet to 'appreciate the advantages of the periodic lease, and makes no effort to obtain it in place of the annual lease.' (Government of Assam 1890: 13). The situation did not change significantly for nearly three more decades.

Why did Assamese peasants resist long-term titles to land, despite what to us would seem to be its obvious advantages? This puzzle provides an important clue to understanding the impact of the colonial land settlement project on Assam and of the larger meaning of colonial rule in terms of the shifts in the global geography of resource use. These consequences are lost both in the early colonial discourse of civilization and primitivism and the latter-day discourse of economic development. While tea cultivation or commercial agriculture introduced by settlers from outside may have brought 'economic development' to the land called Assam, whether it benefited the people who had historically called Assam their home is more problematical. Indeed the loss of access to resources restricted their gathering activities, which lowered household consumption and shook the foundation of the pre-colonial socio-economic formations. The ostensible purpose of land settlement—probably the most important administrative enterprise of the colonial administration in Assam—was to record pre-existing land rights not only of peasants, but of others, including that of *Xatras* (Assamese Vaishnavite Hindu monasteries) and other religious establishments. But the project of protecting existing land rights was shaped by a whole host of ideas that the British brought with them. Among them were their ideas about 'civilization': a dense population and industry, for instance, were seen as markers of civilization and, settled agriculture belonged to a higher plane than shifting agriculture or hunting and gathering. These ideas shaped the land settlement project in practice, and were key to determining the winners and losers of the project.

The other side of recording land rights was the colonial state's assertion of claims to the vast majority of land in which it assumed, no private rights ever existed. That was the land on which the colonial state made the most far-reaching of decisions. Among them were lands declared wastelands enabling their allocation to tea plantations, or surplus land in which to settle peasant immigrants from more crowded parts of the subcontinent. Even though large amounts of land were also set aside as reserve forests or grazing lands; most of them were later either reclassified as ordinary cultivable land or, in practice, the state—both in colonial and post-colonial times—was ineffective in preserving them as forests or as grazing lands for long.

What were Assamese Peasants up to?

Early colonial officials believed that the reason the Assamese peasants were not interested in land titles beyond a single harvest was because they practised land fallowing on a large scale. But even then the lack of interest of Assamese peasants in acquiring long-term land titles still intrigued colonial officials. Why should a peasant give up his ownership rights to the land that he keeps fallow? The length of time that he left a land fallow also seemed inordinately long. Even more intriguing was the fact that when land left fallow was cultivated again; it was rarely reclaimed by its previous cultivators.

The Land Revenue Administration report for 1884–5 tried to solve the puzzle by making a distinction between two parts of an Assamese peasant's agricultural land: that which he cultivates every year and that which he cultivates occasionally. The Assamese peasant practised very little land fallow in the lands that he cultivates 'permanently' and he practises fallowing on 'an enormous scale' when it comes to his 'fluctuating cultivation,' where he 'leaves the land to go into jungle for years' (Government of Assam 1885: 28). Another official, however, expressed his doubts on whether fallowing practices had anything to do with the Assamese peasant's lack of interest in long-term land titles. After all, the cultivator rarely returns to the original land at the end of the so-called fallowing period. 'Fallowing in the ordinary sense of the term,' he wrote:

... is not ordinarily practised by the Assam cultivator; that is to say, the cultivator does not retain his holding, and, when the land ceases to yield abundantly, and without imposing on him the labour of eradicating the weeds which became prolific after the second or third year of cultivation, he throws up the land altogether and goes in search of fresh soil; in the majority of cases he never contemplates a return to what he has resigned, though others may doubtless take the land up again at some future day, the period after which such land is retaken being longer or shorter as there is or is not plenty of waste virgin so available in the neighbourhood.

In some areas such as Lakhimpur, he pointed out; land was not reclaimed for as long as twenty years, even though in other areas it was shorter. But in all these cases, he concluded, 'it is entirely misleading' to refer to land that is not cultivated for some period and to which a cultivator abandons his ownership claim as a 'period of fallow' or to say that in Lakhimpur the 'cultivator fallows on an enormous scale, as do most uncivilized (sic) tribes' (cited in Government of Assam 1885: 4).

Habits of Abundance? A Dissenting Colonial Memo

A dissenting administrative memo by Colonel Henry Hopkinson in 1872 was closer to figuring out why Assamese peasants were reluctant to accept long-term land titles. The key, he suggested, was the land abundance of Assam, which made possible for a peasant to find fresh soil with little difficulty. In such a situation long-term land titles were little more than an encumbrance: an unnecessary commitment to pay taxes on land even when it is not being cultivated.

In most parts of the world the first hurdle that a cultivator confronts is to find land. But in Assam the difficulty is 'reduced to the minimum.' Here, wrote Hopkinson, 'if land is not absolutely so free and common to all as air, still it has hardly any intrinsic value.' In such conditions, Hopkinson suggested, it is more appropriate to think of what an owner-cultivator pays the government in exchange for his land title as license fee and not as a tax or revenue on land. It is a license 'to extract a certain quantity of produce' out of a plot of land. It is a 'license to labour, so that our land tax is really a tax on labour and the labourer's stock and implements required in cultivation.' It is not surprising therefore that a peasant would be disinclined to accept a decennial land title because that amounted to a ten-year commitment of his and his family's labour and capital. He would not want to make such a commitment because he cannot be sure how long he will be able to put in the necessary labour to cultivate that land. He knows that he can always get land when he wants. But what he is not sure of is whether his family or his cattle will survive illnesses or, in cases where he has debts, whether he can pay them back. In such circumstances why would he 'entangle himself in a covenant which, while only confirming what he is already secure of, will add to his embarrassment if those conditions of his undertaking which are variable and uncertain turn out unfavourably'?

Hopkinson believed that the source of the confusion was the tendency of colonial administrators to think that what they saw in the rest of India is true of Assam as well. He made his point rather colourfully. 'Whether the Assamese of the Valley are Hindus in their manners, customs, and institutions,' he wrote, 'might furnish the subject of an agreeable essay.' Much could be said on both sides of the question. But even if they are, he said, he did 'not see why they should have accepted their agricultural polity from the Hindus also.' Referring to ideas popular at that time about Assamese Hindus being migrants from the Indian heartland he said, 'I have an idea that an emigrant from Surrey would not take his agricultural polity with him to town' (Hopkinson 1872: 7–8).

Transition between Resource use Regimes

Hopkinson was right. Assam's land abundance indeed provides a clue to the puzzle. But no more than a clue. The Assamese peasant could find and cultivate other lands, but that was only partly a function of the physical fact of land abundance. Also relevant are the prevailing norms of land use. The fact that peasants did not have to pay for new land—either in rent or in price—or even register his use of that land with anyone is a function of local norms of land use. Obviously there was no land market; nor was there private property in our sense of the term. It was generally accepted that the peasant was entitled to that land. If he took the trouble of clearing another plot of jungle land no authority could stop him from doing so. While the colonial administrator concentrated on the agricultural use of these lands, far more important than clearing those lands for purposes of cultivation were their non-agricultural uses in ways that were central to Assam's rural economy. Among them were collecting materials like bamboo or wood used for constructing houses, boats, household implements, mats and baskets; raising silk worms—the foundation of the large indigenous silk industry—as well as collecting animal and vegetable products for household consumption and trade.

British colonial rule has been described as a 'crucial watershed' in the ecological history of India (Gadgil and Guha 1993: 5). Colonial rule enabled the global expansion of the resource base of industrial societies as land and natural resources earlier controlled by gatherer and peasant societies came under the control of new rules of property that created the legal foundation for the industrial mode of resource use (see Gadgil and Guha 1993: 39–53). The effect of the colonial land settlement policy was to incorporate Assam into this new global resource use regime. The major effect of the colonial land settlement project was to eliminate the access to these lands of the shifting cultivators and hunter-gatherers of the Brahmaputra Valley and the surrounding hills. The full effects of the denial of access, however, were experienced only gradually. The behaviour of the Assamese peasant— the initial rejection and subsequent acceptance of decennial leases—reflects the uncertainties of the transition between two regimes of resource use.

The new rules of property provided the legal foundation for the new projects—those that the early colonials thought will bring 'civilization' to Assam and in post-colonial times came to be seen as projects that would bring about development, modernization and progress. Whatever its contribution to 'progress', the colonial land settlement project resulted in significant dispossession of the Assamese peasantry and of the shifting cultivators and hunter-gatherers of the Brahmaputra Valley and the surrounding hills. The shift becomes clear when the new rules of property are contrasted with the old rules of access to resources.

Before Colonial Rule: Land Use Under the Ahom Polity

The foundation of the pre-colonial Ahom economy and polity—the state that had controlled the bulk of the Brahmaputra valley—was a system of corvee labour. Leaving aside a significant portion of the population that were servile—*bondi, beti,* etc. who worked in the fields and the households of the aristocracy and of the religious establishments—the entire non-servile population had to contribute labour to the state. Males in this segment of the population were divided into groups of three or four persons, each called a *paik* and the units called *got.* A paik from each got was obligated to serve the state for three or four months a year in times of peace. They were assigned to public works such as constructing roads, tanks, embankments or to the royal household or the households of the nobility.

The gots in turn were divided into *khels* that consisted of one to five thousand paiks. A khel could be responsible for tasks such as catching and supplying elephants, supplying particular needs of the royal court such as hand-fans and umbrellas. The khel organization extended to some of the surrounding hills as well. Access to lands and forests—well beyond what colonial administrators saw as the family plot—was crucial for this political economy.

Each paik family got free of rent two *puras* (about 2.66 acres) of wetland and another piece of homestead and garden land. This was called their *ga-mati*—literally body-land.[3] In addition, paiks were free to reclaim unculti-vated land. During a paik's time away from his home as contributor of corvee labour, other members of the got looked after the cultivation of his ga mati. During times of war when all paiks of a got could be called for state service, cultivation became the responsibility of women and children.

Despite the change in the rules of access, the Assamese peasantry continued to utilize lands apart from their ga-mati well into the colonial period. This is apparent from economic historian Amalendu Guha's observation on late nineteenth century Assam based on British colonial documents. After distinguishing between the modes of cultivation of Assam in three belts: the flood plains, transplanted rice belt and the submontane belt, Guha describes how the transplanted rice cultivators—the bulk of paiks—also had an interest in the two other belts.

They collected all sorts of materials for making their houses, boats, implements, mats and baskets, from these tracks. At selected spots on these tracts, often several miles away from settled villages, peasants would erect their temporary clusters of huts known as *pam basti* to carry on shifting cultivation of mustard, pulses and *ahu* rice [Guha 1991: 13].

There is a common perception that only 'tribal' peasants were shifting cultivators while what we would now call the ethnic Assamese—both Hindu and Muslim—peasants were settled cultivators. This perception—premised on the notion that whether a community practised settled agriculture or shifting cultivation was a function of its location on the continuum between the 'civilized' and the 'primitive'—has little foundation in the reality of agricultural practices in Assam. Most peasants did some amount of shifting cultivation, apart from using those lands for non-agricultural purposes.

Goals of Land Settlement

The goal of the British land settlement policy was ostensibly to recognize all traditional rights to land and create long-term hereditary and transferable rights in land. But even if one assumes that the colonial authorities had managed to recognize the property rights of all peasant families to their ga mati, this would still have radically restricted the peasants' traditional access to other lands. In making his proposals on the new rules of land settlement Moffatt Mills in 1853, for instance, had this to say on whether the Assamese cultivator had the right to dispose of his land by sale, gift, or by mortgage. He noted that it was 'generally understood' that the cultivator had that right and argued for its recognition. But he noted: 'I would restrict his rights to his paternal acres [i.e., his ga-mati] or to such lands he occupies in his or her own village. He cannot have, and has not, any hereditary rights of occupancy of lands in other villages, which he cultivates one year and throws up the next' (Moffatt Mills 1984: 6). The privileging of land in a peasant's 'native village'—his so-called 'paternal acres'—and his exclusion from lands supposedly outside his 'native village' was obviously a clever device to exclude the peasants from land other than his ga-mati. The idea also anticipates the notion of the self-sufficient Indian village that would later become a part of the repertoire of colonial knowledge of India.

But the ga-mati, as I have said before, was only a small part of the land to which peasant households had access. Peasants had access to surrounding land both for occasional cultivation, to collect fish, fruits, and vegetables and for essential non-agricultural purposes such as collecting house-building material and raw material for basket-weaving, etc. and to raise silkworms. His ga-mati was not the only 'property' from which a family had to make a living. Peasants in pre-colonial Assam were not agricultural specialists—a division of labour that was yet to be created. Therefore even under the best of assumptions—of colonial authorities succeeding in recognising and recording all rights to ga-mati—the new rules of property resulted in enormous dispossession of the Assamese peasantry. Much of the land that he had access to for occasional cultivation or for purposes other than cultivation suddenly became state land that the colonial state could reallocate.

The apparent inability of the Assamese peasant to understand the value of long-term land titles can be understood only with reference to the land-use norms of the old order. In a world where a peasant could cultivate any previously uncultivated land, it made perfect sense that he would not be interested in claiming ten-year rights to land and assume responsibility for paying taxes for it.

Why did Peasants Finally 'Learn?'

From the perspective of colonial officials, the Assamese peasant did eventually 'learn' the value of long-term land titles. It happened during the second and third decades of the twentieth century with the arrival of East Bengali settlers.[4] Officials gave a scientific gloss to this process of what they saw as Assamese peasants 'learning' from their enterprising new neighbours. According to this view Assamese peasants were uninterested in decennial titles because of their misperceptions about land fertility. They had the false perception that land fertility gets exhausted in three or four years. Indeed according to a colonial report, the 'backward people' in the submontane belt were so 'superstitious' that they even moved their homesteads 'on a mere suspicion that a site was getting unhealthy.' It was impossible for the colonial mind to see the social construction of a house as a temporary rather than a permanent place of residence—consistent with the local resource use regime—as anything but a sign of primitive ignorance. According to this view therefore, on seeing the enterprising East Bengali cultivator produce successive harvests in these lands, the Assamese peasant, learnt the scientific truth that 'only adventitious fertility is exhausted, intrinsic fertility still determines yields' (Government of Assam 1928: 10).

But this 'scientific' explanation is hardly persuasive. While we don't know whether indigenous knowledge made a distinction analogous to adventitious fertility and intrinsic fertility, the assumption that people would simply give up their land just because they don't know about different kinds of fertility is unconvincing. A more plausible explanation is that the colonial policy of settling East Bengali cultivators in these so-called uncultivated lands changed the ground reality. Amalendu Guha notes that in the district of Kamrup shifting cultivation (which as I have said before was done by tribal as well as non-tribal peasants) begins to disappear in the early decades of the twentieth century. 'One misses the scene of burning grass jungles as described by Butler.'[5] The new factor that was responsible for the change, he writes, was that immigrants from East Bengal were now settled in the *chapori* belt (Guha 1991: 13)—i.e. the flood plains. With the arrival of the East Bengali peasants and the policy to settle them in belts that the Assamese peasant had traditionally used for shifting cultivation, the most significant feature of the new land regime—the peasant's exclusion from land other than his ga mati—became a fait accompli.

Making Room for Tea: Enclosure in a Colonial Context

The most dramatic aspect of the colonial land settlement project in nineteenth century Assam was the allocation of vast tracts of land to tea plantations. When the viability of the commercial production of tea in Assam became established, according to Percival Griffiths, historian of the Indian tea industry, 'a madness comparable in intensity with that of the South Sea Bubble' hit the London stock exchange as 'normally level-headed financiers and speculators began to scramble wildly for tea shares in tea lands' (Griffiths 1967: 96).

But even prior to that, Assam's land abundance next to the densely populated Indian heartland—and especially more populous Bengal— appeared striking to early British visitors to Assam. Indeed the idea of settling

Assam's 'wastelands' with Englishmen with capital was mooted as early as 1833—seven years after the British conquest of Assam, and even before the prospects of tea production in Assam were established. To Francis Jenkins, one of the earliest colonial officials in charge of making land policy in Assam, it appeared that a scheme of colonization 'offered a better prospect for the speedy realization of improvements than any measure that could be adopted in the present ignorant and demoralized state of native inhabitants.' He proposed that a class of European planters with capital be encouraged to settle in Assam and produce sugarcane, indigo and other plantation crops. 'To obtain the full advantage that could accrue from European settlers,' he proposed that lands should be 'absolutely unencumbered by tenants and sub-tenants' (cited in Guha 1991: 149).

The Waste Land Grant Rule of 1838 was the earlier law under which land was given to tea plantations. The conditions of the grants were very liberal. For instance, one-fourth of the area was perpetually revenue-free and no revenue had to be paid on the remaining land for twenty years if it was under forest and for fewer years if it was under reeds and high grass. The land revenue rates to be paid after the expiry of that period was very low—lower compared to even what Assam's impoverished peasant cultivators were paying (Gangopadhyay 1990: 134).

Moffatt Mills in his magisterial report on Assam in 1853 recommended even more liberal terms. 'When land is taken up by speculators, involving outlay and a distant return,' he said, 'the terms cannot be too liberal.' He noted that European speculators had not found the existing terms attractive enough and that 'nothing but the absolute rent-free tenure of the land will induce people to bring English capital largely into the market.' The goal of wasteland grants, he said, should not be immediate returns in terms of government revenue, 'the object is to clear those vast tracts of forest, and promote immigration' (Moffatt Mills 1984: 17). In 1854 new rules were introduced to give ninety-nine years' lease and to raise the minimum area of a grant to five hundred acres. The new rules stimulated a land rush, though the terms were even further liberalized in subsequent years (Guha 1991: 167). Some of the tea planters in Assam became not only 'the biggest landlords in the countryside they dominated, but they paid the lowest average rates per acre of holdings' (Guha 1977: 15).

Only a small part of the land acquired by tea gardens, however, was actually used for growing tea. For instance, the Assam Company founded in 1839 and the first Indian tea company had the grant of an area of 33,

665 acres under the Waste Land Grant Rules of 1838. In 1859 the Company had planted tea in only about 4000 acres of land (Gangopadhyay 1990: 132–3). In the 1870s the acreage under tea was only eight to ten per cent of the area occupied by tea gardens and the percentage was about 29 per cent when British rule ended in 1947 (Guha 1991: 191). Tea planters even settled some tenant cultivators on their lands to ensure temporary labour supply during peak seasons (Guha 1977: 15).

Whose Land was it Anyway?

By 1901, tea gardens enclosed 'some one-fourth of the total settled area (or five per cent of the total area) of Assam proper under their exclusive property rights' (Guha 1991: 191). The disruption that the land grab caused to the old order was anything but subtle. Even communication between villages was disrupted as parts of public roads were fenced off and villagers were denied access. This included ancient public roads like Rajgarh Ali, Lahdoi Garh, Kharikotia Road, and Raja Ali. Even many weekly bazaars and *hats*, where the villagers brought their farm products for sale came within the limits of tea gardens. Planters exercised exclusive control over these markets. Indeed the right of way through tea plantations became a major issue during the anti-colonial struggle in the twentieth century. For in many parts of Assam, a villager had to walk many miles around tea gardens. The use of roads that went through the gardens was restricted. For instance, Indians could not go through a tea plantation on a bicycle or on horseback, or with an umbrella open. When the automobile arrived on the scene there were cases when bullock carts were not allowed on these roads for they might damage the roads and make them unfit for the automobile. During the Non-Cooperation movement of the 1930s tea planters sought to prohibit the Indian National Congress activists from entering the plantations (Guha 1977: 134–5).

'As one mode of resource use comes into contact with another mode organized on very different social and ecological principles,' writes ecological historians Gadgil and Guha, 'we expect the occurrence of substantial social strife. In fact the clash of two modes has invariably resulted in massive bursts of violent and sometimes genocidal conflict' (Gadgil and Guha 1993: 53). The violent encounter between the Nagas and the British—a process that colonial rulers described as the 'pacification' of the Naga 'savages'—can be best understood in these terms. There were ten 'punitive expeditions' between 1835 and 1851. After a period of relative quiet, there was an uprising by Angami Nagas in 1879, when they seized the British military base in Kohima, leading to the last major military encounter.

The land grab by tea planters had profoundly disrupted the hunting and gathering economies of the Naga peoples who live on the hills that border the Assamese plains where the first generation of tea plantations were established. The decision in 1873 to introduce the Inner Line, which, in some parts of the Northeast continues till this day, was partly a response to the reckless expansion of British entrepreneurs into new lands, which threatened British political relations with the hill tribes. Among the British adventurers were tea planters as well as speculators in raw rubber who tried to enclose as many tracts of new land as they could. The Bengal Eastern Frontier Regulation of 1873 therefore empowered the colonial government to 'prescribe, and from time to time, alter by notification ... a line to be called the Inner Line.' The line was drawn along the foothills and the peoples living beyond this line were supposedly 'left to manage their own affairs with only such interference on the part of the frontier officers in their political capacity as may be considered advisable with the view to establishing a personal influence for good among the chiefs and the tribes' (Mackenzie 1979: 89–90).

The colonial government laid down rules to bring 'under more stringent control the commercial relations of our own subjects with the frontier tribes living on the borders of our jurisdiction.' These rules governed activities by British subjects beyond the Inner Line; no British subject or foreign citizens could cross the line without a license, and trade or possession of land beyond the line was severely restricted (Mackenzie 1979: 55). The following account of the process of drawing the Inner Line illustrates the substantive role of the expansion of tea plantations in the conflicts between the Nagas and the British:

The question of laying down of the Inner Line for the Luckimpore [Lakhimpur] district generally was taken up by the Chief Commissioner of Assam in 1875. South of Jeipur it was found necessary to enclose within it a tract of country, which had not up to that time been subject to the formal and plenary authority of the district officer. The object of enclosing the tract was to bring into the ordinary jurisdiction the tea gardens of Namsang, Taurack and Hukanjuri [Xukanjuri]. For the Taurack Garden compensation was paid to Mithonia Nagas. For the Hukanjuri and Namsang Gardens similar compensation was paid to the Namsang and Borduwaria Nagas. The sums thus paid are of course recovered as revenue from the occupiers of the gardens (Mackenzie 1979: 89).

The violence of the Naga-British encounter and the tensions in the relations between tea plantations and Assamese society during the anti-British struggle, however, were only some of the early consequences of the new property regime imposed by the colonial land settlement project. The fall-out of this shift continued to be a sub-text in the political instability in the area till this day; notably the insurgencies that blame the Indian government for its economic underdevelopment and indeed sometimes of treating the area as a colony, the perennial tensions between immigrants and the indigenous peoples and unrest among 'tribal' people such as the Bodos and Karbis whose reliance on shifting cultivation had historically been more pronounced than that of the rest of the population. Indeed one reason why the economic grievances of the Bodo people did not come to a head till the 1980s was that for nearly a century many of them were able to move around cultivating lands formally designated as protected forests. Only in the 1980s, following Assam's long campaign against 'foreigners' (see Baruah 1999: 135–43), these most indigenous of Assam's inhabitants came to be treated as encroachers by the Assam government—provoking the anger of many Bodo activists.

Resource Use Under the New Owners

Like their shifting cultivator predecessors, the major new owners of Assam's vast land and forest resources, the tea planters also found the extraordinary fertility of land cleared of forests very attractive. In a 'standard instruction' William Roberts of the Jorehaut Tea Company, for instance, recommended to new planters the superiority of forest lands. 'Forest lands,' he said are 'to be preferred to grass lands, in consequence of the fine rich deposits of decayed vegetable matter which are found on the surface, and which stimulates the lusty growth of the young tea plants, better than any other description of manure.' Given the large tracts of land available to them many planters had a choice in the matter of which lands to use for growing tea. Even though the indentured labour recruited by the tea planters was not exactly expensive, the instruction made the case for forestlands on grounds of costs well. 'The cost of clearing forest land and preparing it for sowing,' said the instruction, 'is about the same as that attending the preparation of grass land' since in order to remove the grass roots, those lands had to be deeply trenched or hoed. Roberts then proceeded to detail the 'standard practice' for clearing forestlands for tea. One can see why the new owners of these lands would be proud of their 'civilized' methods of cutting down forests compared to the 'slash and burn' ways of their shifting cultivating predecessors.

The usual practice of making a forest clearance is by cutting down and burning the small-sized trees and under-wood, and only 'ringing' the large trees about five feet from the ground, in order that a certain amount of shade may be afforded to the young plants; and in the course of about three years these large trees decay and fall down without, however, doing much injury to the tea plants beyond lying in inconvenient positions .... It is strongly recommended that the clearance should be thoroughly completed in the first instance, by felling all the forest trees, cutting the stems close to the ground, by means of either an American axe, or a cross-cut saw, having a rope attached to the upper part of the tree, in order to direct it in the falling.

Of course, unlike their shifting cultivating predecessors who cleared only small amounts of land for cultivating for short periods before returning them to the jungle once again, the deforestation by tea planters was much larger in scale and was permanent. In an era when environmental sensitivity was not seen as a marker of 'civilization,' the first generation of tea planters were even proud of their ability to convert trees into charcoal. Indeed the standard instruction was impressively precise on how to make use of the burnt trees as charcoal:

The whole of the timber can be profitably utilized by cutting the large trees with the smaller lengths, and collecting and packing them properly into smaller branches, in large heaps, say thirty feet in length, fifteen feet in width, and ten feet in height, covering the whole over with small branches, leaves, and clay, and then burning the mass and converting it into charcoal; which can be carted away and stored, either in a godown, or collected in a heap and protected with covering of thatch; where it will remain in good condition for years, or until it is required for manufacturing operations [Roberts 1947: 345–6].

This standard instruction illustrates the ultimate meaning of the project of land settlement in Assam: to shift large amounts of Assam's land and forest resources from the control of the peasantry—both settled and shifting cultivators—and hunter gatherers to the colonial state. The state then reallocated that land; and tea planters were the most significant beneficiaries of this largess.

Returning now to the puzzle, the Assamese peasants' initial reluctance to accept long-term titles was a reflection of the clash between two resource use regimes. Under the pre-colonial local resource use regime, the peasant had access to much of the uncultivated or seasonally cultivated land both for agricultural and non-agricultural purposes. That access was the foundation of Assam's pre-colonial economic formations. The effect of the colonial land settlement project was to incorporate Assam into the emerging global resource use regime. As a consequence, land and resources controlled by the hunter-gatherer and peasant societies of the region under local resource use regimes came under the control of a new industrial and global regime of resource use. The rhetoric of civilization and primitivism that marked colonial theory and practice, only served to obscure this large-scale transfer of resources. In Assam one of the most dramatic examples of this shift was the transfer of large amounts of land from the control of settled and shifting cultivators and hunter-gatherers to tea plantations. The initial reluctance of the Assamese peasants to accept long-term land titles can be explained by habits formed by the pre-colonial resource use regime. Once the nature of their dispossession became a ground reality as the effects of the colonial land settlement project slowly became apparent, Assamese peasants began accepting the virtues of long-term titles—a value that makes sense only under the hegemony of the new resource use regime.

Notes

[1] This chapter originally appeared in *Journal of Peasant Studies*. Reprinted by permission of Frank Cass Publishers from Sanjib Baruah, 'Clash of Resource Use Regimes in Colonial Assam: A Nineteenth Century Puzzle Revisited', *Journal of Peasant Studies* 28 (3) April 2001: 109–24 © Frank Cass Publishers 2001.

[2] Most of Assam was under *ryotwari* and not *zamindari* settlement. In a formal sense, ryotwari settlements were land-revenue arrangements directly between the colonial state and the owner-cultivator (ryot), while zamindari settlements were land-revenue arrangements between an intermediary class of landlords (zamindars) and the state. In practice, however, complex patterns of tenancy developed under both arrangements.

[3] One British official, Captain Brodie, believed that the right to ga-mati was vested in the khel and that on the death of a paik the land reverted to the khel. Moffatt Mills, however, found that Brodie's judgement was not shared by other British officials. Mills himself concluded that ga-mati was 'the property of the state and neither hereditary, nor transferable.' Moffatt Mills [1984]. Moffatt Mills's report shaped colonial land policies.

[4] On the British colonial view of Assam as a land frontier and the history of immigration to Assam—including the settlement of East Bengali peasants in Assam—and its relationship to the political unrest in Assam, see Baruah (1999).

[5] The reference to Butler in Guha's account is to Captain John Butler. His best-known work is Butler (1978).

5

Confronting Constructionism
Ending the Naga War[1]

The Naga Conflict and a Faltering Peace Process

Since 1997, the Government of India and the leading political organization fighting for Naga independence—a faction of the National Socialist Council of Nagalim led by Thuingaleh Muivah and Isaak Chisi Swu [hereafter NSCN-IM]—have had a cease fire and there have been intermittent talks to end one of the world's least known longest-running and bloody armed conflicts that has cost thousands of lives.[2] The Naga conflict began with India's independence in 1947: Naga leaders rejected the idea that their land, which was under a special dispensation during British colonial rule, could simply pass on to Indian hands at the end of British colonial rule. In the 1950s it turned into an armed conflict. In 1963, the Government of India created the state of Nagaland as a full-fledged state of the Indian Union. The territory of the new state coincided with what was then the centrally administered Naga Hills Tuensang Area. As an administrative unit the Naga Hills Tuensang Area was formed in 1957, bringing together the Naga Hills district of Assam and the Tuensang district of North East Frontier Agency. Since the formation of Nagaland many Nagas have participated in the Indian political process while the independentists have remained opposed to it. But the line between the independentist and the integrationist factions in Naga politics have remained blurred, and the armed conflict has persisted with two interruptions prior to the current one: a failed peace process in the mid 1960s and an accord signed in 1975—between the Indian government and a few individual leaders—which was interpreted as a sell-out by many and as a result, it re-energized the rebellion.

The Nagas live on both sides of the hilly border region between India and Burma—in the northeast Indian states of Nagaland, Manipur, Assam, and Arunachal Pradesh—and in Burma's Sagaing Division and Kachin state. Their total population is estimated to be between three-and-a-half and four million people. There are no precise official figures, not only because there is no good census data on Burma, but also because the Indian census data do not correspond with the category 'Naga' and, as we shall see, whether or not some of these groups are to be considered Naga is a highly contested matter. The Indian census uses the names of particular tribes (communities)[3] and not the category Naga, which is an amalgamation of various tribes; the official names of only some tribes have the appelative Naga attached to them. For instance, Manipur has a large population that considers itself Naga. But the largest of the group, the Tangkhuls—the tribe to which rebel leader T. Muivah belongs—is simply referred to as Tangkhuls in Indian census. Among the Naga tribes of Manipur, only the Katcha Naga has the name 'Naga' appended to their official name. Yet the pan-Naga organization, Naga Hoho lists 16 tribes in Manipur as Naga. Since 'Naga' is not a linguistic category, the census data on language are not very helpful. Nagas speak as many as thirty different languages that linguists classify as falling into 'at least two, and possibly several, completely distinct branches of Tibeto-Burman' (Burling 2003: 172).

The expression Naga, wrote John Henry Hutton in his introduction to J.P. Mills' classic ethnographic account of the Lhota Nagas published in 1922, 'is useful as an arbitrary term to denote the tribes living in certain parts of the Assam hills, which may be roughly defined as bounded by the Hokong valley in the north-east, the plain of the Brahmaputra Valley to the north-west, of Cachar to the south-west and of the Chindwin to east. The south of the Manipur Valley roughly marks the point of contact between the "Naga" tribes and the very much more closely interrelated group of Kuki tribes—Thao, Lushei, Chin, etc.' (Hutton 1922: xv–xvi). The website of the NSCN-IM quotes the passage from Hutton to introduce the Naga people and their territories without the qualifications that Hutton had added to his formulation more than eighty years ago. Rather than calling the expression Naga a 'useful' but 'arbitrary' term, and saying that they lived 'in certain parts of the Assam hills' that Hutton ventured to describe only 'roughly', the NSCN-IM's website makes Hutton sound very precise about the Nagas and their lands. 'Mr Hutton defines the land of the Naga people thus', it says, and then it goes on to describe 'the area inhabited by the Naga tribes' quoting Hutton. Indeed the quotation forms part of a paragraph that begins with a precise geographical description of the territory belonging to, what the NSCN-IM calls the Naga Nation:

Nagaland (Nagalim) has always been a sovereign nation occupying a compact area of 120,000 sq. km of the Patkai Range in between the longitude 93º E and 97º E and the latitude 23.5º N and 28.3º N. It lies at the tri-junction of China, India and Burma. Nagalim, without the knowledge and consent of the Naga people, was apportioned between India and Burma after their respective declaration of independence. The part, which India illegally claims is subdivided and placed under four different administrative units, viz., Assam, Arunachal Pradesh, Manipur and Nagaland states. The eastern part, which Burma unlawfully claims, is placed under two administrative units, viz., Kachin State and Sagaing Division (formerly known as the Naga Hills). Nagalim, however, transcends all these arbitrary demarcations of boundary (NSCN-IM 2002).

All Nagas may not fully share this view of Naga history and territoriality. Yet there is little doubt that in the eight decades since Hutton wrote his essay Nagas have developed a strong sense of themselves as a collectivity. Most students of ethnic and national conflicts are familiar with the tension between the constructivist understanding of identities among most contemporary theorists and the practice of nationalists or ethnic activists who engage in the construction of such identities (Suny 2001). While constructivism is the common sense of contemporary theorists of ethno-nationalism, when people talk about their own identities, they are unlikely to include a sense of the 'historical construction or provisionality' about them (Suny 2001: 6). Instead they assume that the identities of today have been fixed and bounded since time immemorial.

Confronting the constructivism that these days, theorists of nationalism typically emphasize and its practioners deny is at the core of what needs to be done to save the faltering Naga peace process today. Whether or not a large segment of the tribes of Manipur are Nagas has become a highly charged issue. Arguably, in matters of identity the only thing that should matter is how a group itself wishes to be known and there is little doubt that most of the communities in question consider themselves Nagas. But the question is not merely whether the Tangkhuls and fifteen other communities of Manipur that consider themselves Naga should be recognized as Naga, it is complicated by the territorial politics in which the Naga politics of recognition is embedded. The goal of creating a single political unit out of all Naga-inhabited areas puts the Naga project of nationhood in collision course with a parallel Manipuri project.

Indeed the issue is so sensitive that until June 2001, the Indian government left the territorial scope of the 1997 ceasefire deliberately vague. Since the NSCN-IM is active in Manipur and other parts of the Northeast, apart from the state of Nagaland, it would have made sense for the ceasefire to apply to all those areas. But given the sub-text that could be read into the territorial scope of the ceasefire, it was not that simple. The government and the NSCN-IM took conflicting positions on whether the ceasefire held only in the state of Nagaland or in other parts of the Northeast, and the Indian government's public statements were contradictory. Eventually things came to a head when the NSCN-IM insisted on a clarification and in June 2001, a joint statement confirmed that the ceasefire was 'between the Government of India and the NSCN-IM as two entities without territorial limits'. The announcement led to a veritable political explosion in Manipur and significant expression of anger in the other affected states. Seeking guarantees from the Indian government that Manipur's territorial integrity would not be sacrificed in the altar of Naga peace has now become a major theme in Manipuri politics. In order to take the peace process further it is now essential to directly address that concern.

The politics of recognition is often an underlying theme in ethno-national conflicts. Identities, as Charles Taylor puts it, are 'partly shaped by recognition or its absence, often by the misrecognition of others' (Taylor 1994: 25). Since recognition or misrecognition causes harm, groups seeking recognition, whether in the form of the demand for self-government or for cultural rights deserve our sympathy. But projects about recognition are also simultaneously projects that involve constructing identities. Thus in our era, the projects of nationhood frequently rely on censuses and other modern forms of enumeration and classification and a modern technology of representation—the map—in order to connect territoriality and collective selfhood (see Winichakul 1994). The notion of territorially rooted collectivities living in their supposedly traditional national homelands relies on a very different spatial discourse than the one of overlapping frontiers and hierarchical polities that precedes it. In Northeast India, I would argue, the historical relations between hill peoples and the lowland states had an especially complex spatial, cultural, and political dynamic. As a result there is a serious collision between competing projects of identity assertion today (see Chapter 9). Only a constructivist understanding of identities can make promoters and supporters of such projects aware of the dangers of these colliding projects. Even when the rhetoric of identity projects is civic and pluralistic, such projects can be on a disastrous road to ethnic violence and ethnic cleansing unless they confront their constructedness.

The Naga desire for a homeland that would bring together all Nagas into one political unit can come into being only at the expense of Manipur, as well as Assam and Arunachal Pradesh. But if the summer of 2001 is any guide, another phase of bloody ethnic conflict may not be far off and it is inconceivable that a solution to the Naga conflict on these lines can be found in the face of the opposition in the region. Key to a political settlement is the recognition on the part of all parties that there is an inherent crisis of territoriality in northeast India. Such recognition, of course, will have to occur within a framework of a process that the Nagas can see as reconciliation, among themselves, with their neighbours and with the Indian government.

Strange Multiplicity: Hill Peoples and Lowland States[4]

In order to understand the collision between the Naga and the Manipuri projects, it is necessary to consider the relatively recent history of a profound transformation of identities and of political ideas and structures in the region. The Naga hills, where a multiplicity of cultural forms had historically reigned supreme are best seen as, what James C. Scott terms, a non-state space—an 'illegible space' from the perspective of the states in the lowlands.[5] Scott's argument, developed in the context of Southeast Asia is eminently applicable to northeast India—a region that is an extension of Southeast Asia in terms of this dynamic of large groups of culturally diverse minority hill peoples living in uneasy coexistence with culturally different neighbours in the lowlands. The ethnic landscape of the hills, writes Scott, has always confused outsiders—states as well as ethnographers. The taxonomies about the hill peoples have been almost always wrong, groups identified as distinct were later found to be not 'uniform, coherent, or stable through time'. The ethnic landscape has had a 'bewildering and intercalated 'gradients' of cultural traits'. Whether it was linguistic practice, dress, rituals, diet or body decoration, neat boundary lines had been impossible to draw. Tri-lingualism, for example, is fairly common (Scott 2000: 21–2). Thus in the case of the Nagas, ethnographers and missionaries engaged in what Julian Jacobs and his colleagues describe as a struggle 'to make sense of the ethnographic chaos they perceived around them: hundreds, if not thousands, of small villages seemed to be somewhat similar to each other but also very different, by no means always sharing the same customs, political system, art or even language' (Jacobs *et al.*, 1990: 23).

Such an unfamiliar and confusing ethnic landscape, Scott suggests, fits well with slash and burn agriculture—the common mode of livelihood in these hills—which means dispersed and mobile populations that could not be captured for corvee labour and military service by the labour-starved states of the plains; nor could tax-collectors monitor either the number of potential subjects or their holdings and income. It is from the perspective of the surveillance systems of states that the ethnic landscape of the hills appears so non-transparent. Of course, not all hill peoples had been shifting cultivators, just as the lowlanders were not all exclusively settled agriculturalists. The Angami Nagas, for instance, are well known for having transformed steep hills into rice fields through terracing and irrigation. Nevertheless, it is hardly surprising that sedentarization, fixing such population in space—'in settlements in which they can be easily monitored'—has been the state project par-excellence and why the state, in Scott's words, have always been the 'enemy of the people who move around' (Scott 2000: 2).

At the same time the non-state spaces in the hills and the state spaces in the lowlands had been anything but separate. Indeed the categories 'hill tribes' and 'valley peoples', says Scott, are 'leaky vessels'. People had continually moved from the hills to the plains and from the plains to the hills. Since manpower was always in short supply, wars in this region were not about territory, but about capturing slaves. If wars produced movements in either direction, the attractions of commerce and what the lowlanders call civilization may have generated a flow of hill peoples downwards. On the other hand, the extortionist labour demands of the lowland states and, the vulnerability of wet-rice cultivation to crop failure, epidemics, and famines produced flight to the hills where there were more subsistence alternatives. While in other parts of the world, such movements may have produced broader cultural formations, here the 'lived essentialism' between hill 'tribes' and valley civilizations—their stereotypes about each other— remained powerful organizer of peoples lives and thoughts. The cultural distance between lowlanders and highlanders were thus reproduced over time, even though this has always been a continuum rather than a sharp line of demarcation (Scott 2000: 3–4).

Northeast India came under the control as the British East India Company in 1826, at the end of the Anglo-Burmese war, when, according to the Yandabo Treaty, the king of Ava (Burma) renounced 'all claims upon' and agreed to 'abstain from all future interferences with, the principality of Assam and its dependencies, and also with the contiguous petty states of Cachar and Jyntea (Jaintia)' and to recognize British-supported Gambhir Singh as the king of Manipur (Bose 1979: 61–2). When the lands in the valleys and the foothills were found suitable for the large-scale commercial production of tea, a mad scramble for land—by entrepreneurs and speculators alike—followed, and the British came in direct confrontation with the Nagas. The land grab profoundly disrupted the hunting and gathering activities and the exchange networks of the Naga people. The Nagas resisted the land grab with numerous raids on the newly established tea plantations and other valley settlements, and the British responded with relentless brutality. The Naga-British encounter was one of the most violent chapters in the history of British conquest of the sub-continent. There were ten violent 'punitive expeditions' against Nagas between 1835 and 1851. After a period of relative quiet, there was an uprising by Angami Nagas in 1879, when they seized the British military base in Kohima, leading to the last major military encounter.

The lowland states and principalities that became part of the British East India Company at the end of the Anglo-Burmese war eventually all became territories of British India. Manipur retained its status as a kingdom under British protection, even though its autonomy eroded over time and Manipuri kings were constantly anxious about the possibility of direct annexation. In their early encounter colonial officials recognized the complex relationship between the Nagas and the lowland states. An early colonial pronouncement described them as having been under the authority of the lowland states, and the treaty with the Burmese, according to this understanding, had made the British successor to those relationships. 'The wild tribes who inhabit the southern slopes of those ranges are subject to Burmah (Burma) and Manipur', said the pronouncement, and 'those who inhabit the northern slopes are subject to the British government' (cited in Mackenzie 2001: 119). Among those Nagas, early colonial officials observed that those occupying the low hills were at times 'claimed' as subjects by the Tai-Ahom state of Assam. The Ahom king Purandar Singha 'asserted successfully his right to share with the Nagas the produce of the salt manufacturing of the low hills. The hill chiefs, when the Native Government was strong, came down annually bringing gifts that may perhaps have been considered a tribute .... (I)t is certain that several of the chiefs had received grants of *khats* or lands, and of *bheels* or fishing waters on the plains and enjoyed assignment of paiks (corvee labour) like the ordinary Assamese nobility' (Mackenzie 2001: 91).

Over the southern parts of the Naga Hills, the period immediately following the conquest, 'it came to be supposed in a general kind of way that Manipur exercised some sort of authority' (Mackenzie 2001: 102). Since the Government was not prepared to take over the Naga country, it was 'inclined to regard the Manipuris as the de facto masters of the hills'. Only in 1837, after the Company rejected the policy of 'making over to Manipur fresh tracts of mountain country for conquest or management', a European officer was ordered to occupy a post in Naga country (Mackenzie 2001: 103–4). The hills of Manipur, like those of the rest of today's northeast India, however, remained much less administered than the plains through much of the colonial period. The weak presence of the state is a major factor in the outbreak of the Naga rebellion.

Initially when the British came in direct contact with the Nagas in the course of their expeditions, they were met with many surprises about the workings of the Naga polities and their relationship with the lowland states. First, any notion of establishing treaty-like relationship with the Nagas had to be given up; for their political systems so confused colonial officials they could not figure out whom to negotiate with and whether chiefs could deliver on their promises. Thus in 1845, when Captain Butler travelled to the Naga Hills with an armed force, he made his way through the country 'conciliating the tribes and mapping the country'. The chiefs came and met him, and even 'paid up their tribute in ivory, cloth and spears'. But they also told Butler that 'they had no real control over their people, and had absolute authority only on the war-path'. A number of villages eagerly sought British protection, but it was only to 'induce us to exterminate their neighbours'. As soon as Butler's expedition left the hills, 'the tribes recommenced their raids on the plains and on one another' (Mackenzie 2001: 108–9). The nature of Naga relations with Manipur was an endless source of confusion to colonial officials. In 1840, one officer in marching toward Manipur found to his astonishment that in one area Nagas were 'avowedly hostile to Manipur and not tributary as had been given out by that State' (Mackenzie 2001: 106). In 1844 another expedition found that Manipur was 'helping one Naga clan to attack another' and that it was 'impossible to get Manipur to carry out honestly the orders of the Government' (Mackenzie 2001: 108). After two expeditions to the Angami Naga country, Lieutenant Vincent reported in 1850 that 'in every Angami village, there were two parties, one attached to the interests of Manipur and the other to the British, but each only working for an alliance to get aid in crushing the opposite faction' (Mackenzie 2001: 112). Nevertheless, the British, laid down a boundary between their territory and Manipur in 1842 and reasserted it in 1867, but it was 'little regarded by Manipur' (Mackenzie 2001: 122).

As colonial officials came to know Manipur, they speculated on the relations between the Nagas and the Manipuris. The political rituals of the Manipuri court pointed to ties that were close, but difficult to fathom. For example, James Johnstone observed that the installation ceremony of the Manipuri kings called for the queen to appear in Naga costume; the royal palace always had a house built in Naga style; and when the king travelled, two or three Manipuris with Naga arms, dress, and ornaments accompanied him. It is not clear why Johnstone assumed that they were Manipuris, dressed as Nagas for these occasions rather than being Nagas themselves. In any case, he took them as evidence that like the Manchus of China, the Manipuri kings may have been Nagas who adopted the civilization of Manipur (Johnstone 1971: 82). While early colonial officials were far from successful in decoding a political system of militarized villages with apparently random ties among them and with the lowland states, they tried hard to make sense of the clear evidence of cultural, political, and ethnic ties across these divides.

Colonial Transformation and the Naga Construction of Collective Selfhood

The story of the emergence of Nagas as a people—the Naga nation in the words of the independentists—is one of the most remarkable twentieth century stories of a radical transformation of political structures and world-views within a relatively short period of time. In the early part of the century most Nagas continued to live in mountain top villages with signs of fortification still intact and head-hunting—an institutionalized form of inter-village warfare—was occasionally still taking place, even though it was criminalized by the colonial state. Neighbouring villages spoke 'dialects or languages totally incomprehensible to one another', and in their communications involving war-making or alliance-building, they relied on sign language, which 'reached a high state of development' (Hutton 1921: 291). As anthropologist Fürer-Haimendorf, who studied the Nagas in the 1930s, puts it, 'a Naga village could not even ideally remain at peace as long as there prevailed the belief that the occasional capture of a human head was essential for maintaining the fertility of the crops and the well being of the community' (cited in Eaton 1997: 249n).

Reading colonial accounts against the grain, one can see how the resistance to colonial conquest produced some of the early alliances. One of the most violent military operations was against Khonoma and allied villages in 1879 and 1880, after a British officer and a large group of accompanying soldiers and policemen were killed. After the operations were over, it was discovered that 'the punishment inflicted by our troops had been far more severe in its results than was at first supposed'. The dispossessed villagers lived as 'houseless wanderers, dependent to a great extent on the charity of their neighbours, and living in temporary huts in the jungles'. The British policy was to get the 'dispossessed clans' to settle either in Manipur or on fresh land in the Naga Hills. But the Nagas could not be persuaded to settle anywhere else, nor were other Nagas willing to take up the 'confiscated lands' (Mackenzie 2001: 139). The colonial interpretation of these difficulties was that those Nagas feared retribution, but a more plausible reading is that they were gestures of solidarity. In 1880, there was a 'daring raid' on a tea plantation. The men, who were from Khonoma, had 'marched down the bed of the Barak through Manipuri territory, ... requisitioned food from some of the Katcha Naga villages on the way'. These villages, wrote Mackenzie, 'though in Manipuri territory are so profoundly dominated by the terror of the Angamis that no resistance was to be expected from them' (Mackenzie 2001: 138). Here again it is hard to miss the evidence of Naga solidarity and coordinated resistance.

The road to Naga nationhood, however, did not open up till the twentieth century. It perhaps began when during the First World War a Labour Corps of 4,000 Nagas, were sent to France, where they saw great 'civilized nations' fighting for 'their ends and interests while Nagas were condemned as barbarous for their head hunting ways' (Yunuo 1974: 125; cited in Eaton 1997: 256). Twenty Nagas came together to form the Naga Club and in 1929, they submitted a memorandum to the Simon Commission that was considering political reforms in India to respond to rising Indian anti-colonial mobilization. The signatories claimed to 'represent all those tribes to which we belong—Angamis, Katcha Nagas,

Kukis, Semas, Lothas, and Rangmas' (Simon Memorandum 1999: 166). The memorandum asked that the Nagas not be included in any reform scheme because they were not unified as a group, educational levels were poor, and because given their small numbers, in any electoral system based on numbers their interests were sure to be overwhelmed. The memorandum interpreted the pre-colonial past of the Nagas as that of an unvanquished people. 'Before the British Government conquered our country in 1879– 80', said the memorandum, 'we were living in a state of intermittent warfare with Assamese of the Assam valley to the North and West of our country and the Manipuris to the South. They never conquered us, nor were we ever subjected to their rule' (Simon Memorandum 1999: 165–6).

In April 1945, the Naga Hills District Tribal Council was established at the initiative of the British Deputy Commissioner. In February 1946, the council renamed itself the Naga National Council—organized as a federation of several tribal councils—and brought out a small newspaper called the *Naga Nation*.

The single most important development that made the imagining of Nagas as a collectivity possible was their conversion to Christianity—'the most massive movement to Christianity in all of Asia, second only to that of the Philippines', in the words of historian Richard Eaton (Eaton 1997: 245). Today Christianity is an essential part of Naga identity. Except for the Zeilongrong Nagas, most Nagas are Christians. Eaton estimates the percentage of Christians to be 90 per cent (though his study is limited to the state of Nagaland) and the NSCN-IM puts the figure at 95 per cent. It was the American Baptist Mission that accounted for most of the proselytizing among Nagas; but the conversions of a number of Naga communities happened after the end of colonial rule and even after the Indian government expelled foreign missionaries from India. The profound destabilization of traditional Naga institutions during colonial rule, however, had set the stage for this profound cultural transformation. The village chiefs were the leaders of the community when Naga society was organized on a war footing. But when head-hunting was criminalized by colonial rulers and inter-village warfare ended, the traditional leaders lost their hold over younger warriors and it was these 'would-be warriors' who, according to Richard Eaton, responded most readily to Christian teachings (Eaton 1997: 256).

Missionaries printed the Bible in selected Naga dialects such as Ao, Angami and Sema and in the process gave those dialects a written form using the Roman script. This meant a simplification of the Naga linguistic landscape—for while the chosen dialects became recognized as standard, many other dialects disappeared. As literacy and education became a key to social mobility, Nagas realized the advantage of learning those standard dialects (Eaton 1997: 252). Hundreds of young men from different areas, who were trained in the secondary schools and missionary training schools run by missionaries were able to communicate with each other (Jacobs et al., 1990:156). To this generation, the idea of Nagas as a single community of fate became real.

The Naga conflict helped make Christianity a part of Naga identity. It is not accidental that nearly half the conversions among Nagas happened after India's independence. The Christian identity which marks the Nagas apart from the mostly Hindu and Muslim population of the Indian heartland has been partly an act of cultural resistance that parallel the political and armed resistance.

An astonishing number of marginalized hill peoples in northeast India today want to be included in the Naga fold; partly because they find the five-decade-old Naga struggle for recognition inspiring. In a recent article on the languages of northeast India, anthropologist Robbins Burling had to take the trouble to separate the political project of Naga unity from the languages spoken by the people who call themselves Naga. 'Today, the people known as "Nagas" certainly recognize some common "Naga" ethnicity', Burling writes, 'but this recognition may have come only after the British gave them the name "Naga". Most of the indigenous people of Nagaland, together with some ethnic groups in the bordering areas of Manipur, Assam, Arunachal Pradesh, and Myanmar are, by general consensus, now accepted as "Nagas", but this term should not fool us into believing that they must have some linguistic unity'. Naga, Burling emphasized, 'is not a linguistic label' (Burling 2003: 172). Particularly striking to Burling was that some groups, 'whose language a linguist would, without hesitation, classify as "Kuki", have declared themselves to be "Nagas"'. Yet, adds Burling, 'everyone agrees that Nagas and Kukis are sharply distinct ethnically. Indeed, they have been killing each other from time to time' (Burling 2003: 188).

When anthropologist Fürer-Haimendorf returned to the Konyak Nagas in the 1970s after three decades, he saw elections taking place in Naga villages and a new breed of ambitious Naga politicians looking beyond their villages for support. His observations graphically capture the transformation of the Naga world. 'Only those who have experienced traditional Naga society', Fürer-Haimendorf wrote, 'can appreciate the magnitude of the transformation'. To an older generation of Nagas mankind was 'divided between a small inner circle of co-villagers, clansmen, and allied villages, on whose support he could depend and to whom he owed assistance in emergencies'. The entire outside world, consisting not only of people belonging to other tribes, but even Konyaks living in other villages, were all potential enemies and legitimate targets of head-hunting. A category such as 'allies from among communities outside the narrow circle of the in-group', he recalled, 'had no place in the Naga's picture of the world'. The notion of 'cooperation between formerly hostile village and even across tribal boundaries' could not have been more alien to the world of the Nagas he knew (Fürer-Haimendorf 1976: 251).

If the Naga conversion to Christianity was the result of their incorpo-ration into a larger political, economic, and cultural universe, so was their journey on the road to nationhood. Paying close attention to Naga cosmologies and to the translation strategies of the Bible into Naga languages, Richard Eaton finds that the particular local gods that missionaries translated as the Christian god, along with the pace of change affecting particular Naga communities, made a difference in the scope and timing of the conversion to Christianity. As Nagas confronted a reality that could no longer be seen as being under the control of their local spirits, they were beginning to pay more attention to the high gods in their own cosmologies who 'as sovereign of the entire universe, was seen as more clearly in charge'. It was in the context of a radically transformed world, that the missionary translation strategy of making the indigenous high god stand for the Christian god that began to yield converts (Eaton 1997: 270). If Nagas had to abandon their many local religions in favour of a world religion to morally negotiate the larger world into which they were incorporated, nationhood was the global idiom that seemed most appropriate to negotiate the rough political terrain that the Nagas have found themselves in all through the second half of the twentieth century.

Confronting Constructionism: Nagas Debate their Past

Earlier in the Chapter 1 have outlined the NSCN-IM view of the Naga past: that it had 'always been a sovereign nation' and is now divided into many political units—decisions over which Nagas have had little say. In the summer of 2000, a remarkable pamphlet appeared in Nagaland's capital

Kohima that explicitly took on this view of the Naga past. The pamphlet entitled *Bedrock of Naga Society* was published by the Nagaland state Congress party and, by all accounts, it was the brainchild of the state's then Chief Minister S.C. Jamir (NPCC 2000). Indeed some Indian newspapers reproduced excerpts from the pamphlet naming Jamir as the author.

The pamphlet was a defence of the 16 points agreement between the Naga People's Convention and the Government of India of 1960 that led to the formation of the state of Nagaland. This is new territory in Naga political debates. *Bedrock* took on the independentist argument that the formation of Nagaland compromised the sovereignty of Nagas. The idea that the Nagas have been a separate independent entity from time immemorial may be an 'attractive proposition' but 'is it really true?' The authors asked, 'were we really an independent nation?' In words never heard before in Naga political discourse, the pamphlet gave this answer:

The stark and inescapable truth is that neither did we have a definite and unified political structure and nor did we exist as a nation. We were actually a group of heterogeneous, primitive and diverse tribes living in far-flung villages that had very little in common and negligible contact with each other.... Each village was practically an entity in itself. The main 'contact' between villages was through the savage practice of headhunting. Mutual suspicion and distrust was rife. Internecine warfare was the order of the day. There was no trust or interaction between different tribes. In these circumstances, the question of a unified 'Naga nation' did not arise (NPCC 2000).

In this version of Naga history, the idea of Naga nationhood gained momentum in the 1950s. The plebiscite of 1951, when volunteers of the Naga National Council went to far-flung villages to collect thumb prints of every Naga to announce that 99.9 per cent of the Nagas want independence 'emotionally integrated the various Naga tribes'. The 16 points agreement was the result of an impasse. It had become evident that under no circumstances the Indian Government would have conceded the Naga demand for sovereignty and the Naga movement had reached a dead end. Some Nagas took stock of the situation, and resolved that 'even if independence was not possible, the land, identity, and individuality of the Naga people should never be compromised'. The result was the agreement that led to the creation of Nagaland in 1963, which 'gave the Nagas worth and significance in the eyes of the world' (NPCC 2000).

Bedrock is undoubtedly a political document with the signature of the Congress party and of former Chief Minister Jamir, who was known to be firmly opposed to the NSCN-IM leader Muivah. Yet its broader significance should not be underestimated. The lines between independentist and integrationist factions in Naga politics have always been blurred; in that sense this intervention is part of a debate among Naga nationalists. It is rare in the history of the practice of nationalism for a constructionist position of a group's identity to be presented with such candor.

The pamphlet, not surprisingly, led to an enormous controversy among Nagas. The NSCN-IM published a pamphlet labelling Jamir an 'Indian stooge' out to destroy Naga solidarity. It denounced the 16 points agreement as a betrayal of the Naga people and expressed surprise that 'a man calling himself a Naga can fall this low that he is willing to disown his own history' (Karmakar 2000). There has been a lively debate in Naga newspapers as well. Other political and civil society groups entered the fray. The Naga People's Movement for Human Rights, for instance, called the pamphlet a distortion of Naga history.

What is not said in the pamphlet is also quite significant. Independentist and integrationist Nagas share the goal of bringing together Nagas under one entity. In recent years many Nagas have begun using the term Nagalim to describe the Naga homeland to distinguish it from the state of Nagaland. 'Lim' is a word in the Ao dialect that refers to land. While the term Nagalim had been used by Naga student leaders for a while, in 1999, the NSCN-IM began formally calling itself the National Socialist Council of Nagalim—instead of Nagaland (Angami et al., 2002). The new term distinguishes between the state of Nagaland and what is seen as the territory of the Nagas without the expansive connotation of the term Greater Nagaland used by the Indian media.

While the integration of the Naga areas of Burma with the areas in India has not been high on the Naga political agenda, bringing the Nagas of India together has been an issue that unites most Nagas. Even the Nagaland Assembly has passed a number of resolutions expressing support for that cause and the 16 points agreement includes a clause articulating this position. *Bedrock* did not abandon that commitment. However, the position that the state of Nagaland 'gave the Nagas worth and significance in the eyes of the world' can also be seen as an attempt to downplay the Nagalim theme. Indeed in many public statements Jamir and his supporters have described the NSCN-IM leadership as 'outsiders', and have asserted that solving the Naga political problem should be up to the 'Nagas of Nagaland'. Such statements clearly are targeted at Muivah.

In response to the ferment caused by the pamphlet, the Nagaland Pradesh Congress Committee (NPCC) in a statement clarified that 'at no point of time the party had said the Naga political problem was resolved with the signing of the 1960 pact'. The pamphlet, it said, was not designed to 'sabotage' the peace-talks between the Indian Government and the NSCN-IM (*Assam Tribune* 2000b). Despite the ambiguities and silences of the pamphlet, as a critique of the view that Nagas have always been a sovereign nation and its embrace of what amounts to a constructionist position on Naga identity, *Bedrock* marks an important turning point that can change the framework in which the Naga problem has historically been framed.

The Manipur Factor and the Peace Process

The issue of the Nagas of Manipur poses the most formidable obstacle to the peace process today. To understand the depth of the Manipuri anger, apart from the complex pre-colonial relations between the lowland state of Manipur and the Nagas outlined above, one has to consider Manipur's sense of growing alienation from India. The circumstances of Manipur's merger with India in October 1949, when it was stripped of the autonomy it had enjoyed, has haunted the post-colonial politics of Manipur. Like the much better known case of Jammu and Kashmir, Manipur during the British colonial period was ruled as a princely state. Four days before India's independence on 15 August 1947, the king of Manipur had signed the instrument of accession entrusting defence, communication, and foreign affairs to the Government of India. Manipur then adopted a new state Constitution under which elections to a state assembly took place and Manipur had a democratically elected state government. Independent India's new leaders made public commitments to preserving Manipur's autonomy. But in September 1949, the Manipuri king, held incommunicado—with no access to his democratically elected Council of Ministers and Manipuri public opinion—and under the pressure of considerable misinformation, false promises, and intimidation, was made to sign a merger agreement. Consequently, Manipur lost its autonomy, the elected ministry was dissolved and an Indian official was appointed to run the state. The merger was never ratified by a popular vote.

A number of militant Manipuri independentist groups regard the merger as illegal and unconstitutional and many in the Manipuri intelligentsia express bitterness about the way it was brought about. Manipur, with its long and unbroken history as an independent kingdom was to be incorporated into India not as an equal member state of the Indian Union, but as a 'Part C state', subsequently 'upgraded' into a Union Territory. The politics of recognition has been a persistent theme in Manipur's troubled politics. Illustrative of the recognition theme are the protest movements demanding the status of a full-fledged state for Manipur under India's federal framework, which it acquired only in 1972—and, quite significantly, from the Manipuri point of view, nine years after Nagaland—and those seeking the recognition of Meiteilon or Manipuri as one of India's official languages—a status granted only in 1992. The possibility that their state might now be radically split behind their backs in secret negotiations between the Government of India and Naga rebel leaders is a source of enormous anxiety in Manipur. That Manipur geographically is a small valley surrounded by hills that make up the bulk of its territory—and that is where most Nagas live—adds to this sense of anxiety.

The Meiteis—an ethnic term that distinguishes the Manipur's lowlanders from the hill peoples—are proud of the long history of their state in the Imphal Valley. Meiteis, who live mostly in the Imphal Valley, number about 1.4 million, and they constitute 57 per cent of the state's population. Among the hill peoples are those that are considered Naga by pan-Naga organizations, e.g. the Tangkhuls (113 thousands), Mao (80 thousands), the Kabui (62 thousands), and fourteen smaller groups. In addition, there are 13 communities that are by some classification placed in the Kuki-Chin-Zomi group. Together Manipur's tribal population of 714 thousands amount to about 30 per cent of the state's population of 2.4 million people, though the hills comprise about 90 per cent of the state's territory.

It has been said by a Manipuri scholar that the 'essence' of the long history of Manipur is the interactions between the Meitei and the surrounding hill peoples and that the culture of the Meiteis is little more than the product of these 'interactions, struggle for supremacy and subsequent fusion into a common ethno-linguistic entity' (R. Singh 1990: 238). It is perhaps a sign of the gulf between the old and the new ways in which identities are negotiated that a recent article could claim that, 'the name Manipur is only applicable to the Hindu dweller of the plains areas' (Shimray 2001: 3675).

Meiteis today feel embattled and embittered by the identity discourse of the Nagas that threatens a radical diminution of the state's territory. Meitei narratives of Manipur stress the state's historical pluralism. A publication brought out to publicize the Manipuri point of view during the controversy over the ceasefire puts it this way: 'It is an undeniable fact that there are many similarities in customs, habits, and manners between the Meiteis and the hill people'. The term 'Naga', it points out, quite accurately about a period that is now past, 'had never been applied to the hill people of Manipur', but it was a term used by the Tai-Ahom kings of Assam and the British to refer only to the people who inhabit the territory that is today called Nagaland. It points out that two Tangkhul Naga politicians, Yangmasho Shaiza and Rishang Keishang have been Chief Ministers of Manipur. And Meiteilon or Manipuri, it claims, is 'the language of all Manipuris' since it is both the language of the Meiteis and the lingua franca of the hill peoples (AMCTA 2001: 35–47). Such claims, of course, are challenged by the Naga and by other hill peoples (see Shimray 2001: 3676).

Meiteis resent that Nagas are supposedly trying to 'destroy' their state. Since Nagas acquired 'a state of its own within a short span of time', even when 'historical states like Manipur' did not, their aspirations have now 'run wild' even 'threatening the territorial integrity of other historical and advanced states like Manipur and Assam' (AMCTA 2001: 23). Meiteis are critical of Manipuri Nagas who identify with NSCN-IM: 'it is most unfortunate' that sections of some tribes who 'claim' to be Nagas and 'whose roots are deeply embodied in Manipur and whose parents shed blood for Manipur are now working in tandem with an outfit (i.e. the NSCN-IM) whose ambition is to destroy Manipur' (AMCTA 2001: 27).

Manipur's anxiety about the Naga claims on its territory long precedes the current controversy. In 1994, when the Nagaland Assembly called for the unification of all Naga areas, the Manipur Assembly unanimously adopted a resolution to uphold the territorial integrity of Manipur. Interestingly enough, the Chief Minister of Manipur at that time was a Tangkhul Naga, Rishang Keishing. Ethnic Naga politicians of Manipur have had to negotiate a difficult line between the claims on their loyalty as Manipuris and as Nagas, given the popularity of the pan-Naga cause.

Manipuri street protests against the cease-fire began as soon as the present ceasefire came to effect on 1 August 1997. On 4 August 1997, thousands of people participated in a protest rally in Imphal and the Manipur

Legislative Assembly passed a resolution protesting the extension of the ceasefire. The mood that animated the spectacular protest in Manipur after the June 2001 announcement of the ceasefire having 'no territorial limits' is best captured in the words of a Manipuri activist. 'The people of Manipur naturally felt that their apprehension was now coming true', wrote Khumajam Ratan, presumably referring to the fear of a potential break-up of Manipur. 'Feeling deeply betrayed, they rose in protest against the central government's decision. When the news of the signing of the 14 June agreement in Bangkok reached Manipur there was a general disbelief. Gloom was writ large on the people's faces. The initial general disbelief and gloom soon turned to an unprecedented demonstration of strong, powerful protests' (Ratan 2001: 1).

The protest included general strikes, social boycott of the political parties, burnings of the Indian national flag and of effigies of Indian political leaders. There were police firings, deaths and injuries and significant destruction of public property including symbolically important ones such as the State Legislative Assembly building. Many Manipuri Nagas left the tense Imphal Valley for the hills. The protests died down only after India's Home Minister announced on 27 July 2001, that the three words 'without territorial limits' would be dropped from the agreement signed with the NSCN-IM regarding the scope of the cease-fire. There is a demand now for an amendment of the Indian Constitution to guarantee the inviolability of Manipur's borders. Like Jammu and Kashmir, Manipur, merged with India as a distinct entity, says a Manipuri publication. Since it had a 'definite historical international boundary at the time of the merger' India should not destroy those boundaries. 'No alien force nor internal contradictions can break the territorial integrity of Manipur' (AMCTA 2001: 38, 48).

Conclusion: Towards an Alternative Institutional Imagination

To those who had expected the long-running Naga conflict to end as a result of the current peace process, the impasse created by the Manipuri protest is disappointing However, the protest also served to bring to light the history of the region's 'strange multiplicity' and the tensions between the spatial discourse that had historically enabled the hill peoples and lowland states of the region to coexist and the spatial discourse of exclusive territorially rooted collectivities that frame today's politics of recognition among Nagas, Meiteis, and other communities.

By stressing the need to confront constructionism, I do not wish to de-emphasize the power of these identities. To say that 'communities are social constructions: imagined, invented, put together', as Michael Walzer puts it, does not make them 'less real or less authentic than some other' (Walzer 1995: 324). Nor do I wish to suggest that confronting constructionism is something that only the Nagas would have to do; it applies to the Manipuris and to the Government of India as well. Some senior Indian security experts, for instance, believe that Naga unity is only a 'secessionist fiction'. As one of these experts puts it, there are 'nearly 40 major tribes, sub-tribes among the people categorized as Nagas, each of which speaks a different language ... and many of whom have unrelenting histories of internecine conflict' (Gill 2001). In its inability to see Naga nationhood as a work in progress, this mind-set is remarkably reminiscent of colonial writings that sought to deny the status of nationhood to colonized peoples on account of their supposedly perpetual state of conflict and disunity.

Indian official attitude towards the Naga conflict, unfortunately, has been dominated by a security mindset. There is a belief that weaknesses on the Naga side—military defeat, an aging leadership, and pressure from the grassroots—have pushed the rebels to the negotiating table, and that time is on the government's side to seek a resolution in its own terms. Apart from a lack of appreciation of how Nagas have come to see themselves as a collectivity—partly because of their long history of confrontation with the Indian state—there is little appreciation in the security discourse, of the Indian government's responsibility in the Naga nightmare or, at least, of the need to acknowledge the Naga sense of being wronged. Hindu nationalist myths and ill-informed ideas making Christian missionaries responsible for the Naga conflict may further stand in the way of creating an atmosphere conducive to reconciliation on the Indian side.

By contrast, Naga civic and intellectual life today shows remarkable signs of vitality, openness, and flexibility. Perhaps because Nagas are free of the burden of a frozen hegemonic national narrative—thanks to the lack of a long literary history—Naga narratives are willing to live with remarkable ambiguity and uncertainty about their past. In that sense *Bedrock of Naga Society* was not an aberration. 'The Nagas are not even sure of their numbers or the physical land areas they occupy', writes a contemporary Naga intellectual known for his non-partisan appeal, 'but whatever scraps of history have been handed down through the generations, they hold on with a tenacity that would escape the casual observer and surprise the serious researcher'. The absence of a common language or shared values, poor education, poor economic conditions or 'the containment and control policies' of the government in order to manage the Naga rebellion, says Chassie, 'have proved futile in tearing the Nagas apart' (Chassie 1999: 21).

It is clear by now that secret bilateral meetings between the Government of India and the rebel leaders cannot produce a solution to the Naga conflict. Manipur surely has as serious a stake as any in the Naga conflict. If it is not a part of the way the Naga conflict is conventionally mapped, it is a function of how most observers have got accustomed to India's centralized style of governing and deciding the fate of this frontier region. Yet stripping the political arenas of the region of substantive powers has been the major cause of the unrelenting political turmoil in the region. The Manipuri outburst is a product of decision-making at far-away places by bureaucrats with no knowledge or interest in the region's history.

At the same time it cannot be argued that the Naga talks can be suddenly expanded to include Manipur as a stakeholder. Before anything like that can happen, all parties would have to come to terms with the limits of the territorial discourse in northeast India that the collision between the Naga and Manipuri projects of recognition underscores. There needs to be an alternative institutional imagination and a source of fresh ideas may be an entirely different political discourse than that of making and breaking states (see Baruah 1997). The Government of India in the past has resisted pressures to accept the international discourse of the rights of indigenous peoples. While there is a lot to be said for a distinction between the predicament of indigenous peoples in settler societies and in India, debates within this global discourse can also bring to the table new ideas for addressing the Naga conflict. The principle of the right to self-determination of indigenous peoples under international law, for instance, has led to concepts like separate polities within shared territories, which have been tried in societies, where relations between settlers and indigenous peoples are based on treaties between a government and particular indigenous nations.

Even if these parties had vastly asymmetric power relations when these treaties were signed, and for a long time such treaties did not protect these peoples against assimilative policies and practices, in recent years they have provided the basis for challenging the foundational myths of the national communities created by settler communities. But most significantly, slowly but steadily they are modifying the architecture of federalism in countries like Australia, Canada, and the United States. The 'native' peoples have been able to claim a place in the federal table *alongside* states. In the Indian mainland, the linguistic reorganization of states has created states or, what can be called nation provinces where particular nationalities constitute majorities capable of defining the public identity of those states. In many cases these nation-provinces are seen as legitimate partly because they pay symbolic homage to the history of India's pre-colonial political formations. Given that experience, it is remarkable that there has been such a dismissive attitude towards the pre-colonial history of Manipur and its hold on the Manipuri political imagination. Whatever institutional structures are designed to resolve the Naga conflict will have to coexist alongside Manipur and not at the expense of Manipur.

Fortunately, in recent months, ideas about alternative institutional arrangements have become a part of Indian discussions of the Naga conflict. Indian journalist and policy thinker B.G. Verghese has suggested a non-territorial approach that would 'strengthen the Naga way of life' and would not affect the integrity of other states. He recommends the formation of a Naga Regional Council that would give Nagas outside Nagaland a say in Naga cultural matters (cited in S. Hazarika 2002). Noted anthropologist B.K. Roy Burman has suggested an institution modeled on the Saami Council where the Saami people living in Sweden, Finland, and Norway are represented (*Times of India* 2001). To be sure, both Roy Burman's and Verghese's concepts are rather preliminary at this stage and they seem to address exclusively cultural issues. Given the history of the past five decades, it would be too much to expect the Naga conflict to suddenly end on a whimper of some vague promise of cultural autonomy. A proposal that might have the power to capture the Naga imagination at the moment might take the Burmese government into confidence and bring the Nagas of Burma into the picture as well. This can be the first step towards a comprehensive dialogue that includes Nagas as well as the other stakeholders to consider an arrangement that crosses both transnational and inter-state borders which recognizes Naga identity, *alongside* both the sovereignty of India and Burma and the territorially embodied identities of states like Manipur and Assam. The concept can combine the Saami Council with the indigenous peoples' institutions of Canada that exercise increasing powers *alongside* the provinces of Canada. Without such a significant shifting of gears, it is unlikely that the current five-year-old Naga peace process can overcome the formidable obstacles it currently faces to end one of world's most protracted and tragic armed conflicts.

Notes

[1] The chapter originally appeared in the *Journal of Peace Research*. Reprinted by permission of Sage Publications Ltd From Sanjib Baruah, 'Confronting Constructionism: Ending India's Naga War,' *Journal of Peace Research* 40 (3) May 2003: 321–38. © International Peace Research Institute (Oslo) PRIO, 2003.

[2] Sahadevan (2000) shows that compared to most internal/civil wars in the world, those in South Asia have been unusually protracted. Using Roy Licklider's definitions (Licklider, 1995), Sahadevan finds that while of the 84 wars included in the Licklider study only 18 or 21 per cent were protracted in the sense that they went on for more than ten years, 63 per cent of the wars in South Asia belonged to this category—three times higher than the global average. The nearly five decades old Naga war, undoubtedly qualifies as one of the longest wars in the world.

[3] The category 'tribe,' despite all its conceptual problems is part of Indian political discourse primarily because of a system of protective discrimination that exists in favour of groups of people listed as tribes. Article 342 of Indian Constitution provides for the President of India by public notification to specify the 'tribes or tribal communities or parts of or groups within tribes or tribal communities which shall for the purposes of the Constitution be deemed to be Scheduled Tribes.' In this chapter, I have used the term 'tribe' to mean groups included in that list. According to a scholar who has examined how the Indian government arrives at the list, the tribes are 'defined partly by habitat and geographic isolation, but even more on the basis of social, religious, linguistic, and cultural distinctiveness—their "tribal characteristics". Just where the line between "tribals" and "non-tribals" should be drawn has not always been free from doubt' (Galanter 1984: 150).

[4] I have borrowed the phrase 'strange multiplicity' from Tully (1995).

[5] The argument of this section extends James C. Scott's (2000) hypothesis about Southeast Asia to northeast India. This and the following two paragraphs are mostly a summary of Scott's hypothesis.

The Life and Times of
the United Liberation Front of Assam

6

Society versus State in Assam[1]

By and large the Indian state can claim significant success in its 'nation-building' project—it has been able to incorporate subnationalist dissent of a number of peoples by using persuasive and coercive means at its disposal.[2] Subnational conflicts that appear stubborn at one time turn out to be surprisingly amenable to negotiated settlement. The assumption that nationalisms have a *telos* that inevitably leads to a demand for separation relies on a rather lazy naturalist theory of the nature and origins of nations, nationalities, and nation-states. What the Indian experience forces us to confront is the fate of nationalism and the nation-state as they spread worldwide as modal forms. In the Indian subcontinent these new forms that privilege 'formal boundedness over substantive interrelationships' (Handler 1985: 198) come face to face with a civilization that represents a particularly complex way of ordering diversity (Cohn 1987). In a subcontinent where the historical legacy of state formation is marked by intermittent tensions between the imperial state and regional kingdoms, nationalisms and the nation-state may have proven to be rather unfortunate modern transplants (Rudolph and Rudolph 1985).

I will use the term nationality, not ethnic group, to refer to the Assamese and the term subnationalism to refer to their politics of 'identity'.[3] The use of the term ethnicity to describe an inordinately wide range of phenomena has not helped our understanding of 'ethnic polities'. Nations and nationalities give rise to nationalisms. 'Ethnic polities' of groups with a connection to a real or imagined homeland is part of the history of the rise of the modern phenomenon of nationalism worldwide. This type, of 'ethnic polities' is radically different from the politics of identity that is not grounded in homelands—the latter is often easily incorporated within a larger ideology of state nationalism. In the US, for instance, ethnic politics takes place within the ideological framework of a national political community—'one nation under God'. The paradigmatic form of this kind of ethnic politics is perhaps the ethnic parades—an organized celebration of 'multi-culturalism'—that would be the envy of anyone engaged in the project of 'nation-building' in India.

Since Assamese and other nationalisms in India coexist with a pan-Indian nationalism, I generally add the qualifier 'sub' to refer to the former, though occasionally, where the qualifier sounds awkward, I simply use the terms nation and nationalism. The term subnationalism designates, what M. Crawford Young aptly describes as identities that 'meet some of the criteria of politicization and mobilization' associated with nationalism, 'but are not firmly committed to separate statehood' (Young 1976: 72). Walker Connor, however, writes quite persuasively that the term subnation, like terms such as ethnic group, can sometimes only be a euphemism that obscures the essentially multinational nature of the vast majority of contemporary states. While the users of the term at least indicate an awareness that they are confronting some 'approximation of nationalism', writes Connor, 'in its clear presumption that nationalism is in the employ of the state and in its relegation of loyalty to the ethnonational group to a subordinate order of phenomena, subnationalism has no peer' (Connor 1994: 111). I agree with much of Connor's argument, but I do not accept his underlying positivist conception of nations. I use the term subnationalism not to refer to some stable essence that makes it distinct from nationalism, but to describe a situation at a particular historical moment.

This chapter attempts to understand the recurrent politics of sub-nationalism in Assam. The Assamese have been engaged in subnationalist politics intermittently in the past, but quite continuously since the 1980s. Assam is among India's economically more underdeveloped areas. However, it is not in per capita GNP that the state lags particularly behind, but in the lack of industrial capacity. With tea gardens occupying a major part of the state's total cultivable land, Assam is probably more of a primary commodity producing colonial economy that dependancy theorists had in mind in their critique of modernization theory, than most other parts of India. As South Asia's last major land frontier, the region—Assam as well as some other parts of Northeast India—has attracted exceptionally high immigration from other parts of South Asia, especially from the densely populated East Bengal. After the partition of India in 1947, not only did the flow of economic migration from East Bengal continue, but added to this flow were a large number of political migrants—Hindu refugees leaving Pakistan. In 1979–85 protests against what was claimed to be illegal immigration and a de facto government policy of enfranchisement of these immigrants led to five years of political turmoil and major outbreaks of violence in the state. Earlier subnationalist political mobilization had focused on cultural policy demands such as the use of Assamese as the official language and as the language of education, and on economic demands for projects that were seen as means toward progress—bridges over the Brahmaputra, refineries and railway lines. Thus when the United Liberation Front of Assam (ULFA) in the late 1980s described India's relationship with Assam as colonial and demanded that multinational and Indian-owned tea companies do more for the development of the state, it intervened in a long debate within Assamese subnationalist intellectual life. In some ways, if Assamese subnationalism before ULFA was shaped by orthodox ideas on what it takes to achieve development and progress, the rise of ULFA marks the advent of critical ideas about development, not unlike, say the relationship between the dependancy and other critical paradigms of development and the old modernization paradigm.

Theoretical Considerations

The politics of subnationalism can be located in the theoretical space that is usually referred to as civil society. It is from its roots in civil society that subnationalist politics derives much of its power and its potential for generating political turmoil; for subnationalism, unlike some other forms of ethnic politics, is not politics within the rules of 'normal' politics, but it often challenges those rules. Well-meaning commentators who counsel moderation and compromise in resolving disputes arising from sub-nationalist mobilization often miss the rupture between civil society and the state that gives subnationalist politics its momentum. Subnationalisms arouse higher-order obligations that compete with the obligations of national citizenship whose unquestioned primacy is best construed as a given social life, but as a project of the modern state. That does not mean that subnationalist demands are necessarily engaged in a zero-sum conflict with the state. As we know, demands generated by subnationalist political mobilization in India have often been settled through negotiation. But such resolutions may obscure the continued capacity of subnationalisms to maintain their autonomous visions and agendas and resist complete incorporation into the 'normal' political process. For long-term solutions to India's dilemma of subnationalist politics, therefore, one would have to look beyond the cliches of the ideologues of modernization and nation-building. It is not the absence of a politics of reason and civility on the part of citizens that sustains subnationalist conflicts. Where a modern state formation is a project rather than an accomplished fact, what may be at issue is a conflict between the will of the state and the dreams and aspirations that grow in the space of civil society.

Albert Hirschman's critique of development economics as a field that expects the Third World to act like wind-up toys pursuing interests and no passions (Hirschman 1981: 23–4) applies to much of social science theorizing about the 'Third World'. In the eagerness to see 'development' and 'progress', social science work on the 'Third World' has shown little interest in the collective imaginings that shape people's engagement with, and dreams of, modernity. The politics of sub-nationalism is premised on a poetics about a homeland and its people. If nations and nationalities are 'imagined communities', it is a poetics that transforms the geography of an area into a primal, 'home-like' or sacred space and transforms a people into a collectivity with imagined ties of shared origins and kinship.[4] In order to illustrate Gaston Bachelard's notion of the poetics of space, Edward Said notes:

The objective space of a house—its corners, corridors, cellar, rooms—is far less important than what poetically it is endowed with, which is usually a quality with an imaginative or figurative value we can name and feel: thus a house may be haunted, or homelike, or prison-like, or magical. So space acquires emotional and even rational sense by a kind of poetic process, whereby the vacant or anonymous reaches of distance are converted into meaning for us (Said 1979: 54–5).

The power of subnationalisms lies in such meanings.

The modern nation-state seeks a monopoly of the collective imagination of all its citizens. It would like the state-defined broad political community to be the sole repository of the poetics of a homeland and of the memories and dreams of a people—defined singularly, even if there may be gestures towards acknowledging diversity. However, the state in India—a legatee to a subcontinental empire and the product of an anti-colonial political project—must come to terms with competing collective imaginings. A dense social space weakly penetrated by the state allows the reproduction of subnational 'imagined communities' that co-exist with the pan-Indian national 'imagined community'. Nationalities with a collective memory and a collective will combined with an autonomous organizational capacity are best thought of as civil societies. India's problem of subnationalism then, is the problem of developing political forms that are more in tune with her evolving forms of civil society. If the Eastern European revolution pitted states against civil societies, subnationalist politics in India sometimes pits particular segments of civil society against the Indian state.

The Indian state's fire-fighting approach to Sikh, Kashmiri, or Assamese, Manipuri or Naga dissent takes very little account of the collective memories and aspirations that shape subnationalist politics. Members of a 'imagined community' and subnationalist political entrepreneurs share the same social space—the intellectual, social, cultural and political world of the nationality. To borrow from Mao Zedong's description of guerilla warfare, subnationalist political activists are like fish in water. Principles of accountability can be found in the relationship between political entrepreneurs and the 'imagined community'. Policy responses to subnationalist dissent must take this relationship seriously. Firefighting tactics might lead to short-term peace that might steal the momentum from a particular group of leaders, but they are unlikely to achieve longer-term resolutions. In Assam, for instance, the unfulfilled promises of the Assam Accord of 1985 between Rajiv Gandhi and leaders of the Assam movement opened the political space for the rise of the United Liberation Front of Assam—a more militant and radical organization ready to avenge the perceived betrayal of the Assamese people by the central government.

The Poetics of Assamese Subnationalism

Assamese subnationalism began in the middle of the nineteenth century as an assertion of the autonomy and distinctiveness of Assamese language and culture against the British colonial view of Assam as a periphery of Bengal. To some extent autonomy and distinctiveness is a continuing theme in post-colonial Assamese subnationalism, accentuated by heavy immigration into the area that has produced fears of minoritization among the Assamese and other indigenous peoples (see Baruah 1999, Chapters 3 and 6). The economic 'underdevelopment' of the state has been the other major theme in Assamese subnationalism. In order to reconstruct the poetics of contemporary Assamese subnationalism, I will now turn to a genre of

Assamese popular music: the songs of Dr Bhupen Hazarika. To say that his music is very popular among the Assamese is an understatement. He is probably the most influential figure in contemporary Assamese cultural life. Born in 1926, Hazarika earned a Ph.D. from Columbia University in 1950. I propose to read his songs as texts that provide clues to the poetics of contemporary Assamese sub-nationalism. While most of his songs are his own compositions, occasionally he sings songs composed by others. In the present discussion, when I refer to Bhupen Hazarika's music, I include both categories of songs. Hazarika's music has a remarkable resonance with the national narrative of the Assamese. Using his songs one can construct an unofficial history of the Assamese nationality—its hopes, aspirations and disappointments.

Until the 1960s the radio and record players were the main means by which Bhupen Hazarika's audience heard his music. However, records in India are more often played in public than private space. People also come to his concerts. People used to wait for his new songs at annual public celebrations of festivals like *Bihu* in spring or the *Durga Puja* in autumn. In recent years audio cassettes have made his music more widely available and readily accessible. Most Assamese know at least some of Hazarika's songs by heart. In a culture where singing is not seen as a function of professional expertise, his songs are sung by innumerable singers in hundreds of 'public' and 'private' events. The nature of public space in India, I will argue below, which incorporates quite a bit of what may be thought of as private space in some other contexts, is an important factor to be considered in understanding the politics of subnationalism.

Hazarika's music can be read as texts that both reflect and constitute the Assamese national imagination. Their power, I suggest, lies in their inter-textuality—their connection with conversations in Assamese 'public' and 'private' life about what can be called the 'state of the nation'. One finds in his music the constant reflection of the political moods of the Assamese. Even the most recent radical and militant turn that Assamese subnationalism took in the form of the rise of ULFA, found more than its pale reflection in Hazarika's music. This is especially interesting because Hazarika enjoys significant recognition on the pan-Indian stage; he has received numerous awards and other forms of recognition from the Government of India, including the Dadasaheb Phalke award. In drawing attention to the subnationalist themes in his music, there is a danger of falling into cosmopolitan stereotypes about the parochial concerns of the nationalist 'mood' in a distant land. It is important to stress therefore that there are many other themes in Hazarika's music. He is part of a familiar tradition of influential progressive cultural figures in India. Internationalism, tolerance, and a radical solidarity with the subaltern as well as romantic love are among the other themes in his music.

The idea of the nation as mother is a familiar motif in national narratives. The motif appears constantly in Hazarika's music. The mother motif achieves a number of things—it makes the connection of a people to its homeland primal, the implied idea of a common womb gives members of the nation a sense of shared origins that minimizes difference. In Hazarika's song 'Mother, what offering can I make at your feet?' (composition by Mukul Barua), the relationship gets imbued with the sacredness of the symbolism of the mother goddess and the sacred obligation to repay through sacrifice. Benedict Anderson has pointed out the affinity between nationalist and religious imaginings. If religious thought 'transforms fatality into continuity', nationalist thought offered 'a secular transformation of fatality into continuity, contingency into meaning' (Anderson 1983: 19). In Hazarika's song the rhetorical question about 'what offering can I make?' is answered with the offer of the sacrifice of life. The territory of Assam is imbued with the significance of the body of the mother. The river Luit (the Brahmaputra) becomes the flow of motherly affection and the river's eventual merging into 'the sea of peace and into the great unit' evokes the Hindu cultural notion of life's unity with the great soul (Hazarika n.d.).[5]

The song 'Bohag is not just a season' (composition by Hazarika 1980) constructs Assamese nationality as a collectivity—with a memory and a will. Bohag is the first month of the Assamese calender. It is the time of the Assamese spring and new year festival Bihu. The song extends the Bihu traditions to the life of the people as a whole and imbues Bohag Bihu with the significance of a national day when the nation takes stock of its past and its future. This notion is similar to the idea of a national birthday, such as the Indian Independence Day and Republic Day or the American 4th July. But what is interesting about the notion of Bihu as a national day is that its origins are in 'time immemorial' and that unlike national birthdays Bihu is celebrated in the social space that is independent from and potentially in conflict with, the state.

Bohag is not just a season or a month; for the Assamese it is a crucial moment in the nation's life-line—it is when the collective life gathers its strength and courage. Bohag is not just about the celebration of the Bihu festival, nor is Bohag about the flowers that bloom at night. It is Bohag that brings processions that transcend caste and creed and it is Bohag that destroys difference.

Drawing on the rituals of Bihu the song makes Bihu a time for national renewal: 'In Bohag the nation takes its ritual bath, and gets rid of its old clothing. And with Bohag comes the pre-monsoon storm that inspires us in our battles to get rid of the shackles of sorrow' (Dutta 1984: 310–11). The idea of a nation reviewing its past and its plans for future is a powerfully constitutive one. If a nation is an act of will, then such texts may be what constitute a nation.

Hazarika's songs register the hopes and disappointments of the Assamese. For instance a song (composed by Hazarika in 1954) celebrates the founding of the first university in the state in 1954—an institution that evoked much hope about the future. The song is a good example of the promises of modernity that accompanied the early years of India's independence from British rule.

Breaking the barriers of darkness, there flows a bright ray of light in Pragjyotishpur (the old name of the city of Guwahati) that will brighten up the banks of Luit (the river Brahmaputra). A festival of a hundred lights of knowledge will brighten up the banks of Luit. The old manuscripts, written on *Sanchi* barks, will find voice, the sound of the traditional flute, die Siphung, will give new hopes and the old royal palace, the Rangghar (the pleasure palace of the Ahom kings) will reopen its doors. Our society will embrace humanity and science will bring tidal waves (of progress) (Dutta 1984: 306–7).

Unfortunately universities in India and the 'Third World' rarely fulfill such expectations. Except for token gestures, research agendas and teaching priorities shaped by a global and pan-Indian academic culture have little room for such 'provincial' dreams.

Through much of the 1960s, a weakness of will was an important theme in Assamese self-perception of the sources of their problems. If nineteenth century nationalists blamed themselves for their economic underdevelopment, the post-colonial generation began to explain Assam's 'backwardness' by their perceived powerlessness. A recurrent theme in Assamese discussions of their conditions is the neglect of their far-away state by policy-makers in Delhi. From 1979 to 1985, Assamese subnationalism came out to the streets with a vengeance to protest against illegal immigration and a de facto policy of enfranchisement of non-citizens.

A song by Hazarika composed in 1968 anticipates the turmoil of the late 1970s and 1980s. The song establishes a continuity with a poem by a late-nineteenth and early-twentieth century literary figure Lakkhinath Bezbarua: 'We Assamese are not [culturally] poor. In what sense are we poor? We had everything and we have everything, but we don't know it and we don't take stock of it.' The notion of taking stock of what a nation *has* or *owns*—culture as property as it were—perhaps indicates nationalism's connection with modernity and capitalism. Hazarika's song begins by referring to the words in Bezbarua's poem, known to many Assamese: 'It won't do to take solace in the words that we Assamese are not poor; today's Assamese must know themselves [become self-aware as a people], or else Assam will be doomed. Today's Assamese must save themselves or else they will become destitutes in their own land.' This song revives the sayings of Assamese historical and cultural heroes. The song stresses Assam's multi-culturalism and talks about 'those who have come from afar and have called the land of the Luit mother are the neo-Assamese'. Here is the anguish of a cosmopolitan cultural figure who cannot be unconcerned with Assam's fate— even if this may be interpreted as provincialism—and yet shares the values of pan-Indian nationalism and internationalism: 'Unless you wipe the tears of your mother eyes, your love for the world will be wasted. If you become a crippled limb in the world's body, the world will not love you for that.' While the 1968 version of the song was a reminder that the calls to action by successive Assamese heroes were unanswered, a 1980 version of the same song is a celebration of what was then happening in the streets of Assam. Instead of the rebuke for non-action of a decade ago, there is now a new-found pride in the new generation of Assamese: 'Today we have martyrs who can say that if Assam die, we too will die' (Dutta 1984: 345–7, 392). By constructing the sacrifices of the youth of the 1980s as a response to calls by an earlier generation of Assamese cultural heroes, the Assamese collectivity is constructed panachronically as well.

The 1979–85 political turmoil in Assam centred on the question of illegal immigration from Bangladesh that was allegedly turning the Assamese into a minority in Assam. The year 1983 was particularly violent. An election that was held against the wishes of the leadership of the Assam movement became a test of will between the leaders of the movement and the Indian state. The leaders of the movement called for a boycott of the election and since participation in the election divided the population of the state in the

middle—mainly, but not exclusively along the indigeneous-migrant divide—
it led to enormous violence.

A song about the violence of the 1983 elections (composition by
Hazarika 1984) seeks to build a collective Assamese connection to a 'martyr'
of 1983 by evoking the ties of family and of a village community, the martyr
becomes every parent's son, every sibling's little brother and every person's
friend. The song '1983—the year of the devastating fire—the year of the
election' is a ballad of a little brother who was killed in the violence of the
election. 'My little brother disappeared that year; do you have any news of
him?' The song praises his accomplishments: 'He wanted to build his country
and to secure a happy future for those who live in Assam. He did not want
to become a stranger in his own land'—the latter being a reference to the
Assamese fear of minoritization. There is a evocation of a family grieving
the death of a young son: 'Mother does not eat her food, the village youth
all wait for you each day, your sister lights an earthen lamp in your room
every day and poor old dad goes to the railway station every day hoping to
find you in one of the trains.' The song concludes with a determination
never to let such violence occur again and, reflecting the Assamese interpretation of the causes of that violence—the state's attempt to hold elections
against the wishes of Assamese civil society—it warns that those who seek
to divide the Assamese will invite the wrath of the Gods and meet their end
(Hazarika n.d.).

Benedict Anderson draws attention to the cenotaphs and tombs of
unknown soldiers as among the most 'arresting emblems of the modern
culture of nationalism'. 'Void as these tombs are of identifiable mortal
remains or immortal souls, they are nonetheless saturated with ghostly
national imaginings' (Anderson 1983: 17). Martyrdom has been an
important theme in the poetics of Assamese nationalism. A student killed
by the police in the campaign for Assamese as the official language in 1960
is referred to as 'the first martyr of the mother language'. There are many
recent songs by Hazarika that are memorials to Assamese martyrs—victims
of the violence of the recent episodes of political turmoil.

By the late 1980s, Assamese nationalism took a militant turn with the
rise of the United Liberation Front of Assam. ULFA was organized as a
liberation army with modern weapons and trained cadres that would liberate
Assam. A song by Hazarika of that period (not Hazarika's composition; the
composer's name is not indicated in the cassette tape) has a martial spirit; it
applauds bravery, sacrifice, and heroism: 'I salute mother Assam and I dress

up to go to war. I salute the river Luit and give *puja* to Goddess *Kamakshya;* with your blessings and an oath I am off to war.' The Kamakshya temple in Guwahati is Assam's most important Hindu temple and an important place in Hinduism's sacred geography. Hazarika's song echoes the Assamese sense of how things came to this; persuasion had failed and there are few alternatives but battle to avenge past wrongs: 'It is no time to teach history lessons, it is no time to take it easy: the enemy taunts us at our gates, leave aside your daily tasks, get ready for war and be prepared to lay down your lives' (Hazarika n.d.).

The ideology of ULFA emphasizes the unity of the indigenous peoples of the area—both the Assamese of Assam and those who live in the areas that have been separated out. The process of fragmentation of the territory of Assam in the 1960s and 1970s is seen as a reflection of Assam's powerlessness. The term 'united' in the name United Liberation Front of Assam reflects this emphasis. One of Hazarika's songs from this period dwells on the unity theme; the seven states of Northeast India become seven sisters born of the same mother. The undivided territory of Assam is the mother and the song (again not Hazarika's composition; the composer is not indicated in the cassette tape) tells the story of the fragmentation in terms of seven sisters being 'married away'. 'Mother, we are seven sisters who once played together in 'the sunny sands of the river Luit.' Here is how the song depicts three of the new states: 'Meghalaya went her own way as soon as she was old enough, Arunachal too separated and Mizoram appeared in Assam's gateway as a groom to marry another daughter.' The portrait of Tripura is interesting: 'I have built my home in the frontier of Bengal to keep an eye on the enemy's movements .... Mother, please don't leave me out.' Of all the north-eastern states Tripura, which borders on Bangladesh, has changed its demographic picture the most as a result of immigration from East Bengal—the indigenous Tripuris are a now a small minority and hence the motif of recognition and identity. The song ends with a determination to keep the unity of the Assamese with other smaller nationalities that are left in present-day Assam—'the Karbis and the Mising brothers and sisters are our dear ones.' Echoing a theme in the ideology of ULFA, Hazarika's song celebrates the reunion of the seven sisters in a new 'emotional unity' that is more powerful than state-drawn modern boundaries. The song ends with a warning against those—the state seems to be the obvious referent—who attempt to break this great unity (Hazarika n.d.).

The images in Hazarika's songs—for example the obligations to 'mother Assam', the stock-taking about the Assamese collective past and the determination to act on its historically constituted collective will, the obligations to honour the memory of martyrs—provide important clues to the 'imaginative geography and history' (Said 1979: 55) that animate Assamese subnationalism.

The State, Civil Society and the Politics of Subnationalism

Assamese subnationalist politics, I have said, originates in and is sustained by civil society and not political society—to use Antonio Gramsci's distinction. It is not accidental that organizations that have led subnationalist protests in Assam often perceive themselves as being 'non-political'. The point seems to be that they see their concerns to be different from and of a higher order than those of 'politicians'. In this view, the concerns of nationality are obviously of a higher order than the imperatives of electoral politics. As we will see organizations and individuals that play a key role in subnationalist protest typically belong to the cultural realm; they see themselves as reluctant entrants to the political realm. The notion of a higher-order concern for the life of the nationality has the capacity of incorporating all Assamese irrespective of their lower-order engagements as it were, into subnationalist projects—membership, even leadership positions, in a political party or in the civil service does not disengage an Assamese from the concerns of the collectivity.

Jean-Francois Bayart in applying the concept of civil society to Africa uses it in two different senses. Following Robert Fossaert he initially defines civil society not as a set of institutions but as social space. He defines it provisionally as 'society in its relation with the state ... in so far as it is in confrontation with the state' or the process by which society seeks to 'breach' and counteract the 'simultaneous totalization unleashed by the state'. But for him there are also situations when civil society becomes the collective will of a people—say as in Iran during the revolution or Poland at the height of the solidarity movement—when it is meaningful to speak of entire civil societies being in opposition to states. It is possible to speak of a civil society in the second sense when societies have the capacity to bridge what he calls certain epistemic gulfs across cultural, religious, and linguistic rifts and 'to confront the state with appropriate conceptual weapons'. It is civil society in the second sense that he finds absent in African societies: 'The concept of civil society seems best to explain—by its absence—the continuing existence of African autocracy (Bayart 1986: 111–12).

I will use the term social space in the first sense of the term and reserve the term civil society for the second sense. However, since what separates social space from civil society is organizational capacity, civil society cannot be an all or nothing phenomenon. It is perhaps best to speak of civil society in India in the plural. That may be the reason why India's subnationalist dissents—each of them located in particular civil societies—have never posed a unified challenge to the Indian state. At the same time it makes sense to speak of stand-offs between the state and, say blocs of civil society—Assamese, Kashmiri, or Sikh, not unlike those in Iran and Poland that leads Bayart to speak of them as illustrations of civil society in the organized sense. There are, of course, also political moments in India when it may be possible to speak of a pan-Indian civil society—at least of an incipient one—say when a Gandhi launches a civil disobedience movement or J.P. Narayan launches a pan-Indian movement against corruption.

Social Space: Some Comparative Considerations

How does a social space become available for the reproduction of subnational imaginings and political projects? Such a space is uncaptured or incompletely captured by the project of the modern state—the creation of a national political community as the framework that defines the limits of legitimate political discourse. From the Assam case it would seem that in India what would conventionally be called modernization—urbanization, expansion of communications, literacy, newspapers and magazines, educational institutions or the electronic revolution and the expansion of the audio cassette and more recently the video cassette—have brought about a social space that has proven to be unexpectedly user-friendly to the reproduction of subnationalism. It has linked villages with towns and cities; and the cultural and literary elites and the newly educated youth with the Assamese peasantry and the urban middle and working classes. In Assam's fast growing urban space there is evidenced not only what modernization theories would have predicted, but also a mode of urban living that reproduces and intensifies ties of family and kinship—both imagined and real. Among the specificities of this mode of urbanization, for instance, is the relative weakness of the bourgeois idea of a home. The Indian middle class home is perhaps closer to the medieval European home, which as Witold Rybczynski says, was 'a public, not a private place'. The houses were full of people and the 'crush and hubbub of life', he says, was partly accounted for by the fact that 'they served as public meeting places for entertaining and transacting business' (Rybczynski 1986: 26–8). The home is part of the social space that sustains the Assamese collective imagination and the projects of Assamese civil society. I had a glimpse of this in January 1991. My brother, a medical doctor who treated patients that were thought to be ULFA militants, was arrested by the Indian army for his alleged ties with ULFA, and our home in Guwahati was soon full of people—relatives, neighbours, friends, and well-wishers—who came to inquire and express sympathy and solidarity. In chat social space, the rupture between state and civil society in Assam was rather apparent.

There was other evidence of this rupture during that period. The Governor and senior civil and military officers in charge of Assam—all of them non-Assamese—for instance were sensitive to Assamese sensibilities and gave orders on how to respect the rituals of Assamese *Magh Bihu* festivities in January. Yet Magh Bihu in Assam that year was not a private event—it was full of public significance. The All Assam Students Union (AASU)'announced that that year's Magh Bihu called for a more sombre celebration because the army operations against ULFA can be no occasion for celebration. It did not particularly serve the interest of the state to have a gloomy Magh Bihu echo the Assamese mood.

In order to understand this social space it may be useful to contrast it with the organization of space under advanced capitalism. For analytical purposes, at the risk of exaggeration, two distinctions can be made. First, the organization of life into the private—the domain of domestic bliss— and the public as the domain of the political seem to be at fundamental odds with the ethos of middle class life in Assam. This bourgeois ordering, of course, is under some threat in advanced capitalist countries too say, by the feminist agenda of making 'the personal political'. Second, compared to conditions in Assam, the space designated as public under advanced capitalism would seem to be rather restricted. If the bourgeois home is about the private—love, affection and family—schools and colleges are about education and a preparation for the bourgeois life—and not about politics—and sanitized shopping malls are about private consumption— not about a whole range of public activities that Indian bazaars are known for—the space for the public in contrast with Assam seems woefully limited. That ethnic parades or political demonstrations in the US often take place in carefully designated public space that is authorized for such a purpose on a particular day illustrates the restricted nature of public space under advanced capitalism. This contrasts sharply with the use of public space in India. The colonial state tried to impose a little more bourgeois ordering of public space in India. The post-colonial state too makes some attempts at order, but it seems too weak to achieve such order in the absence of help from capital. Capitalist modernization of a more destructive kind that eludes the 'Third World' might have put more resources in the hands of the state to achieve such an ordering of public space. Perhaps, if an eight-hour day gets further universalized—as the ideologues of modernization would like— that too might achieve more privatization of the Indian home and further restrictions on the home as public space.

Organizational Capacity and Assamese Civil Society

While the organization of social space under peripheral capitalism may be user-friendly to India's subnationalist projects, one still has to explain how Assamese civil society has come to acquire its remarkable organizational capacity. As I said before, civil society in Bayart's second sense is a function of organization; a collective imagination has to come together with organizational capacity. Organization involves consent as well as coercion. Assamese civil society clearly has its dissenters. In the 1979–85 period, the Assamese who were unfriendly to the subnationalist project faced social boycotts. Coercion played a role in ensuring support for that political project of Assamese civil society. For instance, Assamese government officials managed to reconcile obligations to Assamese civil society with the demands of their jobs by temporarily appropriating the bourgeois idea of individual choice—senior state government officials (most of whom are men) had their wives and children join the processions and demonstrations and avoided the costs of reneging on their higher order obligations to civil society. When the state increased the costs of complicity with the project of Assamese civil society, it became harder to balance the competing demands. But the balance was usually tipped on the side of civil society. Nonetheless, considering Assam's diverse population there has always been significant dissent from Assamese subnationalist projects in Assam. But despite dissent, Assamese civil society has the ideological and organizational capacity of defining and pursuing its political agendas. The year 1983, saw the violent consequences of a test of will between Assamese civil society and the Indian state.

Two key organizations that play a central role in the constitution of Assamese civil society are: the Asom Sahitya Sabha (The Assam Literary Society) and the All Assam Students Union. That both organizations call themselves 'non-political' is significant in order to understand their location in civil society.

The Asom Sahitya Sabha with its motto 'My mother language—my eternal love' had its first session in 1917. The Sabha meets every year and there are culture, music, science, and history sessions. The president of the Sabha in 1967, referred to the meetings of the Asom Sahitya Sabha as Assam's *Jatiya Yagna* ('the great national sacrifice') and thanked members for honouring him with the 'most respected chair of the nation' (Bhuyan 1967: 26–8). The Sabha has consistently sought to promote the Assamese language in Assam—the fact that it is an issue at all is a reflection of the continued contested nature of the cultural definition of the state as a result of demographic change. Writing about the role that the Sabha played in 1959–60 in the campaign to recognize Assamese as the official language of the state, Maheswar Neog—who was a major figure in that organization—wrote, 'These events have raised the institution in the general esteem and marks the start of another phase, when the Sabha began attracting crowds like the National Congress sessions and other political festivals' (cited in Misra 1988: 123). The general secretary of the Sabha in 1971 responded to the criticism that the Asom Sahitya Sabha meetings instead of being gatherings of writers and critics had become like carnivals 'national festivals' where thousands participate (Goswami 1971: 123–4).

The Sabha has an agenda of aggressive cultural nationalism. As early as 1950, it demanded that Assamese be made the official language of the state and that barring those in the Khasi and Jaintia Hills, Mizo Hills and Garo Hills, all schools should switch to Assamese. According to Udayon Misra, 'the Sabha's rigid stand on the question of Assamese being recognized as the sole official language of the state', contributed significantly to the alienation of Assam's smaller nationalities and their demand for separation. He believes that 'a more imaginative language policy of the Sabha could perhaps have slowed down the alienation of the hill tribes from the Assamese people' (Misra 1988: 114).

I have examined the proceedings of seven annual meetings of the Sabha from 1964 to 1972 (Asom Sahitya Sabha *Barshiki,* various sessions*)*. At every session there were resolutions demanding the implementation of Assamese as the official language of Assam and the language of education.

As I had said earlier, the Sabha was the major organization that mobilized public opinion for the adoption of the Official Language Act in 1960. During 1964 to 1972, the Sabha's resolutions complained of the tardiness in the implementation of the act. A 1968 resolution dealt with the implementation of Assamese as the language of the High Court. Its concern ranged from the inadequate supply of Assamese language typewriters, the absence of Assamese signs in government offices to the need for Assamese language training for non-Assamese officials. Other resolutions sought the adoption of Assamese as the medium of education at various levels. The Sabha was concerned about the status of Assamese in the two universities, its use as the language for doctoral research in order that the language 'develops'. It was concerned about the availability of Assamese language texts, the training in Assamese of non-Assamese teachers and the inclusion of Assamese in the curriculum of non-Assamese educational institutions in the state. One of its resolutions suggested the introduction of Assamese language lessons through state-owned radio stations. One resolution warned the state government of state-wide protest unless it showed its seriousness about the use of Assamese. Other resolutions of the meetings include condolences at the passing away of prominent Assamese personalities, plans for public celebration of birth anniversaries of major figures of Assamese cultural nationalism.

In 1971, the Sabha had 169 branches and six affiliates—some of them scattered in the most remote countryside and towns (Goswami 1971: 140–6). The power and influence of the Sabha has been quite apparent in Assam's politics. Its annual meetings are attended by senior ministers of Assam and the state government has supported the Sabha with major financial grants and other forms of assistance (Misra 1988: 126). During the 1979–85 campaign for stopping illegal immigration into Assam, the Sabha gave up its official 'non-political' posture and formally became part of the Gana Sangram Parishad (The Organization for People's Struggle) that led the campaign. This seriously strained its relations with the government and the Sabha lost the government's patronage, which it called an 'indelible stain on the national life of the people'.

The Sabha is not an interest group. Interest groups that try to influence policy usually accept the rules of the political game—itself an indication of the success of the state's project of ordering the political process—and make demands that are negotiable. The Sabha on the other hand, sees itself as non-political—it claims the moral ground to make demands that are of a higher order; and it seems to succeed in claiming the right to make the consent of the governed conditional on the fulfillment of their higher order demands. Thus even if the state attempts to cultivate the Sabha—and the Sabha is financially dependent on the state government—the state does not succeed in influencing the shaping of the Sabha's projects, or to get it to act as an interest group that makes negotiable demands within the accepted rules of the democratic political game.

The other important body that accounts for the organizational capacity of Assamese civil society is the All Assam Students Union. The post-Independence expansion of schools and colleges has led to the emergence of a space where young people from different parts of Assam can meet. This is probably the most important segment of the new social space that has proven favourable to the growth of subnationalist politics. AASU started as a voluntary federation of the students unions of schools and colleges. Organizationally it consists of elected secretaries of students unions. That gives it an extraordinary organizational base. Now there are schools in the most remote small towns and villages; colleges too are numerous. Through a remarkable process of self-selection, only predominantly Assamese-speaking schools and colleges seem to have become part of this federation—Assam's numerous Bengali or Hindi schools are not part of the AASU. It is not surprising that the explosion of subnationalist politics in Assam coincides with the founding and consolidation of this organization. In 1979–85 it led the campaign against illegal immigration into Assam and the student leaders of the campaign, who formed the Asom Gana Parishad, were later elected to power in the state.

Like the Sabha, the AASU too claims to be non-political—a curious claim for a body that brought normal politics in the stare to a standstill for five years from 1979 to 1985 and whose leaders then proceeded to win elections and form the government of the state. Here too the notion seems to be that it is the trustee of interests that are of a higher order than the wheeling and dealing of normal politics. One might add that there is also a notion of the obligations to civil society being of a higher order than a careerist notion of education as a means to achieve individual mobility. As soon as the Asom Gana Parishad—the political party formed by student leaders—came to power in 1985, AASU announced that it was not a student wing of the new party. AASU subsequently took on an independent stance from the AGP government and even organized strikes against the state government. True, the state government tried to influence AASU's politics.

But AASU has continued to assert its independence. Many of the ULFA militants were AASU activists and AASU protested some early police actions against ULFA (Misra 1988: 144–51). A slogan I noticed on a wall in Guwahati in January 1991—'AASU is a relentless procession'—captures AASU's self-perception: it is the custodian of Assamese civil society and with the procession as its preferred mode of political action, it promises never to subordinate the interests of civil society to the powers that be. The Sahitya Sabha and AASU therefore are institutions that give Assamese civil society its organizational capacity.

Conclusion

Given the power of the poetics of subnationalism and the social space that sustains subnational projects, what are the prospects for India's project of 'nation-building'? How does the state–society struggle embodied in the politics of subnationalism in India appear in comparative perspective? The poetics that shape national projects is, of course, not unique to the 'Third World'. The Western national political community is hardly Jurgen Habermas's 'ideal speech community'. The reproduction of the national political community as the hegemonic 'imagined community' is achieved not through the power of reason, but partly through coercion implied in the status of the state as a compulsory association and through political rituals such as, in the US case, elections, Fourth of July parades, the pledge of allegiance or welcoming troops back home. American analysts use terms like civil religion to describe the poetics underlying these political rituals. The history of how this has come about and the difference with the history of post-colonial formations is worth exploring. I cannot go into it here. But very briefly, in Western Europe this seems to have come about as the result of a historical 'shift from society organized around local community to one in which individuals identified with 'the nation' and the accompanying creation of a 'public sphere' as 'an important corollary of the nation-state' that ultimately mediated collective participation in the emerging nation-state (Freitag 1989).[6]

The vibrancy of subnationalisms in India does not mean that they have a telos that must inevitably lead to separation. Analytically one can contrast two extreme resolutions to India's problem with subnationalist dissent within the framework of the Indian union: one authoritarian, the other democratic. The authoritarian resolution may be to destroy through relentless modernization and political repression, the social space that sustains subnationalist politics. In that impoverished social space the state can then take on the project of establishing a monopoly on the national imagination. However, in the 'Third World', neither capital nor the state has that capability. Hence the state may be left with the option of responding to subnationalist protest through periodic repression. A more humane and democratic resolution will involve the state coming to terms with the evolving forms of social space and civil society in India.

The crisis of the Indian national project today may be, above all, a crisis of imagination. There is no inherent reason why a poetics of pan-Indian nationalism cannot subsume subnationalisms—there is enough of a tradition of sacred geography and shared history to do that. There obviously does exist a powerful poetics of Indian nationalism. However, the twentieth century has also shown the dangers of such a poetics—it can divide as well as unite. In an age of nationalism, 'one man's imagined community is another man's political prison' (Appadurai 1990: 6). Nonetheless let me cite another song by Bhupen Hazarika (composition by Hazarika 1984) to illustrate the imaginative possibilities that exist to make subnationalisms compatible with the larger Indian nationalist project. In a tribute to Assamese martyrs, he sings, 'We salute you, O' martyr. In order to save *Bharati's* youngest daughter, you have embraced death' (Hazarika n.d.). Bharati—a feminized name for India—now becomes the mother; *Asomi*—a feminized name for Assam that appears in some of Hazarika's other songs—is the daughter.

The rise of Hindu nationalism in India seems to be an effort to fill the pan-Indian national project—that seems to have lost much of its passion—with a more charged poetics. The modern *imaginaire*[7] of a homeland seems finally to have subsumed the Hindus. If Muslims can have Pakistan, Jews can have Israel, why cannot India be more of a Hindu homeland? Understandably Indian secularists reject that project because in this Hinduized definition of the Indian nation, Muslims are either symbolically excluded or culturally subordinated. The crisis, to some extent, is a crisis of modernity: the age of nationalism everywhere has produced national projects that privilege 'formal boundedness over substantive interrelationships' (Handler 1985: 198). But how does one make the imaginaire of homelands fit into a political formation that is a legatee to a subcontinental empire made up of regional kingdoms and a cultural formation that despite its diversity does not easily yield to territorial boundedness? The violent partition of India in 1947, the subsequent breakaway of Bangladesh from

Pakistan in 1971 and the often bloody history of subnationalist politics in India and Pakistan are signs of the subcontinent's difficulties with the modern imaginaire of homelands. The idea has been especially problematical in north-eastern India. Even after a process of reorganization that has led to the formation of seven states, there are other movements that seek further fragmentation of Assam in order to accommodate more homelands. Some of competing homeland projects make claims to the same land making the politics of homelands very violence prone.

The challenge for India then is to reinvent a poetics that rejects the imaginaire of homelands and of peoples with exclusive cultures and histories—one that privileges interrelationships over boundedness. Such a poetics of space would perhaps be closer to the publicness of Indian homes than the privateness of the Western bourgeois home. If nationalist discourse has been a response to the geographical violence of colonialism, a truly emancipatory discourse will have to be able to develop a different relationship to culture and history than that of cultural property that is owned by nations and nationalities.

Notes

[1] The original version of this chapter was published in *Modern Asian Studies*. Reprinted by permission of Cambridge University Press from Sanjib Baruah, '"Ethnic" Conflict as State-Society Struggle: The Poetics and Politics of Assamese Micronationalism', *Modern Asian Studies*, Vol. 28 (3) July 1994: 649–71 © Cambridge University Press 1994. Apart from the change in the title, this version has a few other changes.

[2] The role of coercion in 'nation-building' has not received much scholarly attention, partly because of the state-centric bias of political science discourse. A number of writers, of course, have drawn attention to this bias. The concept of nation-building, in P.T. Bauer's words, treats people as 'lifeless bricks, to be moved by some master builder'. Donald McCloskey's explication of this point is rather memorably phrased. The metaphor, he says, is of a 'handsome neoclassical building in which political prisoners scream in the basement'. As McCloskey puts it, such metaphors are not 'merely ornamental rhetoric, but a political argument put into a world' (McCloskey 1990: 154). The quotation from P.T. Bauer is cited by McCloskey.

[3] In the original version of this chapter published in *Modem Asian Studies* I had used the term micro-nationalism. A number of readers pointed out to me that the use of term micro was very misleading. Benedict Anderson wrote that there are, after all, 'dozens of nation-states in the UN with smaller populations and smaller geographical terrains' than Assam (Benedict Anderson, personal correspondence, 10 December 1994). I have

also been struck by the fact that in Assamese the term used to refer to this cultural and political tendency is simply *Jatiyotabad* or nationalism—it has no qualifier.

[4] The phrase 'imagined communities' is of course from Benedict Anderson (1983). The notion of poetics is an extension of Gaston Bachelard's idea of the poetics of space (Bachelard 1964).

[5] Hazarika, n.d. The source for the lyrics of this song is a cassette tape. I rely on cassette tapes, widely available in Assam, for the lyrics of a number of his songs. This particular song is sung but not composed by Hazarika. However, his songs are usually his own compositions. For a collection of Hazarika's songs until 1980, see D. Dutta 1984.

[6] Freitag uses Jürgen Habermas' notion of the public sphere.

[7] Arjun Appadurai writes about 'the French idea of the imaginary *(imaginaire)* as a constructed landscape of collective aspirations'. See Appadurai, 1990: 5.

7

The Indian State and ULFA
Winning a Battle and Losing the War?[1]

The independentist militancy that rocked Assam in the late 1980s began to come under control by the 1990s. This was the result of two counter-insurgency campaigns by the Indian Army and a series of clever political moves widely credited to the Congress (I) Chief Minister of the period, late Hiteswar Saikia. A report in April 1993 by Human Rights Watch drew attention to human rights abuses in Assam during the army operations (Asia Watch 1993: 13). However, by that time Indian officials could claim that their strategy in Assam had 'worked'. Major groups of insurgents—members of the United Liberation Front of Assam [ULFA]—surrendered their weapons and renounced the path of armed struggle as well as the goal of an independent Assam. In many ways, political life and life on the streets returned to 'normal', and influential segments of public opinion in India sided with the government's position.

While human rights violation in India's troubled regions receive attention in scholarly and policy circles, the impact of the use of coercion on the legitimacy and longer-term viability of India's political and legal institutions are rarely examined in any systematic manner. Most discussions go little beyond charges made by human rights groups on one hand, and on the other, attempts by government and defenders of its anti-insurgency policies to frame the issue in terms of the challenge posted by independentist militants and the role of foreign governments in supporting such groups. An old intellectual tradition that systematically examined the effects of the use of coercion as an instrument of statecraft, however, would have had much more to say on the subject.

Vilfredo Pareto was a scholar in that old tradition and he wrote at length on the use of force and determination of its effects. 'A few dreamers reject the use of force in general, on whatever side', wrote Pareto, 'but their theories either have no influence at all or else serve merely to weaken resistance on the part of the people in power, so clearing the field for violence on the part of the governed'. Pareto also believed that 'all the advantages and all the drawbacks, direct and indirect' of the use of coercion can be systematically computed (Pareto 1942: 1527, 1512–13). Most of us today lack Pareto's faith in the 'logico-empirical method'. Nevertheless, in order to assess the results of the Indian government's strategy in Assam, one would have to consider, in the spirit of Pareto, possible long-term consequences as well as those that are immediately apparent. The use of coercion, of course is part of a strategy that has other components. In particular, I will refer to some of the de facto and *de jure* bargaining between factions among the militants and the government.

A Localized Regime Crisis

The political configuration of Assam at the height of ULFA's popularity was not a simple confrontation between the forces of political order and anti-system militants. What Assam faced was not only an independentist movement but also a localized regime crisis in the sense that the dynamics of independentist politics disrupted the functioning of political and legal institutions. While officials blamed 'extremists' for this state of affairs, to a significant extent it is the less than critical response of mainstream political forces to 'extremist' politics—indeed the very blurring of extremist and mainstream or moderate categories—that explains why the political, legal, and administrative institutions of the state ceased to function under the pressure of such developments.

'One of the central characteristics of a crisis democracy,' writes Juan Linz, 'is that even the parties that have created the system tend to deviate from the ideals of a loyal system party when they encounter hostility among extremists on either side of the spectrum'. Thus parties or political forces loyal to the democratic system may no longer feel committed to making 'the boundary between the system party, broadly defined, and anti-system parties as clear as possible both publicly and privately' (Linz 1978: 35–7). Such a blurring of lines is reflective of the capacity of anti-system forces in certain situations to successfully challenge the ideological hegemony that underlies a governmental regime. A similar process is at work in a localized regime crisis such as that in Assam.

Only if one thinks of the political conjuncture as a localized regime crisis where the lines between pro-system and anti-system parties get blurred, would it make sense for the political situation in Assam to have become such that by November 1990 the Governor of Assam, in his report to New Delhi recommending dismissal of the state government, described the situation thus:

The holders of public offices have been rendered totally ineffective. The statutory authorities are in a state of panic incapable of discharging their functions. The holders of constitutional offices stand totally emasculated so much so that the State Cabinet cannot even discuss the situation. Members of the Council of Ministers cannot express themselves openly since they doubt the bonafides of each other in so far as their attitudes towards ULFA is concerned (Thakur 1991: 22).

The regime crisis can be understood (a) by locating subnationalist politics in the space that is thought of as a civil society that is autonomous from political society, and (b) by locating the particular episode of radical militancy in the ideological field of Assamese subnationalist politics and its particular historical moment. Subnationalist politics in India, unlike some tamer versions of 'ethnic politics' elsewhere, derive their ideological and political force from a capacity to demand higher-order obligations from their constituents. Organizations and individuals that play a key role in subnationalist protest in Assam often belong to the cultural realm; they see themselves as reluctant entrants to the political realm, and their concerns as different from, and of a higher order than those of politicians. In this view, the concerns of the Assamese nationality are of a higher order than the imperatives of the rules of electoral politics. The notion of a higher-order concern for the life of the nationality has the potential capacity of incorporating all Assamese into subnationalist projects, irrespective of their lower-order engagements as it were—membership, even leadership positions in a political party or in the civil service, does not preclude such participation (see Chapter 6).

I am not suggesting that there is something inherent about nations and nationalities causing them to develop such organizational and political capacities and agendas. Ernest Gellner reminds us of the contingent nature of nations. 'Nationalism', he writes, 'is not the awakening and assertion of these mythical, supposedly natural, and given units. It is, on the contrary, the crystallization of new units ... admittedly using as their raw material the cultural, historical, and other inheritances from the pre-nationalist past'. For all the nations and nationalities in the world that present themselves as having been around from time immemorial, but awakened by recent nationalists, there are many potential nations that are 'determined slumberers' (Gellner 1983: 48). Subnationalist politics of the kind elaborated here can only be understood by referring to the particular ideological, organizational, and political history of the 'imagined community' in question (Anderson 1983). Indeed, the historical construction of the Assamese nationality has been challenged in recent years by groups such as the Bodos, Karbis, and Misings, peoples who have been labeled as 'plains tribal' constituents of the composite Assamese nationality until recently, but who are increasingly seeking autonomous political futures, even outside the political framework of Assam.

ULFA and the Assamese Mainstream

In February 1992, the editor of the Assamese magazine *Aamee* (We), introducing the subject of negotiations between ULFA and the government of India, wrote: 'ULFA did not drop from the sky, nor is ULFA a wild animal. ULFA is our child. [The members of] ULFA are our brothers, they are our kins. [We must understand] why they have chosen the path of the jungle' (*Aamee* 1992). The magazine may have been especially sympathetic to ULFA but the notion that the members of ULFA are 'our boys'—even though they may have gone astray—can be found in numerous commentaries and conversations in Assam. Indeed, Chief Minister Hiteswar Saikia in one of his television speeches spoke of ULFA's surrender as 'the return home of the boys'.

The primary reason for ULFA's influence and the fact that its rise culminated in a regime crisis is the organization's ability to stake out a place for itself in the space that constitutes the mainstream of Assamese public life. The attitude of the Assamese press toward ULFA illustrates this position. Even though many newspapers were critical of ULFA's avowed aim of independence or of its violent methods, they routinely published full texts of statements made by ULFA leaders and engaged the Front in their editorials and other articles. ULFA's position on various issues was, and to some extent continues to be part of the conversation in mainstream Assamese public life. Its popular appeal intrigued many journalists from the rest of the country. For instance, in the *Times of India* Praful Bidwai sought to explain

ULFA's influence by the fear that it inspired. 'Nearly everyone is afraid of ULFA, and in awe of it', he wrote when reporting on the Indian army raids on ULFA's training camps in 1990. People living close to the camps did not answer Bidwai's questions on whether they knew of the existence of the camps or whether they had been harassed.

The graves in ULFA's camps—of people killed for petty 'crimes'—that came to light as a result of the army raids, Bidwai believed, partly explained why people would be frightened. Yet fear alone, he realized, could hardly explain the Front's influence. The goodwill that it enjoyed among wide segments of Assamese society did not appear to him to be the product of fear. 'The truth, however chilling,' he wrote, 'is that ULFA is not a collection of rejects, lumpen and youth from the fringe of society'. Its presence 'looms larger than life in Assam. Many people attribute almost magical qualities to the group. They really believe that ULFA is in some fundamental sense invincible' and 'many Assamese find it hard to think ill of ULFA'. To Bidwai, so impenetrable was the magic of ULFA among the Assamese that he could only express his frustration and anger with ULFA's numerous silent and not-so-silent supporters. 'Touching as this faith is', he said, 'it is at times revolting. The vast majority of Assamese papers have refused to condemn ULFA's self-professed barbarity'. In the local press, the news of the discovery of the graves was overshadowed 'by highly colourful and improbable-sounding stories of Army atrocities'. He found 'a strange kind of inversion of logic and perception' in Assam that had 'to do with the siege mentality that the Assamese, especially of the middle classes have developed' (Bidwai 1990).

Another reporter from the pan-Indian press, Kalpana Sharma, expressed the same astonishment at ULFA's remarkably open style of operation. Writing in June 1990, she found ULFA's presence to be 'ubiquitous', for example, the role of a widely read Assamese newspaper, *Budhbar* (Wednesday), in spreading ULFA's message. The newspaper had a question and answer column designed to educate its readers about ULFA, and according to the editor, it received 150 to 200 questions each week. The editor would select about 15 of these, and the 'ULFA "boys" [would] come to his office and drop in their replies, which are duly published the following week' (Sharma 1990). While *Budhbar*, until a new editor took over in January 1994, was part of the press widely seen as sympathetic to ULFA, even less sympathetic newspapers reported in detail on ULFA's positions on issues and, in their editorials and articles, engaged with it in a dialogue.

ULFA's Beginnings: The Radical Fringe of the 'Assam Movement'

ULFA was founded in 1979 around the same time as the beginning of the 'Assam movement', the six years of political campaigning around the issue of immigration to Assam from present-day Bangladesh that, along with immigration from other parts of India, was turning the indigenous people of Assam into a minority. ULFA was born at a gathering in the historic Rong Ghor in Sivasagar, a palace of the Ahom kings that ruled Assam before the British. Its aim is to 'establish scientific socialism in an independent Assam.' ULFA regards the Yandaboo Treaty of 1826 between Burma and the British rulers of India, which incorporated Assam into British India, as the episode that marked the end of Assam's independence, and it sought the restoration of that 'lost independence' (ULFA 1979: 4).

ULFA's commitment to the idea of an independent Assam, however, may have been mostly a matter of political rhetoric. A seasoned observer of the Northeast, M.S. Prabhakara, pointed out that 'such uncompromising stances are not uncommon among insurgent outfits in the Northeast and have not come in the way of formal and informal talks between them and the Government of India leading, as in the cases of Mizoram and Tripura, to eventual settlements' (Prabhakara 1990). Moreover, by the early to mid 1990s many ULFA leaders repudiated the goal of Assamese independence and instead articulated a commitment to the goal of Assamese *swadhikar* (self-determination).

The Assam movement of 1979–85 protested 'illegal immigration' of 'foreigners' into Assam, primarily from Bangladesh but to a lesser extent from Nepal as well. 'Illegal immigration', however, is only a part of the larger phenomenon of the demographic transformation of Assam and other parts of India's Northeast through migrations from various parts of the Subcontinent since early in the century. Despite the constitutional, legal, and secular couching of the argument against *illegal* immigration in public pronouncements by the movement's organizers, labels such as 'Bangladeshis' and 'foreigners' were commonly used during the movement and they produced insecurity among those minority communities that were seen as harbouring 'illegals'.

In the decades preceding the Assam movement, there were a number of popular campaigns in support of cultural policies that sought to define the state as Assamese—such as declaring Assamese the state language and the language of instruction in educational institutions—and infrastructural demands such as bridges, oil refineries, and railway lines that were seen as key to overcoming Assam's economic underdevelopment. The Assam movement's popularity can be explained only by taking into account the history of Assamese subnationalist political mobilization and the social memory of that sustained 'struggle'. The movement's massive political mobilization became the opportunity for Assamese subnationalism to take a radical and militant turn. The political tendency that eventually took the form of ULFA can be thought of as the radical fringe of Assamese subnationalist politics of the 1980s, even though ULFA did not necessarily share the immediate goals of the Assam movement. Indeed, ULFA sought to distance itself from the immigration issue, and appealed in a number of documents to all *Axom Baxi* (people living in Assam), rather than to the Assamese people, in striking contrast to the mainstream of subnationalist discourse.

A reporter recalls that during his travels in Assam in 1980 at the height of the Assam movement he heard a number of reports of the Assamese youths building ties with insurgent groups in Manipur and Nagaland and crossing over to Burma in order to receive armed training, mostly from the People's Liberation Army (PLA) of Manipur and the Nationalist Socialist Council of Nagaland (NSCN). The militants were activists in Assam agitation even though many of them did not completely share the immediate goals of the Assam movement. In November 1980, for instance, an armed bank robbery in Assam involved both Manipuri and Assamese militants. When the Manipuri PLA leader Biseswar was arrested, one of his associates arrested with him was an Assamese, Naren Gohain. Gohain told a reporter that he chose the path of insurgency in order to oppose the exploitation and oppression of the region—that is, New Delhi's treatment of the region as a 'colony'—and because he had lost faith in the constitutional process (Prabhakara 1985).

Apart from its long-term goal of achieving Assam's independence, ULFA was engaged in what can be called a social agenda, conducting trials of people involved in drugs and prostitution rings. It punished corrupt government officials—though it is alleged that it has as often extorted money from them by blackmail—and those neglecting public responsibilities, such as government doctors who engage in private medical practice or teachers employed in government schools who made money through private tuition at the expense of their classroom commitments. ULFA also intervened in Assamese cultural and social life. In April 1990, on the eve of the Assamese new year festival, Bohag Bihu, it issued a writ asking people not to engage in corruption of the spirit of the traditional festival by playing Hindi film songs and disco music. Such actions reflected ULFA's self-perception as a custodian of the interests of the Assamese nationality in the pattern of more mainstream organizations such as the All Assam Students Union or Asom Sahitya Sabha (Assam Literary Society).

The growth of ULFA can be traced to the changing fortunes of the Assam movement. The February 1983 election was a particularly tense period in the state, as a long series of negotiations between the central government and the student leaders of the Assam movement had failed and the election became a test of wills between the two. By holding the election, the government in effect tried to force a resolution of the controversy over electoral rolls. The rolls, prepared in 1979 and, according to movement leaders, included the names of hundreds and thousands of illegal aliens, had precipitated the Assam movement. The leaders, as expected, called for a boycott of the elections, portraying them as Assam's 'last struggle for survival'. Not unexpectedly, the elections led to enormous violence, and the call for a boycott led to extremely low turnouts in ethnic Assamese strongholds. Nonetheless, a Congress (I) government came to power, one that ethnic Assamese public opinion regarded as illegitimate—a claim later accepted by the Rajiv Gandhi government when it agreed to the demand that the government resign to make room for fresh elections. The 1983 election and the period of the Hiteswar Saikia government that followed was the time when ULFA made the most significant inroads.

A theme in the ideology of Assamese subnationalism in the 1980s was the unity of all 'indigenous' northeasterners, not an unproblematic concept in a region known for heavy immigration. The term 'United' in ULFA's name reflects the importance of this theme, which became more formalized as time went on. In May 1990 ULFA, the NSCN, the United National Liberation Front of Manipur (UNLFM), and some Burmese insurgent organizations signed a memorandum of understanding. According to Indian military intelligence, the objective of these organizations was to establish an independent state comprising the northeastern states of India and northwestern Burma. They formed a common organization called the Indo-Burma Revolutionary Front (IBRF), noting in their agreement that the people living in northeastern India and northwestern Burma are of the same racial stock and that historically and culturally they are set apart from the inhabitants of mainland India and Burma. The governments, they said, have neglected these far-flung regions, 'which must unite and fight their war of independence' (Abdi 1990: 1).

Militancy Under Friendly Conditions:
ULFA Under Regional Party Rule

In August 1985, the Assam Accord was signed by Prime Minister Rajiv Gandhi and the leaders of Assam's campaign against 'foreigners', marking the end to six years of political turmoil in the state. In the election later that year, a new regional party, the Asom Gana Parishad (AGP), formed by the student leaders that ran the anti-immigrant campaign, won a majority of seats in the Assembly and formed the state government. However, once in power there was little the AGP could do to expel or disenfranchise illegal aliens, even though the signing of the Assam Accord would suggest that the Indian government had accepted major parts of this demand. The Indian parliament had passed legislation making it more difficult to prove illegal alien status, and therefore not more than a thousand illegal aliens were detected—less than had been routinely detected in earlier years—even though the agitators claimed numbers in the hundreds of thousands. With the AGP's perceived inefficacy on this issue, its general non-performance, and allegations of corruption against many of its youthful ministers, the appeal of the regional party eroded rather rapidly. Even though the ULFA distanced itself from the issue of 'foreigners', it viewed the non-implementation of the Assam Accord as one more piece of evidence of the central government's apathy in protecting the interests of the Assamese. In one of its documents, ULFA claimed that 'the mass movements of the past and especially the illegal elections of 1983 prove beyond dispute that there is no so-called moderate road available to the people of Assam' (ULFA 1983). The sense of ethnic powerlessness that the non-implementation of the Assam Accord generated was a context in which ULFA's militant stance found a sympathetic constituency.

The AGP was ill-placed to play the role of a system-party that would resist the growth of ULFA militancy. Its response to ULFA was half-hearted, betraying an ideological inhibition that is characteristic of regime crises. As a regional political party wedded to the Assamese cause, the AGP shared a common ideological space with ULFA, and its government was incapable of effectively challenging the Front. Perhaps, ULFA also succeeded in blackmailing AGP ministers against whom there were charges of corruption.

Thus, as the Governor's report of November 1990 put it: 'The loss of faith in the efficacy and the credibility of the government apparatus is so great that the distinction between ULFA, AASU (All Assam Students Union), and AGP, which existed at some stage, stands totally obliterated' (Thakur 1990).

As the AGP sought to shift from a movement to a ruling party in a context where failure to deliver was becoming more and more apparent, defining its relationship with the AASU, its parent body, as well as with the radical fringe of the Assam movement was one of its most difficult problems. New Delhi put pressure on the AGP government to act against militants, who were being charged in rising numbers with murders, kidnappings, and extortions. By November 1990, when President's Rule was imposed in Assam, 113 people had been killed by ULFA, according to government figures, of whom 58 were political party activists and 19 were government officials (Thakur 1990). By now ULFA was virtually running a parallel government in the state. It built a sizable armed organization with sophisticated weapons by extorting huge amounts of funds from local businesses. ULFA's demands put enormous pressure on business, particularly the tea industry—the most important sector of Assam's economy—and the Marwari trading community, mostly people from Rajasthan who have a highly visible presence in the state's commercial life. It is very hard to get reliable figures, but the picture that emerges from various newspaper reports is that the amount of 'taxes' collected by ULFA was staggering.

The Indian army cited documentary evidence of ULFA demanding and possibly getting large amounts of money from major tea corporations—Rs 10 million from MacNeil and Magor, Rs 9 million from Assam Company, Rs 6.5 million from Warren Company, Rs 2 million from Stewart Hall, and Rs 4 million from Doom Dooma Tea. Apart from money, ULFA made other demands of the tea industry including employment of local youth, establishment of high schools and colleges in tea plantations, commitment to the basic needs of neighbouring villages, moving corporate headquarters to Assam, support for higher education for deserving children of tea workers, and improvement in the quality of food and housing provided to tea workers. ULFA made these demands on behalf of the 'people of Assam' (*Sentinel* 1990). The pressure felt by local business was dramatized when on 8 November 1990—just before proclamation of President's Rule—Doom Dooma India Ltd, part of the Unilever group that owns Brooke Bond and Lipton, evacuated nine of its top executives and their families to ensure their safety after the company decided not to yield to ULFA's demand for Rs 3.5 million. In April of that year, the killing of Surendra Paul, chairman of Assam Frontier Tea Ltd, had sent chills through the industry.

The Coercive Face of the State and ULFA's Retreat

The V.P. Singh government in New Delhi fell in November 1990 and a new government led by Chandrasekhar, supported by the Congress (I), came to power. In opposition, the Congress had criticized the Singh government for its ineffectiveness in Assam and implied that the fact that the AGP was a constituent of the coalition that ruled in New Delhi had limited the central government's ability to respond effectively to ULFA. The change of government at the centre created political conditions for the dismissal of the state administration, the imposition of central rule in Assam, and the launching of an anti-insurgency campaign code named Operation Bajrang on 27 November 1990.

Operation Bajrang was not successful. When the army went into the largest of ULFA's camps, the militants had fled, and ULFA managed to sustain its mystique and give the impression that it had out-manoeuvred the Indian army, which continued the military operation until April 1991. The more dramatic change in policy came about with the State Assembly election in June 1991. ULFA decided to be a neutral, a decision that many observers felt reflected the influence of the state's former Congress (I) Chief Minister Hiteswar Saikia on ULFA's decision-making process. Contrary to public expectation, the election was peaceful and fair, ironically due largely to ULFA's announced intention not to intervene. The AGP was defeated and the Congress (I) won a majority of seats in the Assembly.

But now the situation changed dramatically. On 1 July, the day after Congress (I) government led by Saikia was sworn in, ULFA kidnapped ten people, including officials of the Indian government-owned Oil and Natural Gas Commission (ONGC), civil servants working for the state government, and a Soviet citizen who was in Assam as a consultant to the government-owned Coal India. The state government initially acceded to the Front's demand and released more than 400 ULFA members or sympathizers from prison in exchange for the hostages. But the negotiations over hostages did not proceed smoothly. There were more incidents of political violence in Assam, and the Chief Minister after announcing a 'general amnesty' for ULFA detainees, retracted it by saying that it did not apply to those against whom there are 'serious charges'. Two of the hostages, the Soviet engineer and an ONGC official, were killed by ULFA.

On 14 September 1991, on Saikia's recommendation, the centre launched another army operation against ULFA; Operation Rhino continued till January 1992 when the prospect of talks between the government and ULFA led to its temporary suspension. By then the remaining hostages in ULFA's hands had been released. On 12 January 1992, five top ULFA leaders met with Prime Minister P. V. Narasimha Rao, but it was apparent that the armed wing ULFA was not associated with these talks—just the week before, one of its leaders, Hirakjyoti Mahanta, was killed after his arrest by the army in Guwahati. The meeting with the prime minister was symbolic but afterward army operations were suspended temporarily, among other reasons, to enable these 'pro-talks' leaders to meet their rank and file and persuade them to give up arms and take the negotiating path. In April 1992, army operations were resumed in six districts that were specifically targeted because the local leaders opposed the surrender of arms, and negotiations. By then ULFA had become a divided house, with one faction favouring dialogue and arms surrender and another opposing it. Many ULFA activists surrendered arms in exchange for government protection and cash payments for rehabilitation. Suddenly, ULFA ceased to be a serious political actor capable of holding the state to ransom.

Human Rights Abuses

The use of the army involved serious human rights abuses. Asia Watch (today's Human Rights Watch-Asia) sent an investigator to Assam in March 1992 who was 'harassed, questioned and followed by police' all through her travels. Nevertheless, she managed to visit some of the worst affected areas of the state and interview families of victims of army abuses. She confirmed reports of patterns of human rights abuses by security personnel and acts of violence committed by members of ULFA. The Asia Watch report said:

The Indian army has conducted massive search-and-arrest operations in thousands of villages in Assam. Many victims of abuses committed during these operations are civilians, often relatives or neighbours or young men suspected of militant sympathies. Villagers have been threatened, harassed, raped, assaulted and killed by soldiers attempting to frighten them into identifying suspected militants. Arbitrary arrest and lengthy detention of young men picked up in these periodic sweeps, or at random from their homes and from public places are common, and detainees of the armed forces are regularly subjected to severe beatings and torture. Death in custody had occurred as the result of torture, and in alleged encounters and escape attempts (Asia Watch 1993: 1).

The report noted that dissent in Assam was severely curtailed and the human rights activists and journalists were arrested for reporting on abuses. It also said that militant groups were responsible for such human rights abuses as bombings, kidnappings, and the assassination of dissident ULFA members and suspected informers (Asia Watch 1993).

There is evidence that coercion sometimes had a specific political purpose. The killing of Hirakjyoti Mahanta, ULFA's one-time Deputy Commander-in-Chief, after his arrest on 31 December 1991, is a case in point. Local as well as national newspapers reported that he was killed after he was arrested in army custody, while the army claimed, to no one's satisfaction, that he was shot and killed as he tried to escape. It is widely believed that Mahanta, against whom there were a number of murder and other charges, was killed because he was a major obstacle to the pursuit of negotiations between the government and ULFA. It is difficult to determine the truth of such reports but the fact that people may believe them and, in the absence of public investigations of such incidents, they are bound to have the effect of eroding the legitimacy of state institutions. Such reports continue to come out of Assam. In February 1994, the Guwahati High Court, heard a habeas corpus petition on behalf of nine individuals who their relatives claimed were detained by the army; the following day five of them were found murdered. The army denied that it had ever detained those people and claimed they were killed in an 'encounter' between the army and militants (*Sentinel* 1994).

Loss in Regime Legitimacy

Soon the expectation of talks between ULFA and the Government of India had all but disappeared; even if such talks did take place, it was unclear what exactly would be discussed. A section of ULFA, including a couple of top leaders, were opposed to talks. Some leaders of the Front had taken refuge in Bangladesh—an apparent paradox considering Assamese subnationalism's opposition to immigration from Bangladesh but also indicative of the ideological distance between ULFA's brand of radical subnationalism and the mainstream of Assamese subnationalism. Meanwhile

ULFA—or rather some its former members—became integrated into the political process to some extent. This follows the pattern of insurgencies in other parts of the Northeast where former insurgent factions play a role in mainstream politics directly or indirectly. The ULFA card gave political capital to Chief Minister Saikia in the internal factional politics of Congress (I) and in his claim to resources from New Delhi.

Many former ULFA activists in Assam surrendered their weapons and were 'rehabilitated,' many of them receiving attractive financial rewards— a 'golden handshake'. The state's disinclination to ask uncomfortable questions of those who surrender—about the very large sums of money collected by ULFA or about serious offences including murder—is no less attractive than direct financial rewards as an incentive to give up the 'path of the jungle'. Those who surrendered were described as the 'pro-talks' faction of ULFA in that they preferred negotiations to armed struggle. They continue to live openly, some even allowed to carry guns for self-defence. One rather dramatic example of such rehabilitation is ULFA's former Publicity Secretary, Sunil Nath (as an ULFA activist he went by the name of Sidhartha Phukan), who became the editor of a respected Assamese weekly newspaper *Deobar* (Sunday).

Only someone with a naïve faith in a politics-free notion of law and order would expect a full resolution of the numerous cases of political violence in Assam. Assamese subnationalism would frame these incidents in its own terms, which would compete for legitimacy with the interpretations that official legal institutions might, but do not, insist on. One can see it as a strength of the Indian system that it bargains with anti-system political foes such as the ULFA. But that does not mean that the terms of such bargaining do not matter and that there are no costs. The hegemony of legal and political institutions, ever elusive in India, has become even more questionable in today's Assam as a result of such bargaining.

M.S. Prabhakara reported in January 1993 that ULFA's prestige had not diminished and that it had been reorganizing itself since the middle of 1992. ULFA was conducting a critical internal review of its strategy, and contrary to the expectation that it would resume violent activities, it seemed to be pursuing a different course of action. ULFA's district committees have been reconstituted, and civilian cadres have more authority than military cadres inside the organization. The new ULFA places more emphasis on its social agenda, and a number of local development projects in the state are run by organizations with ties to ULFA, such as the *Jatiya Unnayan*

Parishad (National Development Council) that consists of ULFA activists
and sympathizers. There are new local organizations in different parts of
the state made up of former activists and sympathizers dealing with such
issues as flooding and erosion, industrial pollution, illiteracy, eradication of
'social evils' (which in Assam mean drugs, prostitution, corruption, alcohol),
land management, and abuses in the educational system. ULFA cadres have
provided relief to flood victims, and in the post-Ayodhya tensions between
Hindus and Muslims, they intervened successfully to control violence in
certain areas (Prabhakara 1993: 9).

There is evidence, however, that ULFA's prestige took more of a beating
than Prabhakara's report would suggest.[2] A battle was on for the hearts and
minds of the people. The government realized that how the events of those
years are remembered or forgotten would be important in shaping the future
of Assam. On 31 December 1992, the first anniversary of the killing of
Hirakjyoti Mahanta, there were attempts at formal observances. While the
police stopped the holding of a memorial service in the capital city, such
services did take place in other parts of the state. Were ULFA or some other
organization to succeed in shaping the collective memory of the events of
those years, it could widen the gulf between Assamese civil society and the
institutions of the state.

Yet, Assam may not see a recurrence of a regime crisis in the immediate
future. An important factor in this is that the notion of Assameseness itself
is under serious threat from the ferment among the Bodos as well as among
Karbis and other 'tribal' groups. It is unlikely that the political landscape
will become as polarized as it had been during the height of ULFA. While
full-blown regime crisis may be unlikely, the continued appeal of ULFA
and of other militias, the weak assertion of the authority of state institutions,
and a growing tolerance for quasi-political violence point to the likelihood
of a different kind of crisis. *India Today* quoted unnamed trade and industry
sources in Assam as saying that 'under the cover of stage-managed surrenders,'
the government gave 'license to the militant outfits to operate.' Allowing
one-time militants to keep weapons for their self-defence may at least partly
explain a new wave of extortions, and the dividing line between political
and non-political violence grows more blurred each day. The extortions
that took place in Assam in the years following the 'surrenders'—and
continued till much later—were often attributed to what people describe
as SULFA [Surrendered ULFA] (*India Today* 1993: 86–7).

Vaclav Havel, in his days as a dissident writer, wrote to the Communist Party secretary of Czechoslovakia in 1975 that while in the long run he had no fear of 'life in Czechoslovakia coming to a halt, or of history being suspended forever' because of the state's repressive policies, he was worried about policies that 'systematically activate and enlarge the worst in people' (Havel 1989: 34–5). The same can be said about the possible consequences of the Indian state's way of confronting the challenge of ULFA.

Notes

[1] The chapter originally appeared in *Asian Survey*. Reprinted by permission of the University of California Press from Sanjib Baruah, 'Winning a Battle and Losing the War? The State and Separatist Militants in Assam, India,' *Asian Survey* Vol. 34 (10) October, 1994: 863–77 © University of California Press 1994.

[2] For instance, the widely read newspaper *Agradoot* in its editorials regularly critiqued the ideological positions associated with ULFA. See the collection of editorials by Kanaksen Deka published as a book (Deka 1993). First published in 1990, the book was in its tenth printing by February 1993.

8

Twenty-Five Years Later
A Diminished Democracy[1]

After the breakup of the Soviet Union, India, arguably, is the world's most multi-ethnic polity. The constitutional design of India's democratic polity is federal in structure. It has 29 states—with elected legislative assemblies and state governments and Governors appointed by the central government—and six Union Territories. India is an ethnic federation; most Indian states can be described as nation-provinces in the sense that particular nationalities constitute majorities and they define the public identity of these states. India's nation-provinces, however, are far from mono-ethnic places. Yet the nation-province model, by and large, has been able to create legitimate units of governance in large parts of India.

Indian federalism, however, is relatively weak. Indeed, the Constitution even shies away from describing the polity as federal, and instead uses the term Union of India to emphasize the centralized structure. To some extent, managing India's diversity itself has been a reason for this centralized design. For instance, in order to accommodate sub-national demands the Indian parliament can redraw state boundaries—with minimal consultation with the affected state—and it has done so repeatedly. Thus three of India's 29 states—Chattisgarh, Uttaranchal, and Jharkhand—were created only in 2000. While breaking up old states and creating new states has been an effective tool in the hands of the Indian government to respond to subnational demands this has also made for a rather weak form of federalism. States that can be broken up by the legislative fiat of the central government are a far cry from Swiss cantons or American states.

Assam and the Origins of Independentist Politics

Assam can be described as the geographical core of Northeast India. Five of the seven states of today's Northeast India were a part of Assam in colonial times and the break up of Assam into smaller states in post-colonial times is the product of the Government of India's efforts to contain and pre-empt independentist insurgencies in the region. Historically the Northeast India is where South and Southeast Asia meet. While historically the peoples of the region have had different levels of contact with the Indian mainland, the saliency of independentist ideas, has not been a function of cultural proximity or distance. Thus a book on the region's post-colonial political turmoil takes up two case studies of independentist politics: that of the Assamese—a people with a long history of interaction with the Indian mainland—and that of the historically isolated Naga people. In both cases, argues the author, while the independentist movements may look 'decimated' from time to time, they 'continue to hold centre-stage' in each state's politics (Misra 2000: 185).

In the case of ULFA, today even though it has been largely contained, its resilience and the legacy of the Indian government's politico-military strategy of dealing with the challenge have led to an unstable political climate, with significant occurrence of political violence and human rights violations and substantial weaknesses in the legitimacy of governmental institutions. The costs of this festering conflict in terms of the erosion of democratic institutions and values are the focus of this chapter.

Counter-Insurgency and the Growing Democracy-Deficit

An opinion piece on Assam by Sunil Nath, published in December 2001, portrayed the state of the conflict produced by ULFA's independentist politics as involving three parties: the government of Assam, ULFA, and the group of former ULFA militants that has acquired the appellation SULFA. A fourth important node should be added to this picture. As I have argued in Chapter 3, a major player—indeed the crucial node of policy-making towards independentist militant groups like ULFA—is New Delhi, especially the Indian Home Ministry.

Nath argued that the elections to the state Assembly in May 2001, which brought the Congress government to power, had set the stage for a new phase of the conflict. Assam was in 'a lull before it is ripped away by one more surge of violence,' the author predicted (Nath 2001: 23). The

Congress government that came to power in July 2001 was perceived to have a pro-ULFA tilt, while SULFA enjoyed the patronage of the previous Asom Gana Parishad (AGP) government. Counter-insurgency operations against ULFA during the final years of AGP rule had heavily relied on covert collaboration between SULFA and the security forces. Nath's prediction of a new round of violence was premised on this history: so-called 'unknown assailants' or death squads had murdered the relatives of a number of prominent ULFA leaders. It was expected that those murders would be avenged by ULFA. Fortunately, Nath's prediction has not come true.

Nevertheless Nath's narrative, which emphasizes the crucial role of SULFA, is a particularly well-informed account of the public and the not-so-public politics of independentist militancy in Assam. The author, Sunil Nath was one of the first groups of independentist militants to have surrendered in 1992. He had been the central spokesman and publicity secretary of ULFA. Now he is a newspaper editor, an important political commentator and a leader of a new organization, *Asom Jatiyo Mahasabha* (Assam National Conference), formed by former ULFA members. Nath's essay is an exceptional source because it comes close to being an insider's account of some of the events, especially aspects on which public documentation is scarce.[2]

The picture of democracy in Assam that emerges from Nath's account of the Indian state's battle with ULFA is discouraging. While elections have been held in Assam every five years, ULFA's activities and the state's counter-insurgency strategy together have produced a significantly diminished form of democracy in terms of respect for basic freedoms, the rule of law and principles of accountability and transparency. Many of the former militants, for instance, had committed significant crimes including murder and robbery. ULFA, after all, had amassed large amounts of money primarily through extortions. Yet with the active backing of the state, armed SULFA men have squared off with ULFA on city streets. Nath's prediction of a new round of killings and the reference to the killing of innocent citizens by death squads—family members of ULFA leaders being killed as acts of vengeance or as a way of trying to force their kin to change their ways—are hardly the sign of a law-abiding state. 'The killings and violence were such,' wrote Nath, 'that at times the statewide scene resembled that of a banana republic after a military coup' (Nath 2001: 22).

The political role of SULFA and ULFA in the electoral politics of Assam gives no less disturbing a picture of Indian democracy. While they do not officially participate in elections, they seem to play important roles. News reporters routinely speculate on their role in elections. They feature in the campaign rhetoric in ways that seem to confirm their political roles. Thus during the election campaign of 2001, former Chief Minister Prafulla Kumar Mahanta repeatedly accused the Congress party of having ties with ULFA. In the elections of 1996, the roles were reversed; the Congress made similar charges against Mahanta's party, the AGP. The election outcomes and post-election developments suggest that there was some truth to those charges.

At the same time, the threat posed by independentist militancy in Assam is significantly lower today, as a result of military operations that have killed many ULFA cadres, and of a policy that has induced many others to surrender. But arguably, in terms of the quality of India's democracy, as experienced by citizens in Assam, things have not turned any better. The quantitative data on casualties in violence associated with ULFA in Assam, for instance, indicate that the numbers have only increased during this period.

TABLE 8.1   FATALITIES IN VIOLENCE ASSOCIATED WITH
UNITED LIBERATION FRONT OF ASSAM

Year	Civilians	Security Personnel	Suspected Militants	Total
1992	35	10	16	61
1993	48	15	21	84
1994	49	7	53	109
1995	16	14	18	48
1996	59	48	35	142
1997	68	50	111	229
1998	97	42	116	255
1999	55	29	122	206
2000	162	27	218	407
2001	59	27	145	231
2002	7	7	123	137
2003	74	9	108	191
Total	729	285	1086	2100

Source: South Asia Terrorism Portal. Adapted from data in different tables. http://www.satp.org.

To be sure, the data is not unproblematical. For instance, when officials claim that a person killed in an encounter is an ULFA militant, there is no independent means for verifying such a claim. In any case in all the categories of killings—of civilians, security forces and of militants—there was an increase in the mid 1990s, despite a decline in ULFA's strength by then. There has however, been a decline since 2001, though the figures are still higher than those during the early 1990s when ULFA was at its peak. Whether the decline since 2001 represents the decreasing influence of ULFA or reflects a change in the scope of counter-insurgency measures associated with the change in government in June 2001 is unclear. In any case, quantitative data of this sort is a poor representation of the quality of life in a democracy. But the picture of a diminished democracy, while the threat from ULFA has declined, seems to be confirmed by other evidence as well. One of the main reasons for this, I would argue, is the liberty that has been taken with the rule of law in devising the military-political response to the independentist challenge.

The rest of this chapter reviews the last decade of India's engagement with the challenge of ULFA. As I have argued in the last two chapters rather than being the agenda of small group of extremists, ULFA's concerns are continuous with the mainstream social discourse of Assam. That produces a peculiar crisis. Significant interpenetration between state-level politicians and civil servants with militant independentists makes it difficult for the local state to confront the challenge. The burden therefore moves to Delhi. And as the Delhi-led counter-insurgency establishment tries to negotiate the complex web of interconnections, it seeks to insulate as much as possible its actions from the local democratic institutions and processes. While elections continue to play an important role, basic democratic values like the rule of law, accountability, and transparency get thrown out of the window. While this response succeeds in meeting the independentist challenge—in terms of eliminating the likelihood of a break-up of India— in the long term, it significantly diminishes the quality of Indian democracy.

Fish in Water? Independentist Militants and the Assamese Mainstream

ULFA's founding in 1979 coincide with the beginning of the Assam movement—the six years of political campaigning around the issue of 'foreigners', which was the beginning of the gradual worsening of the political situation in Assam. In the last chapter I have shown that ULFA's origins in this political conjuncture explains its close connection with the Asom Gana Parishad—the political party formed by the young student leaders—that has twice been elected to power. The AGP and ULFA grew out of the same political upheaval of 1979–85. ULFA was the radical fringe of the Assamese nationalist political mobilization of this period. However, initially it was more a political tendency than a fully formed group. Yet ULFA did not fully share the immediate goals of the Assam movement. Thus it sought to distance itself from the immigration issue, and in a number of documents it appealed to all *Axom Baxi* (people living in Assam) rather to the Assamese people in contrast to the proponents of the Assam movement.

As I have argued in the last two chapters, the Assam movement's enormous popularity can only be explained by locating it in a long history of Assamese subnationalist mobilization. However, any account of the highly vaunted popular backing for the Assam movement has to be qualified by a reminder of Assam's ethnic heterogeneity. The census classifies Assam's population into the speakers of 68 languages and dialects. The major language, Assamese is claimed as mother tongue by 13 million people or 57.8 per cent of the population. Bengali-speakers are the second largest group: 21.7 per cent, and Bodo-speakers the third largest group—5.3 per cent of the population. As for religious faith, 67.1 per cent of the population is Hindu, 28.4 per cent Muslim and 3.3 per cent is Christians. Muslims include ethnic Assamese Muslims as well as Muslims of Bengali descent and a small number of Muslims of other ethnic backgrounds. Thus even if the ethnic Assamese population may have been mobilized to its fullest, the main issue that the movement raised may have still left at least a third of Assam's population—a variety of minority groups—largely unimpressed. But despite this qualification, the power of the Assam movement as a social force is undisputable.

The demand for autonomy has been a theme in Assamese intellectual and political history for a long time, even though ULFA may have broken new ground in explicitly articulating, as a social movement, the goal of Assam's independence from India. There are significant continuities between ULFA's independentist politics and the ideas held by even the first generation of prominent leaders of the Indian National Congress in Assam, who argued for a pan-Indian federation with powerful autonomous states. At the time of India's independence, Assamese leaders, both in the Indian Constituent Assembly and outside, advocated a far stronger form of federalism than what the rest of India was prepared to have.

The poet and nationalist leader Ambikagiri Roychoudhury, for instance, wanted to see India become a multinational federal state with dual citizenship. Assamese members of the Indian Constituent Assembly argued for giving states much broader powers. Among their proposals were: (a) giving states the right to legislate on immigration, (b) making citizenship matters a part of the concurrent list, (c) leaving residual powers to the states, and not to the Centre, (d) limiting central power over subjects in the concurrent list, (e) not giving the Centre the power to unilaterally redraw state boundaries, (f) making state governorship an elected office, and (g) giving a much larger share of the excise and export duties on tea and petroleum to the producing states. Assam, of course, had important stakes in all these issues, and these positions were ironed out in debates in the Assamese public sphere as India prepared for its post-colonial future (see Misra 2000: 84–104).

At the time of independence, no other issue separated the Assam Congress from the all-India Congress more than the question of where to settle the refugees of partition. Since large-scale immigration from East Bengal had already begun to significantly change Assam's demography, it was already an explosive political issue in Assam by the 1940s. Leaders of the Assam Congress therefore wanted fewer refugees to be settled in Assam, and it was this concern that led them to assert state prerogatives on matters of citizenship and immigration. But the response of the national leaders was patronizing and dismissive. Jawaharlal Nehru, for instance, sarcastically noted in a message to Assam's Chief Minister Gopi Nath Bordoloi: 'I suppose one of these days we might be asked for the independence for Assam' (cited in Barooah 1990: 33). As the controversy over how many refugees were to be settled in Assam continued, Deputy Prime Minister Sardar Vallabbhai Patel called Bordoloi's successor Bisnuram Medhi a narrow-minded parochial person (Barooah 1990: 36). The idea of Assam's independence, of course, did not remain a joke for long, and nor could the label of 'parochialism' smother the desire for independence among a younger generation of Assamese.

In the Constituent Assembly, the Assamese proposals for a federation with strong autonomous states did not succeed. Later during the political mobilization of the Assam movement, these threads were picked up once again by a newer generation of Assamese nationalists. ULFA therefore articulated 'an idea which has long been embedded in Assamese psyche' (Misra 2000: 143). ULFA's ideas are located in a political discourse that has occupied centre-stage of Assamese civil society for more than half a century.

Thus it is hardly surprising that, even after easy military defeat in the hands of the Indian army—with a high death toll in actual and fake encounters with security forces—and the defection of a large numbers of militants, ULFA continues to draw sympathy especially in the rural areas. While ULFA's policies and programmes have been challenged, its ranks have not declined, it has been 'expanding at an alarming rate' (Misra 2000: 147).

This is the context in which 'the Assamese middle class,' Sunil Nath recalls, 'played the role of Frankenstein when it applauded from the gallery at the emerging ULFA, which rapidly grew in strength during the late 1980s in the adulatory atmosphere created by the middle-class led Assamese media' (Nath 2001: 20–21).

A Crisis of Governance

Given that the ideas that inspire ULFA are located in the mainstream of Assamese social, political, and cultural life, it is not surprising that there is no hard boundary between independentist militants and the Assamese 'mainstream'. Many politicians belonging to mainstream parties and ULFA members, or at least members of their families, know one another, or at least their social ties overlap significantly. However, the danger of this kind of political configurations should also be clear. After all, ULFA is committed to achieving Assam's independence through armed rebellion. The blurring of lines between ULFA and the ruling AGP government during the late 1980s provided a fertile ground for the initial growth of ULFA. As I have argued in Chapter 7, there is an affinity between the political conjuncture in Assam in the late 1980s and situations that scholars of democracy associate with a crisis of democratic regimes and their breakdown. The AGP government that came to power in 1986 was ill placed to play the role of a system party and resist their friends and allies who were articulating a radical version of their own political agenda. Assam's situation, however, did not produce a crisis of Indian democracy as such, because the conditions were localized to one state. But it pushed the burden of developing a response to another level of governance—the central government in Delhi.

Since then, as I have argued in Chapter 3, India has created a de facto parallel political system, somewhat autonomous from the democratically elected governmental structure, to deal with the independentist militants of Northeast India. While the apparatus involves the limited participation of state-level political functionaries and senior civil servants, the state level is also perceived as the weakest link in the chain because of the fear that the presence of locals might potentially subvert the counter-insurgency operations. The perceived need to insulate the fight against insurgency from the state level democratic process has led to a preference for covert actions that have steadily eroded democratic principles such as the rule of law, accountability, and transparency. This parallel structure was not in place in Assam in the 1980s, when ULFA got its start.

Yet despite the Assam government's ambivalence, by 1990 ULFA began to be seen as a serious threat by the central government. A change in government in New Delhi created the political conditions for the dismissal of the state government, the imposition of central rule and the launching of a military counter-insurgency campaign in November 1990. However, the military campaign was not very successful, partly because of the high levels of penetration of ULFA sympathizers in the state-level police and bureaucratic hierarchy.

At this point, the imperatives of democratic politics—the need to hold elections at regular intervals—shaped official policy vis-à-vis ULFA. While elected state governments can be dismissed, constitutionally, Indian states cannot be run from Delhi for long periods of time. Moreover, not having an elected state government in place while conducting counter-insurgency operations would make those operations appear illegitimate in Assamese eyes. Given the popular sympathy that ULFA had enjoyed, being able to project the image that the military operations have the support of an elected state government was important. Elections to the Assam Assembly were held in June 1991 as the initial constitutional limit of six months of President's Rule came to an end.

In the election ULFA announced its neutrality; according to Sunil Nath, in order to get a respite from the military pressure. The decision perhaps also reflected the influence of Congress party leader Hiteswar Saikia on ULFA's decision-making process. The AGP was defeated in the election and the Congress won a majority of seats, and Saikia became Assam's Chief Minister.

But once the new government came to power, ULFA struck back by kidnapping a number of senior civil servants on the very day the government was inaugurated. The state government made concessions by releasing many ULFA prisoners. After the initial embarrassment of this hostage crisis, Hiteswar Saikia came upon a strategy of simultaneously increasing the military pressure and, trying to encourage a split in ULFA. On September

1991, on Saikia's recommendation, the centre launched another army operation. In January 1992, when five top ULFA leaders met with the Indian prime minister apparently as a first step towards finding a negotiated settlement, a split in ULFA was apparent. For exactly at that time army operations continued targeting those ULFA leaders known to be opposed to the negotiations.

Clearly the local knowledge of the Congress leader was important in the choice of tactics; especially the attempt to split ULFA. The decision proved momentous for it gave rise to the SULFA phenomenon that changed the ground reality giving the threat of independentist militancy an added dimension. From New Delhi's—and the fledgling counter-insurgency establishment's—point of view, Hiteswar Saikia emerged as an indispensable leader. In Chapter 3 I have shown how the perceived indispensability of another Assamese chief minister led a Governor to face a choice between the imperatives of counter-insurgency and the possibility of making a major symbolic move to strengthen the legitimacy of democratic institutions in Assam.

The SULFA Phenomenon

ULFA militants were encouraged to surrender their weapons and there was a government programme to rehabilitate them. Many of those who surrendered received attractive financial assistance ostensibly for starting businesses. In Sunil Nath's words,

Saikia bestowed 'blue-eyed' status to the surrendered boys, granting them all kinds of proper and improper favours .... Though the majority of the surrendered ULFA members returned to their homes and rejoined normal lives, there were quite a few who took advantage of the state government's patronage and barged into all avenues of moneymaking. Their status as the favoured brats of the Chief Minister made it easy for them to enter into collusion with unscrupulous bureaucrats and police officers, thus evading the normal process of the law. Their conspicuous consumption and open display of suddenly acquired riches, meanwhile helped the government in getting more surrenders from the disillusioned ULFA ranks (Nath 2001: 21).

Since then, SULFA has been a controversial presence in Assam and a tool in government's fight against independentist militancy. A statement made in the Indian parliament the Indian Home Minister in 2000 gives an account of the process and the formal aspect of what it entails. Officially the programme is called 'Scheme for Surrender-Cum-Rehabilitation of Militants in the North East.' According to it those who surrender are initially kept at a Rehabilitation Camp—where board and lodging is free—for training in some trade or vocation, paid a monthly stipend for 12 months not to exceed Rs 2000 per month. In addition, explained the minister, the Assam government had a scheme of providing substantial finance for business projects by former militants. 4,843 ULFA and Bodo former militants were paid Rs 30.30 crores of margin money—or down payment for starting businesses—by the Assam government. It also guaranteed 69 crores of loans given to them by various banks. These are very substantial amounts of money given to individuals with little or no business experience. The number of 'surrendered militants' who were 'registered' in Assam, said the minister, was 251 in 1998, 675 in 1999 and 1900 until 12 June 2000 (Government of India 2000).

Apart from the financial rewards, an important aspect of the surrender policy is that since the former militants are considered to be in danger from their former comrades, they are allowed to carry weapons and the state takes responsibility for their security. The particular way the state has gone about providing security is both expensive and not conducive to public order. The surrendered militants are provided with armed security guards— typically recruited explicitly for this purpose. The sight of armed former militants going about their business in public places and protected by armed guards is one of the most curious sights in the streets of Assam today. A press statement by the Chief Minister Mahanta in January 1999 touched on the financial aspect of this arrangement. The rehabilitation of former militants within the state, he said, meant that they required security adding significantly to the amount of money needed (*Times of India* 1999). An editorial in a Guwahati-based newspaper suggests that the personal security officers are seen as the most attractive benefit that comes with surrender since they could be 'used for illegal and unlawful activities' (*Sentinel* 2001). But perhaps an even more attractive part is an aspect that is not even formally stated: the government's disinclination to ask questions—about the very large sums of money collected by ULFA or about the serious offences that many of them had committed as militants. This allows some former militant leaders to live off their substantial ill-gotten wealth.

The potential for abuse of this policy of encouraging surrender is enormous. Law enforcement officials, apparently viewed the surrendered militants with special favour and they are not arrested no matter what they do in order 'to make a very comfortable living'. In fact, according to an editorial in an authoritative local newspaper, 'many of them are actually helped to get involved in unlawful and anti-people money-making activities while the authorities merely look the other way' (*Sentinel* 2001b).

A press report of March 2001, illustrates the SULFA phenomenon at work and the public ire that it provokes. The example is interesting also because here the SULFA individual is engaged not in a business, but in a supposedly public interest oriented non-governmental organization. Still he manages to use the political patronage for securing lucrative contracts. According to the news report, SULFA leader, Lohit Deori—who was a major figure in ULFA till his surrender a few months earlier—and nine of his associates were involved in dispute in the city's major business district. Apparently they were members of a NGO that was engaged by the city for garbage disposal. While collecting garbage-clearing fees from businesses, a dispute arose between them and a businessman who had the temerity to ask whether the NGO had a valid contract with the city for garbage disposal. This led to the so-called NGO activists and their security guards assaulting the businessman, his employees and ransacking the shop (*Sentinel* 2001a). Old habits die hard. But what is astonishing about this incident is that there is little in their post-surrender conditionalities that apparently require former militants to be circumspect about such habits.

There are hundreds of such stories that make their rounds in Assam. Indeed because the police often turns a blind eye to SULFA's coercive business practices, according to Nath, it has become 'an unwritten code that to engage in any business, construction contract, or trade in Assam, one had to pay a fixed percentage in commission to the local SULFA chief.'

SULFA, Counter-insurgency and Democratic Politics

It is implausible, however, that SULFA would get such indulgence from law enforcement officials without anything in exchange. After all, not long ago they were on opposite sides. As a matter of fact, despite their privileges, many SULFA individuals are quite dependent on the goodwill of their handlers in the security establishment. After all there are real fears of attacks by ULFA, and of their past catching up with them. That produces a dependence on the security establishment that could be easily used by the latter. It is not surprising therefore that, not long after the initial surrenders, SULFA got inducted into counter-insurgency operations. As word of the discrete charm of SULFA life got around, ULFA leaders, according to Nath, faced the possibility of large-scale defections from their ranks. In response,

ULFA attacked some of their former comrades, and SULFA, as Nath puts it, while 'wallowing in their new found riches,' discovered that 'they were now at the top of the ULFA's hit list.' They concluded that it was best to be on the offensive and found that the security establishment was only too eager to help. Indeed, as Nath puts it, 'the military and police officers could hardly suppress their glee when they found eager volunteers among the SULFA boys, with their insider's knowledge, in the fight against ULFA' (Nath 2001: 21–2).

The onslaught on ULFA by the security forces, with support from SULFA, took a significant toll on ULFA. But as the military battle was being won, the public resentment against the wave of crime and coercive business practices by SULFA grew. The illegalities that were central to the SULFA strategy clearly had costs. The costs in terms of the quality of democratic life have been the heaviest. The numerous incidents of seemingly arbitrary and unsolved cases of state and private violence created a chilling atmosphere. Thus even though 'the public was becoming increasingly uneasy,' writes Nath, 'few dared to speak up openly for fear of being branded an active supporter of ULFA—the consequence could be incarceration, or even liquidation' (Nath, 2001: 22).

Under these conditions, elections remained the only way for citizens to express their disapproval of what was going on. The AGP government was thrown out of office in the election of 1996—the familiar phenomenon of voters 'throwing the rascals out'. Negotiations with ULFA have not taken place so far. While the ULFA hard-liners stuck to their independentist position, those who surrendered became irrelevant to a political resolution of the crisis. ULFA's continued resilience—despite the formidable military and political pressures it faced—and the presence of SULFA, armed and protected by the state, are hardly the conditions in which a new state government could suddenly usher in an era of peace. The fires therefore have tended to smoulder till the next opportune moment for it to flare up. Thus after the 1996 elections, when its then patron—the Congress party— was defeated, SULFA initially lay low. But the moment ULFA reappeared on the scene, there was, once again, pressure from the central government on the state government to act, and Chief Minister Mahanta soon changed his stance towards ULFA.

As counter-insurgency operations resumed, SULFA's virtues were rediscovered, and, according to Nath, 'they were brought back to centre-stage on a red carpet.' The late 1990s saw more than a repetition of the earlier cycle of violence. Not only was the scale of blood-letting worse, this phase saw the phenomenon of 'secret killers', death squads who would raid the houses of ULFA members and assassinate them to exact a revenge for their kin's rebellion. According to Nath, this phase also saw a 'sharp rise in the 'syndicate' style monopoly exercised by some SULFA groups over nearly all the high-profit businesses in the state' (Nath 2001: 22).

The consequences of this for the lives of ordinary citizens are illustrated in a news report from Guwahati, Assam's major city. 'Alarming rise in killings spreads terror in Guwahati' was the heading of the news report. In less than a month there were five major 'insurgency-related killings' in busy shopping areas of the city. This was apart from 'other murders, kidnappings and extortion.' While 'a fear psychosis,' had gripped the city, an unnamed senior police official was quoted as admitting that while there was a significant rise in violence, there was not much the police could do because they are not ordinary crimes, but 'insurgency-related violence' in which ULFA men were killing SULFA men or SULFA was retaliating (rediff.com, 1998).

Elections, however, came to the rescue of citizens once again. In the elections of May 2001, the voters once again 'threw the rascals out,' and this time the opposition Congress party came back to power. But if Nath is right, once ULFA acts there will be pressure on the new government to act and the cycle of violence could repeat itself.

Delhi's Choice: Throwing Accountability out of the Window

I have pointed out the difficulties that India's counter-insurgency establishment faces in designing and implementing a counter-insurgency strategy, while negotiating the terrain of Indian federalism. While interpenetration of ULFA and Assam's government no longer produces the kind of paralysis that it did in the 1980s, it has not been easy to keep what are seen as the imperatives of counter-insurgency insulated from local politics.

There are disputes that have come up from time to time. A particularly sensitive subject is the respective role of the state police and the Indian army in counter-insurgency operations. The counter-insurgency establishment prefers what is called a Unified Command under which all forces, including the state police, come under the operational command of the army. But army operations in Assam and the charge of human rights violations that invariably follow cannot but become a problem for elected politicians. Even if military action is regarded as inevitable, there is still a choice to be made between a gentler approach of the Assam police forces that know the locale, and the harsher methods of the Indian army, whose soldiers are mostly from outside the region. Assamese politicians are sensitive to state-level public opinion in such matters. Thus following a failed attempt on his life that sealed his relationship with ULFA, Chief Minister Mahanta supported the Unified Command structure from 1997. Tarun Gogoi, on the other hand, in one of his first statements as Assam's Chief Minister, following the election victory of the Congress in May 2001, said that he would like to see the Assam police play more of a role because of their superior knowledge of local conditions. This was a code for his opposition—albeit mild—to the United Command structure.

As discussed in Chapter 3, in 1998 the Governor of Assam, Lt General Sinha faced a difficult choice when India's Central Bureau of Investigation (CBI) was about to prosecute Chief Minister Mahanta on a serious charge of corruption. A decision to prosecute a chief minister in India requires the consent of the governor. It is an odd and rather undemocratic power for a governor to have. But the decision in this context was even more difficult than usual. The legal pursuit of a serious corruption charge against an elected chief minister could significantly raise the legitimacy of India's democratic governmental institutions in the public eye—a legitimacy they badly need in today's Assam. But letting Mahanta go would be a blow to the imperatives of counter-insurgency, as viewed by the security establishment, given Mahanta's support for the Unified Command structure.

The Governor decided against his prosecution (see Chapter 3). It was difficult to avoid the inference that Chief Minister Mahanta's indispensability as a leader who had consented to the Unified Command Regime was a critical factor in the Governor's decision; that there a *quid pro quo* in the Governor's decision to protect Mahanta from legal prosecution: a way of assuring his continued support for the Unified Command structure. The perceived needs of counter-insurgency had clearly trumped the value of achieving greater transparency in government and of making an important symbolic move that could raise the legitimacy of Indian democratic institutions, in a state where it is seriously challenged by independentists.

Conclusion

The present state of democracy in Assam, brought about by ULFA's brand of militant independentist politics that has had surprising resilience, and the Indian state's politico-military response to it, raises important questions about the theory and practice of democracy. Empirically oriented political scientists usually operate with a minimalist notion of democracy understood in the sense of a few basic procedures such as regular elections. Indian public opinion also displays a commitment to democracy in the minimalist sense. Indeed Indians take great pride in being the world's largest democracy and especially, that democracy in India has been resilient compared to its fluctuating fortunes in Pakistan. The kind of 'aberrations' outlined in this chapter does not feature in such celebratory rhetoric. Most political scientists, however, would acknowledge that this minimalist notion of democracy is a necessary but not a sufficient condition for political life to sustain the substantive values associated with the term democracy. Yet in the world of actually existing democracies, conditions like those in Assam—apparent aberrations—are neither rare, nor do they permit the comfortable assumption that they are examples of democracy as a work in progress.

In Assam engaging independentist militancy during the last decade has meant the de facto suspension of the rule of law, or at least a selective view of legality. While the aberrations may have begun as temporary measures to meet the challenge of ULFA, soon they acquired a life of their own. While these developments are punctuated by democratic elections held at regular intervals, the reality of life on the ground could not be further removed from the substantive values of democracy. Democracy, as Guillermo O'Donnell reminds us, 'is not only a polyarchical political regime but also a particular mode of relationship, between state and citizens, and among citizens themselves, under a kind of rule of law that, in addition to political citizenship, upholds civil citizenship and a full network of accountability' (O'Donnell 1999: 321). Human rights violations are too weak a term to describe what is missing from democratic life in Assam today. Indeed it is perhaps not surprising that while the early 1990s saw great mobilization on the issue of human rights violations, the term has now lost its capacity to express moral outrage. Indeed like most other Indians of the political class the Assamese now regard human rights organizations as at best naïve, or at worse, as front organizations for independentist militants.

Laws like the Armed Forces Special Powers Act [AFSPA] (see Chapters 1 and 3) make the regime of informal illegalities—or at least some of the worse forms of illegalities such as the use of secret killers—possible. Whatever the justification for such laws, the real cost of the way India has chosen to engage with the challenge of independentist militancy is the erosion of the principles of rule of law, accountability, and transparency. Since more than anything else the SULFA phenomenon illustrates this diminishing of democracy in Assam, let me briefly return to the policy of encouraging surrenders. Sunil Nath presents a moral argument in defence of the policy to encourage surrenders. 'The moral question,' he writes, is that 'when somebody is hunted down by the State' it should be a matter of 'natural justice' that he 'should be given a chance to surrender rather than be killed in an encounter.' He then reminds the reader that the people 'hunted down', are not 'hardcore criminals', but misguided youth who are 'bowled over by ideology and the romanticism of holding a gun.' As long as insurgencies remain in Assam, surrenders, he believes, will remain its inevitable by-product since 'it will be morally and tactically unsound to disallow such cadre to return and repent' (Nath 2001: 23).

Repentance is not the word that would immediately come to mind when considering the SULFA phenomenon. However, what is striking about Nath's moral discourse is what is taken for granted. He defends the morality of surrenders against what he sees as the alternative of security forces 'hunting down' independentist militants and killing them in actual or staged encounters. Given this context, one can hardly quarrel with the argument for permitting surrenders. But in this context it is worth remembering that there exists a whole tradition of humanitarian laws of war that require that those who surrender be taken prisoners and be treated humanely. Would it have been impossible for the Indian state to be guided by these traditions in engaging ULFA? In any case even if one agrees with Nath's moral defence of the policy of encouraging surrenders under the given conditions, it does not justify the circumvention of the legal process on matters of crime and punishment. The illegalities permitted to SULFA, and the use of SULFA as a tool of secret violence against ULFA, do not follow from the moral case for permitting surrender.

What raises moral questions then is not the policy of encouraging surrenders as such, but the entire politico-military strategy that has created the SULFA phenomenon. For analytical purposes, it may be useful to contrast Nath's forgiving view of serious but youthful political crimes with an episode involving a similar crime in another legal system—that of the United States. In September 1970 Katherine Ann Powers, then a 21-year-old radical anti-war protestor at Brandies University, participated in a bank robbery. She was in a get-away car waiting for four accomplices who had robbed a bank in Boston. When a police officer arrived at the scene, one of her comrades shot and killed him. While her comrades were arrested and imprisoned, Powers managed to hide for 23 years. She lived in Oregon, where she owned a restaurant and raised a family. Everyone knew her by an assumed name and no one but her husband knew about her radical past. But unable to live with the untruth, in 1993, she decided to turn herself in.

To the extent that her action was prompted not only by the difficulties of living in hiding, but also by a sense of guilt about the illegality of the act, Powers' action perhaps is an illustration of the importance of law as meaning in an ideal conception of democratic citizenship; and law as meaning is not the same as law as power (Cover 1992: 112). The judge found Powers guilty and, despite the political and youthful nature of her crime committed 23 years earlier, he did not see the case as being anything more than a case of a policeman's murder, completely stripped of its politics. In Assam, on the other hand, most SULFA activists have committed crimes that are many times worse, which have been all but forgotten by a political process that has determined that legal amnesia is a necessary incentive to encourage surrenders by independentist militants. The contrast also suggests that the rule of law requires that law has to have sufficient autonomy to be able to control the meaning of an act, and cannot permit a 'continuous renegotiation of the boundaries between these formal and informal legalities' (O'Donnell 1999: 313).

Apart from diminishing Indian democracy through the erosion of the rules of law and the values of accountability and transparency, the policies that have produced the SULFA phenomenon systematically activates and enlarges the worst in people. A newspaper editorial summarized some of those effects early in 2001, while commenting on news reports that major political parties were considering nominating ULFA cadres and SULFA personalities to contest elections as their candidates:

If well-established political parties cannot see the danger to society arising from such unethical practices, there is very little to be said. But the message that is going out loud and clear to the younger generation is that people who take up clandestine weapons, threaten people, extort money at gun-point and then surrender, are indeed better off in every way than youths who have never resorted to violence (*Sentinel* 2001b).

It is clear that the Indian state's political-military response has been successful in meeting the challenge of independentist militancy in Assam, albeit at significant costs to the quality of democratic life. The Indian government has had similar successes in containing or defeating other independentist militancies in Northeast India and in the rest of the country.

In the case of the Naga insurgency, for instance, while the government's military-political tactics have not ended independentist politics, they have significantly changed the reality on the ground. Army actions and the village regroupings wrought havoc to the traditional institutions that were the foundation of the Naga independence movement led by A.Z. Phizo in the 1950s. After that, the formation of the state of Nagaland in 1963, opened up the possibilities of 'sharing the fruits of power' that gave rise of 'tribalism'—competition over the share of the resources among tribes that come under the Naga rubric. As rivalry between 'tribes' became important, Phizo's 'ideal tribal utopia' lost its charm (Misra 2000: 52–5) 'More than half the battle in Nagaland,' according to Udayon Misra, was 'won by market forces' (Misra 2000: 158). But market forces is a misnomer since what Misra is referring to is the informal (and illegal) perquisites of elected office shared among politicians and their clients—over-ground as well as underground—that are heavily subsidized by the Indian state.

Yet the Naga insurgency persists, according to Misra, due to a number of factors. He believes that many political players find it profitable to continue the insurgency. For elected state governments of Nagaland, the insurgency is an excuse to get more resources from New Delhi. Over-ground Naga politicians may not want competition from the leaders of the underground, which would happen if the latter ended the insurgency and staked claims to elected office. The ability of the Naga insurgent group, the National Socialist Council of Nagalim (NSCN), to run a virtual parallel government, especially in remote areas, enables it to continue recruiting cadres. And the human rights violations by security forces during counter-insurgency operations help the militants extend their base by creating sympathy for their side.

In the case of the Sikh militancy in the Punjab, the Government of India perhaps can reasonably claim to have been more successful than its mere containment. The Sikh militancy of the 1980s in Punjab ended in the early 1990s. An estimated 35,000 to 70,000 people were killed during this insurgency—as a result of the violence by the militants and by the State. In an empirical study on the motivations of Punjabi youth in joining Sikh militants, the authors made this chilling observation about its methodology. 'In a majority of empirical studies,' said the authors, 'the standard pattern is to interview the participants in the movement. In the present study this was not feasible. Most of the terrorists were dead' (Puri *et al.*, 1999: 27).

The risks of ULFA breaking up India have never been anything but remote. But the way the Indian state has gone about responding to the challenge has serious long-term costs that would be apparent only if one looks beyond the temporal horizon of the architects of counter-insurgency. After all, to paraphrase Vaclav Havel and to draw on some of his optimism, life in Assam 'cannot come to a halt, or history cannot be suspended for ever.' The 'surcharge' which will be imposed on Assam 'when the moment next arrives for life and history to demand their due' is sure to be incalculable (Havel 1989: 34–5).

Notes

[1] The paper was originally presented at a conference on 'Separatism, Autonomy and Democracy in Asia' on January 22–23, 2002 in Jakarta, Indonesia.

[2] All reference to Sunil Nath in this article refer to Nath, 2001.

SECTION V

*Policy as an Invitation
to Violence*

9

Citizens and Denizens
Ethnicity, Homelands, and the Crisis of Displacement[1]

In 1997, the Khasi Hills Autonomous District Council passed the Khasi Social Custom of Lineage Bill. The body has constitutional jurisdiction over Khasi 'customary law'. The Khasis have a matrilineal kinship system and the bill sought to codify their system of inheritance through the female line. But the bill became highly controversial. A number of organizations, including the influential Khasi Students Union and the Syngkhong Rympei Thymmai (literally, 'Association of New Hearths') opposed the measure and argued that instead of codifying the 'outdated system' of matrilineal succession, the Khasis should 'modernize' their kinship system. They proposed a change that would have allowed only children of two Khasi parents to be regarded as Khasi.

Why did legally establishing who is and who is not a Khasi become so important? Because the Khasis are designated as one of the Scheduled Tribes [STs][2] in Meghalaya and the lion's share of public employment, business, and trade licenses, and even the right to seek elected office are reserved for members of the STs. Nearly 85 per cent of the public employment in Meghalaya is reserved. Fifty-five of the 60 seats in the state Legislative Assembly are reserved for the STs. While the historical disadvantages that the tribal peoples suffered account for this elaborate protective discrimination regime, the status of non-tribals in Meghalaya as well as in the states of Arunachal Pradesh, Mizoram, and Nagaland where such a protective discrimination regime exists, is best described as that of denizens.[3] In all these states, the rights to land ownership and exchange, business, and trade licenses and access to elected office are restricted. This protective discrimination regime is the result of incremental policy-making going back to colonial times when policy instruments were devised to protect vulnerable aboriginal peoples living in isolated enclaves—once described as 'backward tracks'. Under the Sixth Schedule of the India's post-colonial Constitution many of these enclaves became autonomous districts and autonomous regions within those districts—often identified with particular titular STs. Subsequently many of these territories became full-fledged states, and the protected minorities turned into majority groups in these states. However, thanks to the trend of demographic change inherent in economic development policies, their majority status is under increasing stress. In three of the states—Arunachal Pradesh, Mizoram, and Nagaland—the continuation of the colonial institution of the Inner Line gives an even stronger layer of protection against potential settlers. Anyone entering those territories is first required to secure an official permit. One of the unintended effects of this process of incremental policy-making is that the notion of exclusive homelands, where certain ethnically defined groups are privileged, has become normalized in the region.

In recent years internal displacements caused by violent ethnonational conflicts in many parts of Northeast India have attracted the attention of refugee advocates. Most observers agree that there have been episodes of conflict producing significant levels of internal displacement in this region. However, estimating the precise number of internally displaced persons (IDPs) has not been easy. Mahendra Lama describes the nature of the problem in India as a whole. Political sensitivities prevent the government from releasing data on displacement. But without 'a central authority responsible for coordinating data from central and state governments regular monitoring is not possible in such a huge country.' The 'nature, frequency and extent of the causes of internal displacement' in India, are so varied, Lama writes, that it would be a 'herculean task to monitor and record them' (Lama 2000: 24–6). The Norwegian Refugee Council's profile of internal displacement in India in 2000–1, based on its Global IDP Database, is illustrative of the wide divergence that exists between various available estimates of IDPs in Northeast India and it also points to the absence of data in some cases. The available estimates of the number of IDPs in the state of Assam in 2000–1, for instance, varied between more than 200,000 to more than 87,000 persons. The estimates of Reangs displaced from Mizoram and living in the refugee camps of Tripura varied between 31,000 and 41,000. The profile cites one estimate that at least 80,000 Bengalis were uprooted in Tripura since 1993. In Manipur conflicts between tribal groups led to the displacement (at least temporarily) of as many as 130,00 Kukis, Paites, and Nagas since 1992, but there were no estimates of the number of IDPs in Manipur in 2000–1. In Arunachal Pradesh as many as 3000 Chakmas had become internally displaced, but the number of those who have left the area was unknown (Norwegian Refugee Council, 2001: 31–4). The US Committee for Refugees in its report for the year 2000 estimated that there were 157,000 displaced persons in Northeast India (USCR 2000).

Despite the absence of precise figures, these estimates underscore the magnitude of the IDP crisis in Northeast India. In this chapter I will not make a fresh attempt to provide numerical estimates of the number of IDPs in the region. Instead my goal is to describe the particular historical conditions and institutional context in which some of the typical ethno-political conflicts of the region take place and why these conflicts have proven to be particularly conducive to episodes of ethnic violence and displacement.

Northeast India is one of South Asia's last land frontiers and through much of the twentieth century these sparsely populated areas have attracted large-scale migration from the rest of the subcontinent. The protective discrimination regime, outlined earlier, arose partly as a response to these demographic trends. Many of these tribal societies have been going through a process of transition from shifting cultivation to settled agriculture, from clan control of land to commodification of land, urbanization, and cultural change associated with the process of 'modernization'. The new economic niches created in this process of social transformation attract many denizens to the region. I would argue in this chapter that (a) the normalization of the idea of exclusive homelands for ethnically defined groups generates a kind of politics that is in dissonance with the actually existing political economy of the region; (b) the emerging pattern of class differentiation taking place within the framework of the protective discrimination regime of these transitional economies is complex. While some settlers exploit indigenous tribals, others occupy the most marginal of economic niches. While the protective discrimination regime has enabled some tribals to do well, it has not stopped the process of proletarianization of other tribals; (c) This is the context in which the idea of exclusive homelands—expressed in the institutional language of autonomous district councils or separate statehood—has shaped the political imagination of tribal as well as non-tribal activists of the region.

This particular configuration of institutional legacy, demographic trends, and political discourse in Northeast India has shaped an extremely divisive politics of insiders and outsiders that have led to the incidents of displacement. While this combination of circumstances is unique to this part of India, the introduction of similar ideas of exclusive homelands in demographically mixed situations have produced similar conflicts—with the attendant risks of ethnic violence and internal displacement—in other parts of India as well. In the new state of Jharkhand for instance, the summer of 2002 saw significant unrest over the state government's new 'domicile policy', which would have made ancestral roots in the territory based on the 1932 land records a requirement for public employment. The new domicile policy led to protests and political polarization of the state between pro-domicile and anti-domicile groups. A bandh (general strike) called by pro-domicile groups turned violent claiming a number of lives. The scope of this chapter, however, is limited to the seven states of Northeast India: Arunachal Pradesh, Assam, Manipur, Meghalaya, Mizoram, Nagaland, and Tripura. An eighth state, Sikkim that was added to the key policy-making institution, the North Eastern Council in 2001, is outside the scope of the chapter. I argue in the concluding part of the chapter that the way out of the dilemma in Northeast India is not a regime of undifferentiated nation-wide citizenship and the elimination of all controls over immigration into the area. Instead I propose a way of defining political communities in civic rather than ethnic terms that could incorporate the ethnic outsider—at least beyond the first generation—and bring the citizenship regime of the region in line with the actually existing political economy of the region.

Returning to the controversy in Meghalaya over Khasi succession rules, the authority of the Khasi Hills Autonomous District Council to decide on Khasi succession rules is derived from the Sixth Schedule of the Constitution. According to its sponsors, the goal of the Khasi Social Custom of Lineage bill was to stop non-Khasis from adopting Khasi surnames to take advantage of opportunities reserved for STs. The Khasi activists opposed to the measure would hardly disagree with that goal. However, the attempt to codify 'customary practice' drew public attention to the liberal way in which the Khasis have traditionally incorporated outsiders into their fold. The practice by which children of a Khasi mother and a non-Khasi father can become a Khasi came up for special scrutiny. The opponents of the bill argued that the system allows too many people to pass off as Khasi and take advantage of opportunities reserved for Khasis. Thus the President of the Syngkhong, Keith Pariat was quoted in the press as saying that the matrilineal system no longer serves contemporary needs and that, if it was allowed to continue, the 'pure Khasi tribe' will become extinct in another ten to fifteen years (cited in Shridhar 2000). The bill, however, did not become law because it did not receive the Governor's assent—a constitutional requirement aimed at moderating the legislative powers of state legislatures.

By raising questions about the way 'outsiders' have historically been incorporated into the Khasi fold, the controversy had the effect of putting under the cloud the rights—including rights to property ownership, public employment and to seek elected office—of significant numbers of people living in Meghalaya, some for generations. And since the proposed reforms would have denied those rights to people who had some claim to being a Khasi, the climate generated by the controversy could only have been worse for most denizens—residents of Meghalaya who had no claim to being a Khasi or a member of one of the other STs.

This chapter, I wish to emphasize, is not an argument for a universal model of national citizenship. I agree with the view expressed recently by two political theorists who have examined various kinds of differentiated citizenship in the world. 'Critics of minority rights,' write W. Kymlicka and W. Norman, 'can no longer claim that minority rights inherently conflict with citizenship ideals; defenders of minority rights can no longer claim that concerns about civility and civic identity are simply illegitimate attempts to silence or dismiss troublesome minorities' (Kymlicka and Norman 2000: 41). The regime of citizens and denizens that has evolved in Northeast India has to be understood in a historical context. It began as an attempt by the colonial state to insulate some of the peoples organized in pre-capitalist social formations from the devastation that the initial onslaught of global capitalism had brought. Given this history, one can argue that a model of formally equal citizenship would only reinforce discriminatory outcomes and that the only way to protect such vulnerable groups of peoples is a regime of differentiated citizenship. But whether a particular regime of differentiated citizenship can achieve its intended goals has to be a matter for investigation. For the costs of sacrificing the basic principle of equal citizenship are high; and there are intended as well as unintended consequences of regimes of differentiated citizenship.

From Excluded Areas to Exclusive Homelands

Attempts to deal with 'aborigines' by creating protected enclaves where they can be allowed to pursue their 'customary practices' including kinship and clan-based rules of land allocation go back to the earliest period of British colonial rule in India. It is worth remembering, however, that the idea of protection came only after the phase of enormous violence that was let loose on some of the same people by the early colonizers in the course of pacification campaigns of 'savage tribes' and, after it became clear that the initial onslaught of colonial transformation had led to the massive dispossession and displacement of many of these peoples organized in pre-capitalist social formations. For many, whatever protection came along, was too little and too late.

As early as 1874, the Indian legislature had passed a scheduled districts act. The Government of India Act of 1919 empowered the Governor General in Council to declare any territory to be a backward track where laws passed by the Indian legislature would not apply. The Statutory Commission, which in 1930 had examined the political conditions in British India and proposed constitutional reforms, observed that there was a 'complete statutory bar to the legislative authority of legislatures within every backward track' (cited in Ghurye 1980: 109). The Commission did not like the term 'backward tracks', but it agreed with the notion that such tracks should be outside general constitutional arrangements. It proposed a change of name from backward tracks to excluded areas. The Government of India Act of 1935 therefore provided for excluded and partially excluded areas—so called because they were excluded from the operation of laws applicable in the rest of British-controlled India.

Some of the potential problems, especially the dangers to non-aboriginal people living in those areas were anticipated by the debates about these measures even in colonial times. One of the best-known critiques of colonial-era tribal policies is G.S. Ghurye's 1943 book *The Aborigines—So Called—and their Future*. 'The acknowledgement of the right of the so-called aborigines to follow their traditional pursuits, like the practice of shifting cultivation, without any reference to the needs of the general community,' wrote Ghurye in reference to the recommendations of the Statutory Commission, 'was the most dangerous doctrine endorsed by the Commissioners.' The Commissioners, he charged, had not considered the impact on non-aborigines living in those areas and 'much less did they give their thought to the proportions of such people in the various areas, unless we discover it in the distinction of the two categories of excluded areas made by them.' If the distinction between excluded and partially excluded areas was indeed based on the proportions of non-aborigines living in those areas, he wrote, it was too broad a distinction to be useful (Ghurye 1980: 111). About the Government of India Act of 1935, Ghurye wrote that in its 'eagerness to do something for the tribals,' the British parliament barely considered the condition of:

... the non-tribals in whose midst the protected aborigines live and on whom they depend to some extent for their livelihood. That these non-tribals, too, have rights, that their good will and cooperation, next only to the conscious and deliberate internal organization of the tribals themselves, are the most essential factors for the present welfare and future development of the so-called aborigines, failed to receive adequate consideration.

That some non-tribals may have indeed taken 'unfair advantage of the simplicity and ignorance and simplicity of the aborigines,' Ghurye argued, was no reason to write off their contribution to 'socio-economic development,' and much less to treat all of them as a 'right-less population' (Ghurye 1980: 126–9).

Nevertheless the Constitution of India of 1950, retained most of the provisions of the 1935 Act, though the nomenclatures and some of the institutional forms were modified. Not surprisingly, Ghurye could reprint the same book with a few changes and a new title in 1959. Most importantly, from our perspective, the Constitution made a distinction between the tribal areas of Assam (five of the seven states of today's Northeast) and those in the rest of the country. While the tribal peoples of the rest of India came under the Fifth Schedule, the Sixth Schedule provided for the administration of the tribal areas of Northeast India.

The chairman of the subcommittee of the Constituent Assembly that drafted the Sixth Schedule, Gopi Nath Bordoloi in presenting its proposals justified them by referring to the uncertain political conditions in the region at the time of independence. Bordoloi stressed the need for continued protection because of the doubts among the tribal people of what a post-colonial dispensation would bring; he spoke of the need to 'integrate' these peoples in a Gandhian way (cited in Chaube 1973: 86–7)). The fear of being swamped by outsiders, once the colonial era restrictions were suddenly removed, was indeed a concern expressed by leaders of these peoples. That the Naga revolt broke out soon after independence—and continues till this day—indicates that anxiety expressed by Bordoloi was far from theoretical.

The Sixth Schedule distinguished two sets of tribal areas of (undivided) Assam using the administrative categories that were then in effect: (a) the districts of the United Khasi and Jaintia Hills (excluding Shillong), Garo Hills, Lushai Hills, Naga Hills, North Cachar Hills and the Mikir Hills and (b) the North East Frontier Tracts and the Naga Tribal Area. The first set of areas today comprise the states of Meghalaya, Mizoram, Nagaland, and parts of Assam, and the second category consists mostly of the state of Arunachal Pradesh and a part of the state of Nagaland. The Sixth Schedule institutions were meant for both sets of areas, but the latter set of territories—which were mostly un-administered during colonial times—were considered not quite ready at that time for such self-governing institutions. The administration of those areas were going to be carried out directly from Delhi—with the Governor of Assam acting as the agent of the Indian President.

The Sixth Schedule provided for autonomous districts and autonomous regions within those districts with elected councils which enjoy powers to levy some taxes, to constitute courts for the administration of justice involving tribals and law-making powers on subjects including land allotment, occupation or use of land, regulation of shifting cultivation, formation and administration of village and town committees, appointment of chiefs, inheritance of property, marriage, and social customs.

The Sixth Schedule, however, was not intended to protect all the STs of Northeast India. Only those that were considered to be relatively concentrated in the old excluded and partially excluded areas, and for which the Constitution used the term tribal areas, came under the purview of the Sixth Schedule. The Bordoloi sub-committee did not consider the situation of other STs. Among them were groups such as Bodos, Misings, and Tiwas that are described today as plains tribes to distinguish them from the hill tribes that came under the Sixth Schedule. In the Constituent Assembly, the special needs of the plains tribes were the responsibility of a separate subcommittee, which was in charge of minority rights. A Bodo politician, Rupnath Brahma, was a member of the Minority Rights sub-committee.

The process of formation of Autonomous District Councils, however, did not quite proceed the way Constitution-makers had anticipated. The outbreak of the independentist Naga rebellion for instance, meant that political conditions for holding elections to the Naga Hills District Council did not exist. Instead in 1963 the state of Nagaland was created. The North East Frontier Tracts where the Sixth Schedule was eventually supposed to be in place also went through a different process of institutional change than the one anticipated prior to the Indo-China war of 1962. The area is now the state of Arunachal Pradesh, where tribals enjoy protection at the state level. On the other hand, the Sixth Schedule has been extended to Tripura in response to tribal militancy, where the Tripura Tribal Areas District Council was formed.

It is not accidental that Nagaland was created in 1963, a year after India's war with China. I have argued elsewhere that the Chinese invasion exposed India's vulnerabilities in the region. Already the Naga independentist rebellion had begun to make officials of the post-colonial Indian state anxious. There were stirrings of unrest in other parts of the region as well. Beginning with the China war, the managers of the Indian state began to see the external and internal 'enemies' in this frontier region coming together and constituting a looming threat to national security. Extending the institutions of the state all the way into the international border—nationalizing this frontier space—became the thrust of Indian policy ever since. Over the next few years, the governmental structure of the region was fundamentally redesigned to create what I have called a cosmetically federal regional order. Thus with the creation of Nagaland, statehood in Northeast India became de-linked from questions of fiscal viability and of its implications for the constitutional architecture of the larger polity. Building on the elementary apparatus of state institutions created by the Sixth Schedule became a good way to ensure both the penetration of the state and the creation of local stakeholders in the pan-Indian dispensation. Apart from consolidating the idea of exclusive homelands, organizing the region into a number of mini states, all of them with the formal institutions of any other Indian state government, also had the effect of imposing a particular developmentalist paradigm. There is, after all, a standard vision of development which is contained in the routine practices of the bureaucracy of a developmentalist state that allocates funds to departments such as Public Works, Rural Development and Industries; and that vision only gets bolstered by the patronage politics of an electoral democracy. In the sparsely populated parts of this frontier region, these economic trends have invariably meant more immigration (see Chapter 2).

The most significant aspect of this new regional order, from the perspective of the theory and practice of citizenship, however, is that the

vast majority of seats in the state legislatures of the mini states—indeed all
but one seat in the case of three legislatures—are reserved for candidates
belonging to the STs. Table 9.1 gives the number of reserved seats in the
state legislatures of northeastern states and also gives the percentage of the
ST population.

TABLE 9.1   Northeast Indian states: Reserved seats for Scheduled
Tribes in State Legislative Assemblies

States	ST as % of Population*	Leg. Assembly Total Members	Leg. Assembly Seats for STs	Leg. Assembly Unreserved seats
Arunachal	63.7	60	59	1
Assam	12.8	126	16	102 **
Manipur	34.4	60	20	40
Meghalaya	86.6	60	55	5
Mizoram	94.8	40	39	1
Nagaland	87.7	60	59	1
Tripura	31.0	60	20	33 ***

*   based on 1991 census data.
**   8 reserved for scheduled castes.
***   7 reserved for scheduled castes.

In the Legislative Assemblies of Arunachal Pradesh, Mizoram, and
Nagaland all but one seat are reserved for STs. In Meghalaya 55 of the 60
seats are reserved. Apart from the issue of the denizens not being able to
contest elections, the principle of one-person, one-vote, one-value has had
to be undermined in other ways as well in order to achieve such a weighted
system of representation. Generally, the norm about ensuring the equality
of the relative weight of each vote in a democracy requires that in electoral
systems with single-member constituencies, the electorates in all districts
be roughly of the same size. That could not done if the legislative assemblies
were to have such a weighted system of representation. As a result, Nagaland's
largest urban centre, Dimapur, for instance,—which has a very high
concentration of denizens—is divided into two constituencies and one of
them is the sole unreserved (non-tribal) seat in the Nagaland Assembly.
This unreserved constituency has many times the number of voters of each
of the other constituencies in the state.

Through another constitutional amendment the balance between reserved and unreserved seats in the assemblies of Arunachal Pradesh, Meghalaya, Mizoram, and Nagaland has been frozen in order to ensure that delimitation of constituencies in light of demographic changes in future does not change the current balance.

Whatever the philosophical dilemmas these arrangements present to the theorist of citizenship, the emergence of elected state governments under the control of tribal politicians and of a visible well-to-do tribal elite in those states has captured the imagination of tribal as well as non-tribal ethnic activists in the region. There is a perception that the STs in the states with the most comprehensive protective discrimination regimes have done well economically and have been relatively successful in insulating themselves from being swamped by immigrants. While a homeland has become something to aspire for on the part of those ethnic groups (STs as well as others) who don't have one, ethnic activists of the existing homelands have become zealous defenders of what they see as their statutory entitlements. We saw that exemplified in the case of Khasi activists in Meghalaya.

Post-colonial Changes: Economic Transformation and Class Differentiation in a Land Frontier

The idea of protecting the aborigines of excluded or partially excluded areas, as I have said above, was a problematical proposition even when these policies were originally conceived. As Ghurye had argued, the economic structures of those societies were more complex and varied than the image of isolated aboriginal peoples that shaped those policies. In the half century since India's independence, the process of economic and social transformation— significantly propelled by the post-colonial state's development initiatives— has brought about far-reaching changes. One significant change is in the rate of population growth in these areas. For instance, between the 1991 and 2001, the population growth rate in the state of Nagaland was 64.41 per cent—the highest in India. Table 2.1 in Chapter 2 (p. 50) gives the population growth rates of the northeastern states. Except for Assam and Tripura—where the growth rates were very high in earlier censuses—all the other states show growth rates that are above the national average during the 1991–2001 decade. In addition, in the states of Arunachal Pradesh, Meghalaya, Mizoram, and Nagaland as well as in Assam's two autonomous districts (Karbi Anglong and North Cachar hills), STs as a proportion of the total population is on decline. However, at the moment, except for the Karbi Anglong district, the majority status of STs is not immediately under threat. This trend of population growth is, of course, the rationale for freezing the present balance of ST representation in the states' Assemblies.

Too often the demographic change in the region has been seen only from the perspective of what scholars of migration call 'push factors'. But it is important to bring in the 'pull factors' as well—the economic transformation and process of class differentiation in these states that have provided significant economic opportunities to new immigrants—some of which may be hidden from the gaze of the law. Since the protective discrimination regime in place restricts what denizens can legally do, numerous informal arrangements have emerged in the ownership and control of agricultural land and in business practices. Denizens have become integrated into the economies of the region in substantial, but often quite informal ways. Those informal niches are sometimes positions of advantage vis-à-vis a person belonging to a ST and at other times the ST person may be at a position of advantage. In the Karbi Anglong district of Assam, for instance, while there is no transfer of land from tribals in a formal sense, field-studies reveal that agricultural land belonging to STs are often cultivated by non-tribal denizens. In one area, while ownership rights are in the name of tribals, Bengali and Nepali denizens are the real owners (Bordoloi 1986. Cited in Karna 1990: 36). This should hardly be surprising. As shifting cultivation declines, largely as a result of official policy discouraging it, the shifting cultivators of yesterday can hardly be expected to transform themselves overnight into viable settled cultivators without sustained assistance. Under these circumstances selling the land that has been allocated to him or her would have been the obvious option. But since the protective discrimination regime restricts selling of land to denizens, the cash-starved former shifting cultivator tends to turn actual control of his land to immigrant denizens—Nepalis and Biharis in this case—in exchange for cash. These denizens typically are better adapted to cultivate these lands because they bring with them some cash, agricultural implements, and their prior experience in settled cultivation.

Furthermore there are informal ways in which denizens acquire de facto property rights that are likely to become de jure rights in future. A recent report by a local human rights group relates the ethnic violence in parts of Karbi Anglong to the tensions generated by this transition. Even Indian security forces, ostensibly there to deal with the security threat posed by insurgencies, have become appropriated by partisans of the local conflicts generated by the informal practices that govern the emerging pattern of property relations. In the parts of Karbi Anglong that was surveyed, Hindi-speaking denizens whom the indigeneous Karbi people refer to as Biharis (though they are not all from Bihar) have acquired informal control over what is formally designated as public lands. These denizens who have consolidated a 'considerable amount of economic and political power' in Karbi Anglong now are seeking the formal change in the status of those lands and formal land titles (MASS 2002, 11–13).

According to the report, the loss of land by tribals to denizens was the source of ethnic conflicts, rise of insurgent groups, counter-insurgency operations and human rights violations. While the indigenous Karbi youth had come under the influence of the United People's Democratic Solidarity (UPDS)—a rag-tag band of Karbi militants—the Bihari denizens had the informal backing of Indian security personnel stationed in the area to fight the UPDS, because of shared ethnic ties between these soldiers and the denizens. Thus in a violent conflict in July 2000, according to the investigation of this fact-finding team, the central government's elite counter-insurgency force, the Black Panthers 'killed four of the deceased in cold blood and the settlers gunned the other two down' (MASS 2002: 21).

While in this case, Karbis lost actual control of land to Hindi-speaking denizens, the process of transition from shifting to settled cultivation has been far too complex for the tribals/non-tribals dichotomy to neatly coincide with a notion that the former is always exploited by the latter. In Meghalaya, for instance, a class of Khasis has been able to extend substantial control over both urban and agricultural land. There has been a capture of what is formally clan-controlled land by powerful individuals. Chiefs and headmen have been issuing land deeds to non-Khasis and Khasis alike charging a fixed rent and cash payment (Karna 1990: 35). A recent report on rural indebtedness in the Ri-Bhoi district of Meghalaya describes another aspect of the emerging pattern of class differentiation 'The money-lender is no longer the foxy non-tribal taking advantage of the simple tribals as it used to be. Today the *mahajans* (trader-moneylender) are as tribal as the village-folk are and as cunning as the old non-tribal moneylenders of the old days' (*Grassroots Options* 2000: 11).

This is not limited to Meghalaya. In various forms, such a process is occurring in most tribal areas of the Northeast. 'It is no longer surprising,' writes sociologist M.N. Karna of the North Eastern Hill University, 'to come across a Naga or a Garo owning a thousand acres of land. Nowhere in these areas would customary practices have permitted such a concentration of land, but new linkages have brought with them hitherto unknown phenomena like absentee landlordism, realization of rent from land, sharecropping, land mortgage, landlessness and so on' (Karna 1990: 36). Such land grab has also been made possible by official development policies that have encouraged plantation crops such as tea, coffee, and rubber.

In Assam's North Cachar Hills, the Autonomous Councils have been encouraged by official agencies to grant individual deeds of land control to enable banks to extend loans. Villagers in the 1980s formed loose knit 'committees'—headed by influential individuals—with the blessings of official agencies. These committees then secured land deeds from the headman or the Autonomous District Council. According to Sanjoy Barbora, the result of this process at the end of 20 years is that there are today Dimasa (a ST of the area) individuals, 'usually well-heeled in terms of education and access to political power' owning 700 bighas (approximately 233 acres) of land and the experimental homestead plantations abandoned by the tea, coffee and rubber board because of falling prices (Barbora 2001, see also Barbora 2002).

It should come as no surprise then that the other side of this privatization of clan-held lands is the emergence of a poorer group of people eking out a living by working as agricultural workers or sharecroppers or by whatever other means possible. To be sure, most of them are local tribals, who despite the protection given to them as members of STs, lack the social and political resources to benefit from privatization of clan-lands or to be able to hold on to lands allocated to them. But occupying these economic niches, are also a large number of denizens—Nepalis, Biharis, and Bangladeshis among them. Indeed a tribal landowner may even find it safer to informally lease out his land to a denizen because, as Karna puts it, 'it may not be difficult to handle them if disputes arise' (Karna 1990: 34).

Modern India, according to Upendra Baxi, has achieved 'national integration without achieving national integrity.' India's 'developmental politics,' he points out, has forged national markets for large numbers of unorganized migrant labour crisscrossing the country. In these labour markets, he writes, Indian citizens have become, 'subjects without rights' all over again. What Baxi had in mind is migrant construction workers building 'monumental state projects' such as the physical infrastructure for the Asian Games in New Delhi, roads and flyovers in large cities, and housing estates across urban India for wealthy Indians; migrant labour in the power-loom sector of the textile industry in Gujarat; and 'the staggering forms of migrant labour from the destitute regions of east India' that had made the green revolution in Punjab possible. Baxi calls this phenomenon 'unconstitutional national integration' (Baxi 2001: 925–6).

Perhaps the post-colonial social transformation of Northeast India, taking place under the protective cover of the Sixth Schedule, is slowly making the region a part of this grid of 'unconstitutional national integration' in somewhat unexpected ways. The Bangladeshi and Nepali presence in the region points to a significant transnational dimension of this grid as well. At least a part of the significant rise of population of Northeast India has to be explained by this migrating proletariat meeting the labour demands of the building boom in the region—made possibly partly by the state resources pumped into the area and the substantial leakage of funds through corruption—and the class relations in the emerging forms of post-shifting cultivation agriculture. Their presence in these economic roles is certainly very visible to any visitor to Northeast India today.

Slowly but steadily, the dispossessed tribal of Northeast India is sure to join this mass of humanity on the move. Thus if the Bihari denizen in Karbi Anglong takes advantage of the misery of the poor Karbi to take effective control of his land, a tribal landlord in the Naga foothills, often empowered and enriched by positions in or connections to the state government of Nagaland, may be in a position of power and dominance vis-a-vis the Bengali denizen sharecropper informally leasing his land. Questions of social justice in Northeast India are significantly more complex today than what the regime of protection was originally designed to accomplish. The informality of the arrangements exposes a large number of poor people to a more vulnerable legal position than that already implied in the marginal nature of the economic niches they occupy.

Homelands and the Politics of Displacement

There is a disturbing relationship between conflicts over homelands that turn violent and displacement. These conflicts are not only between tribals and non-tribals. The discourse of homelands creates in every territorial entity—existing and potential—groups that belong and those who do not. Thus denizen communities as well as minority groups of all kinds—tribals as well as non-tribals—face the danger of falling victim to this politics of displacement. The urge to protect an existing homeland against the homeland claims of a rival group, the project of creating a new homeland or the fear that one ethnically defined group's homeland or a part of it can be claimed by another are typically the subtexts of these conflicts. The aspirations for homelands are typically expressed in the Sixth Schedule's language of Autonomous Districts and in the newer language of separate statehood since the cosmetically federal regional order came into being. Bringing an ethnically defined group scattered in many states into a homeland, maintaining the territorial integrity of a homeland that exists, creating a new homeland for a group that does not yet have one are all part of this political discourse.

To return to the Meghalaya example, some of the numbers cited by Khasi activists about non-Khasis living in Meghalaya are telling. Keith Pariat, President of the Syngkhong Rympei Thymmai, for instance, said that full two-thirds of the 1.8 million people living in the Khasi hills were non-Khasis (cited in Shridhar 2000). How the figure was arrived at and the categories Pariat used are not above question. But the perception itself is significant. A few years earlier, a Khasi Students Union leader had said that in a number of electoral constituencies in the Khasi Hills, Bangladeshis outnumber locals, while in the Jaintia coal belt Nepalis and Bangladeshis are a majority (cited in Verghese 1996: 203). There is little doubt that there has been a steady influx of people from Bangladesh—with questionable legal status—into Meghalaya and other parts of the Northeast. But the national and ethnic labels are hardly accurate since they do not distinguish between primary immigrants and their descendants who may be even generations removed. This rhetoric—not untypical in today's Northeast—illustrates the potential adverse impact of homeland discourse on hundreds of thousands of ethnically labelled people.

In the 1980s the logic of entitlements for ethnically defined groups and the norms and laws of Indian citizenship laws came to a head as a result of some displacement of ethnic Nepalis in Meghalaya. The displacements became the catalyst for a major political upheaval in the Darjeeling area of north Bengal—which historically has had a large concentration of ethnic Nepalis.

The settlement of ethnic Nepalis in Northeast India as well as the Darjeeling region has an old history that goes back to colonial times. However, quite separately from that history since India's independence, there has also been a significant movement of people across the Indo-Nepal border. This movement of people is governed by the Indo-Nepal Treaty of 1950. According to the treaty, Nepali citizens can freely establish residence, own property and engage in trade and commerce in India just as Indian citizens can do in Nepal. The Gorkha National Liberation Front, an organization of ethnic Nepalis of the Darjeeling region, now interprets the displacement of ethnic Nepalis in Meghalaya as evidence of a danger implicit in the Indo-Nepal treaty for India's ethnic Nepali population.

The treaty said the GNLF, turns the ethnic Nepalis of India into aliens. For in effect, it puts the bonafides of the ethnic Nepali Indian citizen in doubt. Indeed the GNLF's preference for the term Gorkha to describe the ethnic Nepalis of India is significant. The GNLF believes that while the term Nepali implies citizenship of Nepal, the term Gorkha—popularized by the British to describe soldiers recruited from the Gorkha Valley of Nepal—does not carry the same baggage. Along with the creation of Gorkhaland, the GNLF therefore demanded the abrogation of Indo-Nepal Treaty. A separate state called Gorkhaland, the GNLF argued, will demonstrate that 'we are not here in India in accordance with the 1950 Indo-Nepal agreement, but we have been here in this land since 12th century' (cited in Sonntag 2002: 172). Of course, an ethnic homeland for Nepalis in north Bengal that GNLF secured did not quite change the conditions of the ethnic Nepalis in Meghalaya, where the rhetoric of ethnic entitlements portrays all non-tribals as outsiders. Indeed in due course all ethnic Nepalis may even be assumed to belong to Gorkhaland and hence outsiders in other homelands.

Among recent episodes of conflict-induced displacements in Northeast India are: Paites, Kukis, and Nagas who were displaced in Manipur; Reangs displaced in Mizoram; Bengalis and various Tripuri tribes displaced in Tripura; and Chakmas displaced in Arunachal Pradesh. The political upheaval that became a model for the recent wave of ethnic entitlement campaigns in the region is the Assam movement of 1979–85. This episode of political protest was important because it involved a community that was not seen historically as one needing protection.

Let me give some details of a few of these conflicts to show the relationship between the politics of ethnic homelands and displacement. The displacement of Reangs (also known as Brues) in Mizoram relate to the demand by the Brue National Union for an Autonomous District for Reangs in Mizoram. The Reangs have a large presence on the tribal belts in Tripura, as well as in Mizoram. Mizo politicians and organizations like the

Young Mizo Association vehemently oppose the demand and see the Reangs not as indigenous to Mizoram, but the bulk of them as recent immigrants. They see the demand for a Brue homeland as a conspiracy to split up Mizoram. But from the Reang activist's point of view, the demand for a Reang homeland is justified. As a supporter of the Reang demand said, referring to the fact that there already is the Autonomous District Council for Chakmas in Mizoram, 'If the 60,000 Chakmas can have their own Autonomous District Council in Mizoram, why not the Reangs with a population of about 90,000?' (cited in Ali 1998).

One of the major elements in the Kuki-Naga clashes that have led to the displacement of Kukis and Nagas in Manipur is the Kuki demand for the creation of a Sadar Hills (Kangpokpi) district. The demand for a separate district by bifurcating the Senapati district of Manipur is framed in terms of the inconveniences of the people living far away from the present district headquarters. However, the proposal is read by Nagas as the beginning of the process of creating a Kuki homeland in an area of Manipur that the Nagas claim as theirs, and which Naga militants would like to see some day become part of greater Nagalim.

A conflict that has produced some widely reported displacements in the late 1990s centres around the demand for a homeland for the Bodos on the north bank of the Brahmaputra. While the memory of ancient Bodo kingdoms, and of a past when Bodo culture may have been uncontaminated by Assamese or Bengali culture animates the demand, Bodo speakers today are only 1.1 million or 11.5 per cent of the population of the north bank where the Bodos want their homeland to be. Furthermore, while there are areas where Bodo speakers are relatively concentrated, they do not constitute a relatively contiguous area. This reflects both a history of ethnic change and of demographic change as a result of immigration. Indeed today's demographic picture is hardly surprising; after all, it is precisely because of it, that this territory was not designated as either an excluded or a partially excluded area in colonial times; nor did it become part of the Sixth Schedule's tribal areas. True, the inability to extend protection to them was itself to a large extent, a function of demographic changes brought about by colonial transformation when the Bodos had lost control over much of their land to tea plantations, government enclosed forest areas and to migrant groups settled in those areas by official policy. In that sense they were probably one of those groups for whom the colonial discovery that the 'aborigines' might need protection came too late.

Nevertheless in an attempt to respond to the demand for a Bodo homeland, an agreement signed between Bodo activists and the Assam state government in 1993, provided for the formation of a Bodoland Autonomous Council. However, the precise territorial jurisdiction of the Council was left open to be settled later. Disputes over the precise jurisdiction eventually led to the collapse of the agreement. On the other hand, the continuing public discussion about a dissonance between what Bodo activists see as a historically Bodo area and the contemporary demographic reality of overlapping ethnicity has fuelled violence against 'outsiders'. East Bengali Muslims and Hindus, Nepalis and Santhals have been victims of the displacements that have followed.

Now a Homeland for a Non-Tribal Community?

One of the ironies of the career of the idea of protecting tribals in Northeast India is that over time, as the economic and ethnic landscape has become more complex, the not-very-subtle distinctions originally made between tribal groups in different levels of isolation—implied in categories like excluded and partially excluded areas, and the distinction between tribes living in such areas and those living in mixed areas—have been lost. Now traditionally unprotected groups demand the same kinds of protection once extended to groups that were thought of as the most isolated. Perhaps the most interesting example of this process is the current discussion among All Assam Students Union [AASU] and the central and the state governments about ways to extend protection to the 'indigenous peoples' of Assam.

The issue goes back to the Assam movement that ended with an accord signed between the Government of India and the All Assam Students Union in 1985. The Assam Accord signed between Prime Minister Rajiv Gandhi and the AASU leaders not only acknowledged that Assam has a problem with 'foreigners'; it agreed on certain formulas for identifying, expelling, and disenfranchising some of them. After the Accord, the student leaders of the Assam movement formed a political party and contested elections to the state Assembly and won. But since constitutionally citizenship is under the federal government's jurisdiction, there was not much the state government could legally do. A law passed by the Indian parliament in response to the Assam movement made the task of proving that someone is an illegal alien in Assam, extremely difficult, if not impossible. And once faced with the tasks of winning elections and staying in power, the electoral logic of Assam's demography soon made these student leaders significantly modify their position on the issue of 'foreigners'.

The non-implementation of the Assam Accord therefore has remained a live issue in Assam politics. Clause VI of the Assam Accord had promised 'constitutional, legislative and administrative safeguards to protect, preserve and promote the cultural, social, linguistic identity and heritage of the Assamese people.' The formulation had angered Bodo activists in the late 1980s who argued that it might legitimize the imposition of Assamese language and culture on Bodos and other tribal groups. Yet in the most recent discussions on the implementation of the Assam Accord, a proposal made by AASU that was actively considered would reserve hundred per cent of the seats in the local elected bodies, and the state Legislative Assembly in Assam and all the seats for Assam in the national parliament for 'indigenous peoples'.

According to press reports, representatives of the Assam government and of the Government of India had agreed 'in principle' with the proposal. The student leaders have defended their proposal on the ground that Indian citizens from other parts of India living in Assam will continue to have all other rights except that they will not be able to contest elections in the state. Obviously the proposal is modelled on the near-total reservations of seats for STs in the tribal states of Arunachal Pradesh, Meghalaya, Mizoram, and Nagaland, but this time for a category of people that would include non-STs.

The proposal, especially the concept of 'indigenous people', has become highly controversial. Among the most vociferous critics of the proposal, not surprisingly, are Assam's tribal activists. Since the term indigenous people in international human rights discourse has historically been seen as being synonymous with what in India are called scheduled tribes, the extension of the word 'indigenous' to include a non-tribal people—especially one that is itself in loggerheads with some of Assam's STs—has aroused deep suspicion. Daleswar Bodo, Vice President of the Bodo Sahitya Sabha, said that the notion deprives the 'aboriginals/autochthons of Assam, like Bodos and Misings, of their due protection and safeguards from the intrusion of the new-comers under the guise of "*khilonjia*", that is, indigenous' (cited in Das Gupta 2000). In other words, he fears, that the Assamese by calling themselves an 'indigenous people' will manage to obscure their presence in tribal areas. Another important Bodo organization All Bodo Students Union said that the reported understanding has created 'lots of doubts, confusion and misunderstanding' (Das Gupta 2000). Tribal activists from Karbi Anglong and North Cachar districts have challenged AASU credentials to unilaterally engage in a project to defend the interests of 'indigenous peoples' of Assam. It called for a dialogue among different sections of Assam's population to arrive at a consensus definition. ABSU called for a meeting of experts to define the categories indigenous and non-indigenous peoples of the state (Das Gupta 2000).

Organizations representing minority groups such as Bengali Hindus—many of them refugees of the Indian partition of 1947—and Bengali Muslims have also expressed misgivings. A Forum for Linguistic Minorities of Assam was announced in order to 'safeguard the interest of the people belonging to the various linguistic minority communities.' Its public statement emphasized that 'all citizens of the State, irrespective of their language and religious affinity' must continue to 'enjoy equal rights as guaranteed by the Constitution' (Das Gupta 2000).

Yet the AASU proposal has been taken seriously enough for mainstream political parties to develop positions on it. The chief of the state's Congress party, who is now the Chief Minister, Tarun Gogoi said that his definition of indigenous people is simply: those 'who accept the Assamese language and culture and Assam as their own land' (cited in Das Gupta 2000). It is not clear, however, how such a definition would be used to decide who is eligible and who is not, to contest elections in Assam. Other political parties have proposed formulas that were used in the Assam Accord to define a 'foreigner'. No matter how serious the problem of immigration into this frontier region, the cavalier way that a basic political right of citizenship of hundreds and thousands of people—to stand for elections—is becoming a matter of negotiation—is rather extraordinary.

Looking Ahead: From Ethnic Subjects to Citizens

But the formidable difficulties that AASU faces in operationalizing the concept of indigenous peoples show how anachronistic the homeland idea has become in the context of the actually existing political economy of Northeast India today. More than any other case, the displacement of Santhals in Kokrajhar district in the late 1990s—victims of violence by Bodo militants—dramatized this incongruity. The Santhals in Assam are descendants of tea workers brought to Assam as indentured workers—many of them more than a century ago. Their displaced forefathers provided the muscle for the tea industry that marked the arrival of global capitalism in Assam in the nineteenth century. That such a group could be displaced for the second time in the course of an indigenous group's search for an ethnic homeland—no matter how tragic the story of their immiserization—brings home the absurdity of the way insiders and outsiders are framed in the homeland discourse of Northeast India. The discourse today has become a serious challenge to the foundational principles of citizenship. It cannot be expected to provide a framework for the struggles for social justice of today and of the future.

Minimally we need a framework that does not involve the state forever categorizing groups of people in ethnic terms and making descendants of immigrants into perpetual outsiders. While mechanisms to control immigration are no doubt necessary, so are rules about incorporating the descendants of immigrants—no matter how restrictive. And at least a generation or two later, they have to become full citizens. I would suggest that the notion of dual citizenship, not unknown in federal systems—i.e. citizenship both of India and of a state—might be able to provide such a framework. Such a regime of dual citizenship would be a variation in the theme of the differentiated citizenship regime that exists in Northeast India. But its purpose would be to replace the ethnic principle with a civic principle and to give the right to define the rules of inclusion and exclusion to territorially defined political communities.

A quick review of the language in which the citizenship laws of countries are framed illustrates how the logic of the citizenship discourse necessarily differs from that of the discourse of homelands for ethnically defined groups. In principle, most countries recognize three ways of becoming a citizen: birth within the territory of a country (*jus soli*), descent from a citizen (*jus sanguinis*), and naturalization. If jus sanguinis incorporates the principle of citizenship gained through blood ties to citizens, the other two principles can incorporate the ethnically or culturally different outsider. In contrast to that, the homeland discourse tends to define political communities in static and exclusively ethnic terms. Of course, in reality countries vary enormously on how much of the jus soli principle is applied to the claims to citizenship of children of immigrants born in the country and on the degree of difficulties that are involved in obtaining citizenship through naturalization. Indeed in countries like Israel and Japan, jus sanguinis remains the predominant way of acquiring citizenship. Yet the openings for new members that exist in principle makes the discourse of citizenship different from the exclusionary logic of the discourse of exclusive homelands.

Certain recent developments in the citizenship policies in Europe may illustrate my point. Despite the political rhetoric against foreigners in Europe today, the trend in most European countries has been to extend the right of citizenship to second-generation immigrants. The labour demands during the latter half of the twentieth century had induced a major part of Europe's recent immigration. Originally the migration was thought of as temporary— as illustrated by the notion of guest worker that guided official policy in some countries. However, as many temporary migrants became permanent settlers, countries have had to respond creatively to the reality of a growing number of foreign non-citizen residents living in their midst. Most states seem to be 'unwilling to tolerate, generation after generation, large numbers of non-citizens without an entitlement to citizenship' (Hansen and Weil 2001: 12–13). Whatever their degree of economic and social integration, lack of citizenship had tended to separate immigrant groups from the broader community in significant ways and implicitly justified xenophobic and exclusionary rhetoric. Thus it was hard not to see a direct connection between Germany's inability to recognize Turks, Yugoslavs and other former guest workers as potential German citizens and the attacks of Turks as 'foreigners'. Germany, of course, has since 2000 changed the laws of citizenship recognizing the right of second-generation immigrants to citizenship (Hansen and Weil 2001: 12–13).

Indeed except for Austria, Greece, and Luxemburg, the other twelve EU countries now give second-generation immigrants the right to become citizens. Children of immigrant parents, born in the country, can apply to be citizens when they become adults. Of course, there are conditions. Residency in the country is always a condition and sometimes the residency requirement can be as long as 10 years. In some cases there are also conditions such as double jus soli, i.e. apart from the applicant, a parent too has to be born in the country. Of course, for first generation immigrants the access to citizenship through naturalization in EU countries is extremely restricted. But my point is not to defend European citizenship laws that are still remarkably exclusionary, but to draw attention to the fact that, unlike the homeland discourse, it is hard within the discourse of citizenship not to recognize the right to citizenship of second-generation immigrants. In that sense the citizenship discourse is qualitatively different from the homeland discourse of Northeast India that makes denizens (and perpetual foreigners) out of ethnically defined outsiders and their descendants.

The obvious advantages of the framework of dual citizenship, it seems to me, is that it can define political communities in civic terms; introduce a dynamic element of incorporating new members and thereby make a decisive break from the notion of ethnic homelands that is part of the legacy of colonial subject-hood. Dual citizenship would imply that elected state governments and legislatures could make rules by which an internal immigrant becomes a citizen of the state and a member of the political community embodied in that state.

Furthermore, under a strong dual citizenship regime, even national citizenship could become a concurrent subject requiring for instance, that international treaties affecting the flow of people from outside the country into India—for instance the treaties affecting the rights of ethnic Nepalis or East Bengalis in India—would need the concurrence of state governments. Making such treaty making a part of state level political debates could give such treaties the popular legitimacy that they appear to lack in Northeast India. Giving state legislatures a formal say in controlling the flow of people into the region—restrictions that exist today, but primarily through non-transparent colonial-era bureaucratic practices like the Inner Line or as an indirect effect of the protections given to STs—will give legitimacy to the internal immigration into the region that is only likely to increase in coming years.

Indian public opinion, however, is unlikely to be friendly to the idea of dual citizenship. Indeed in the debate in 1999 that followed the autonomy resolution of the Jammu and Kashmir Assembly, commentators specifically pointed at the dangers of the dual citizenship idea. Arvind Lavakare, for instance, argued that if a state had such power, it would 'discriminate in favour of its citizens in matters such as the right to hold public office, to vote, to obtain employment or to secure licenses for practicing law or medicine.' He gave the example of Jammu and Kashmir where the right to acquire immovable property is restricted to the state's permanent residents to illustrate how 'politically explosive' the idea of dual citizenship can be. 'With that solitary exception (sic)', he noted with satisfaction, an exception that could be removed by abrogating Article 370 of the Constitution, 'the Indian federation has largely achieved, and seeks to maintain, uniformity in basic civil and criminal laws' (Lavakare 1999). Like many Indian commentators, Lavakare is, of course, oblivious of the northeast and of Article 371 that gives some of the northeastern states their special forms of autonomy, the article that immediately follows the article on Jammu and Kashmir that offends so many Indians.

The choice in Northeast India today is not between a new set of restrictions that dual citizenship would introduce for the first time and a uniform national citizenship where all Indian citizens have unrestricted rights to movement, residency and property ownership. What exists on the ground is a set of rules that distinguishes between citizens and denizens, rules that have fuelled an increasingly exclusionary politics of homelands and have been prone to generating ethnic violence and recurrent episodes of displacement. Dual citizenship in such a situation would be able to introduce for the first time a regime of civic citizenship that will be in line with the actually existing political economy of the region.

Such a citizenship regime will also be consistent with the traditional liberal incorporative ethos of region. In the controversy over the Khasi Social Custom of Lineage Bill with which I began this chapter, the matrilineal system of succession that Khasi activists would like to 'modernize', has a remarkably liberal and progressive conception of group membership. While descent is traced along the female line, that does not stop children of non-Khasi women married to Khasi men from being absorbed into Khasi society. Children of such marriages typically adopt the non-Khasi mother's given name or occupation as a clan name and over time such names became recognized as Khasi clan names. Indeed there are many Khasi clans today that trace their ancestry to non-Khasi women. They were wives or concubines of Khasi men abducted from the plains in the course of trading expeditions and wars. This also does not discriminate against children married out of wedlock. As Khasi sociologist Tiplut Nongbri points out, while the Khasi rules of descent may render 'the ethnic boundary of the Khasi highly porous, it makes the addition of new members into the society relatively easy and adds to the vibrancy of the system' (Nongbri 1998). Dual citizenship will only return the northeast to the spirit of such progressive traditions of incorporating new members—so dramatically different from the caste sensibilities of mainstream India—and make a clean break from the colonial constructions of ethnic subject-hood that have generated today's lethal politics of homelands.

Notes

[1] The chapter originally appeared in the *Journal of Refugee Studies*. Reprinted by permission of Oxford University Press from Sanjib Baruah, 'Citizens and Denizens: Ethnicity, Homelands, and the Crisis of Displacement in Northeast India', *Journal of Refugee Studies* 16 (1) March 2003: 44–66 © Oxford University Press 2003. The chapter was originally written as the First V.Venkata Rao Memorial Lecture that I gave at the meeting of the Northeast India Political Science Association held in North Lakhimpur, Assam in January 2002.

[2] See endnote 7, Chapter 1.

[3] 'Denizen', of course, is not a contemporary legal category. The term goes back to the power of denization that British monarchs once had to grant some aliens some of the privileges of natural born subjects. Denizens, for instance, could buy land but could not inherit it. At a later stage, the parliament sought to control the royal power of denization by passing laws that disallowed denizens from being members of the privy council and the houses of parliament and from occupying civil or military offices of trust, or from obtaining grants of land from the crown. While the restrictions on the rights of the non-tribal population have a very different history and rationale, the particular limits, e.g. on rights of property ownership, access to public employment and elected office are not dissimilar to those applicable to denizens.

SECTION VI

Epilogue

10

Beyond Durable Disorder
Northeast India and the Look East Policy[1]

At a symposium on global urban problems Jeffrey Sachs, an economist and one of the leading contemporary thinkers on development, referred to Afghanistan's capital city Kabul as 'one of our biggest challenges.' 'We should not pretend,' he said, 'that Afghanistan's problems started with the Taliban and will end with the Taliban.' Its problems, he joked 'started with Vasco de Gama in 1498, when he put the Silk Road out of business by showing the sea route from Europe to Asia and back' (J. Sachs 2002).[2]

Northeast India's recent problems are bad but fortunately no one would say they ever got as bad as Afghanistan's. Yet Jeffrey Sachs' casual remark has more relevance to our region than would be apparent initially. As in the case of Afghanistan, many observers see a relation between Northeast India's political troubles and the region's economic underdevelopment. Successive Indian prime ministers have announced generous financial packages to address the structural obstacles to the region's development. Indeed if money could solve problems Northeast India by now should have been on the cusp of both an economic revolution and a political breakthrough. However, if we go by the experience of Afghanistan whose developmental challenges have attracted considerably more money and the attention of some of the world's most talented development experts, it would be naïve to think that successful counter-insurgency and a lot of money would on their own get the Northeast out of its present predicament.

As my starting point therefore let me paraphrase Jeffrey Sachs and put forward the following proposition: We should not pretend that Northeast India's problems started with ULFA, the PLA, the NDFB or the NSCN[3] and that it will end with them. My scepticism about money or counter-insurgency being able to buy peace and prosperity in the Northeast should not be construed as pessimism. I have taken Sachs's observation as my point of departure because Sachs is known for his relentless engagement with the challenges of development in various corners of the world and for not shying away from the complexity of problems that particular countries or regions confront. In that spirit I take a historical view of the region's under-development and draw attention to the need for a bold vision to link the investments that are being made in Northeast India today with the opportunities that have become available in this era of globalism.

Let me first elaborate what Sachs may have had in mind regarding Afghanistan. His remarks reflect the emphasis on geography as a crucial variable in development that one finds in his writings. As he has said elsewhere 'since sea-navigable regions are generally richer than land-locked regions, regions that are both temperate and easily accessible to sea-based trade almost everywhere have achieved a very high measure of economic development. Tropical and land-locked regions, by contrast ... are among the very poorest in the world' (J. Sachs 2000:2). Ricardo Hausmann put the implications of this new emphasis on geography by Sachs and others somewhat provocatively:

Economic development experts promise that with the correct mix of pro-market policies, poor countries will eventually prosper. But policy isn't the problem—geography is. Tropical, landlocked nations may never enjoy access to the markets and new technologies they need to flourish in the global economy (Hausmann 2001: 45).

Historicising Land-Locked Northeast India

The daunting challenges of development that Northeast India faces because of its landlocked condition are well known. The Partition of 1947, as B.G. Verghese puts it, 'caused the extreme isolation of the Northeast.' He describes the region as South Asia's third landlocked 'state' along with Bhutan and Nepal. The loss of connectivity and market access as a result of the Partition, he said, 'set its economy back by at least a quarter century' (Verghese 2001). Historian David Ludden puts the same point even more forcefully. Partition, he said, referring to its impact on Northeast India:

Cut old routes of communication and mobility across new national borders more dramatically than almost anywhere in the world. The Bengal Assam railway tracks from Guwahati to Dhaka were torn up at the Cachar-Sylhet border, in 1965. Now it is much easier to communicate by phone or mail between Dhaka and London than between Dhaka and Guwahati (Ludden 2003: 21).

However, on the east and the north, Northeast India's isolation from its neighbourhood has much older roots: that which came about as a result of the advent of Western dominance over sea routes and over global trade and more particularly the British conquest of the region and the decisions to draw lines between the hills and plains, to put barriers on trade between Bhutan and Assam and to treat Myanmar as a strategic frontier—British India's buffer against French Indochina and China. While the British colonial rulers built a major new transportation infrastructure, aimed primarily at taking tea and other resources out of Assam, the disruption of old trade routes remained colonialism's most enduring negative legacy.

Northeast India was on the southern trails of the Silk Road.[4] This part of the Northeast Indian story is not well known outside the circle of historians of the ancient and the medieval world. A review of the historical literature on a related theme by Francoise Pommaret, a French historian of Northeast India's neighbour Bhutan, gives a useful picture of Northeast India's place in these trade routes. Pommaret summarizes the state of scholarly consensus as follows: 'Kamrupa was on the trading route between southwest China and India. Even though the existence of this route seems well established, its importance as a trading route and its age are controversial'. Xuanzang or Hsuan-Tsang, the seventh century Chinese pilgrim who visited Kamrupa had learnt from the people he spoke to that the journey to the southwest borders of Szechuan took about two months but that the mountains and rivers were hard to pass (Pommaret 1999: 8). W. Liebenthal believed that there was a route into Kamrupa from Szechuan perhaps much before Xuanzang's time but it did not become a trade route (Liebenthal 1956; cited by Pommaret 1999: 8). But there is evidence that this route was used even as late as the nineteenth century. 'Assamese merchants,' writes N.K. Basu, 'went to Yunnan in China by the line of trade through Sadia, Bisa and across the Patkoi range of mountains' (Basu 1970; cited in Pommaret 1999: 9). The Mon-yul corridor in Arunachal Pradesh was another link between Northeast India and Tibet. It passed through Tshona Dzong and Tawang and was the shortest route between Tibet and the plains of Assam (Pommaret 1999: 10).

Apart from silk and other goods, the Silk Road also carried ideas, art, and culture. It facilitated the spread of Buddhism across Asia. Indeed it is only by taking into account the importance of the southern trails of the Silk Road during ancient and medieval times that it is possible to understand the importance of the Assamese town of Hajo as an important Buddhist pilgrimage site or of Sualkuchi as an important silk centre. There was a time Hajo was believed to be ancient Kusinagara, the site of Buddha's historical death, and a Bhutanese chief and his religious teacher had opened it as a pilgrimage site. Hajo thus became a meeting place of pilgrims from 'all of Bhutan and Tibet and even from as far a-field as Ladakh and Southwest China' (Aris 1979: 113). It was a thriving pilgrimage and trading centre. It had a cosmopolitan population since it was a pilgrimage centre for Hindus, Muslims, and Buddhists. The Muslims practised metal casting and the nearby town of Sualkuchi became an important centre of silk trade (Aris 1979; cited in Pommaret 1999: 11–12).

A piece of trivia from the world of spices bears the traces of Northeast India's place in ancient trade routes. The botanical name for the cultivated cinnamon bark of southern China is *Cinnamomum cassia*. The cultivation of cinnamon in southern China goes back centuries before the Christian era. Yet the most likely etymological source for the term 'cassia' is the Assamese term for the Khasi people, Khasia. Apparently cinnamon found its way from the Khasi hills to southern China in very ancient times. Modern experiments have shown that the cinnamon bark of 'the eastern Himalayas' is 'substantially identical' to Chinese cinnamon bark (Miller 1969: 75). It seems that very early on cinnamon was brought from the Khasi hills to be widely cultivated in the area that later became known as southern China.

Northeast India's place in trade along the southern Silk Road serves as a reminder that the region's recent history as a remote, underdeveloped and troubled hinterland is neither inevitable nor unchangeable. Its marginalization has to be understood only in historical terms as the product of changes brought about by powerful global forces including colonial and post-colonial geopolitics. The emergence of British India and the international political boundaries drawn during colonial rule provided the foundation of the post-colonial political order of nation-states. The Partition of 1947 and the state of diplomatic relations between India and its neighbours turned Northeast India into a 'sensitive border region' requiring special attention based on national security concerns. The condition has not been conducive to the region's economic and political well-being.

Between South and Southeast Asia:
Imagining a Different Future

Counter-insurgency as an intellectual stance, as I have said in Chapter 1, has not produced either good scholarship or ethically and morally defensible political positions on Northeast India. Scholars and observers, who view the region's troubled politics through the lenses of security studies, often explain it by the region's supposed underdevelopment, its poor integration with the pan-Indian 'mainstream' and the actions of malevolent neighbours. One cannot imagine, within this framework, an end to the current troubles except within the failed narratives[5] of national development and nation-building.

In earlier chapters I have referred to the contest over history and memory as an essential theme in the cultural politics that underlie Northeast India's durable disorder. Some of the revisionist local histories—that inspire many independentists—emphasize the region's historical ties with Southeast Asia. The region, of course, is not only the northeastern borderland of South Asia, but it can also be described as the northwestern borderland of Southeast Asia. Indeed a major two-volume work entitled *Southeast Asian Tribes, Minorities and Nations* published by the Princeton University Press in 1967 included a chapter on Assam: the province then more or less coincided with what is called Northeast India today. Peter Kunstadter, the editor of the volume explained the inclusion this way. Assam, he wrote, has a large population of tribal and minority peoples whose languages are more closely related to the languages of Southeast Asia than to those of the Indian subcontinent. Their cultures too resemble the cultures of their neighbours in Southeast Asia. Like the southern boundary of China that does not mark a cultural or linguistic division, India's eastern border, wrote Kunstadter, also does not mark off a cultural or linguistic area (Kunstadter 1967: 205).

The idea that South Asia is a discrete geographical region separated from Southeast Asia is a fiction. There are no 'natural' geographical boundaries separating South and Southeast Asia along the Indo-Myanmarese border. In territorial terms today's 'South Asia' is to a large extent successor to the entity called 'British India'. Northeast India's ties—historical, cultural, social, and economic—therefore do not stop at these international boundaries. We know from the rise and fall of regions like Eastern Europe or Central Asia that regions are not objective geographical realities, but rather contingent and contested entities. If nations can 'come and go', asks political scientist Donald Emerson, 'why not regions' (cited in Acharya 2003: 24)? Or, as political geographer Anssi Paasi puts it, 'the construction of regions and territories is part of the perpetual transformation of the spatial system, in which regions emerge, exist for some time and may finally disappear' (Paasi 2000).

The Japanese occupation of Burma (today's Myanmar) is a critical episode that led to the Indo-Myanmarese border becoming the dividing line between South and Southeast Asia. The Western Alliance formed in 1943—the foundation of the post-war geopolitical category Southeast Asia—subsequently placed Myanmar within the geographical ambit of the South East Asian Command [SEAC]. A lot has happened since then. What gives Southeast Asia its coherence, writes a scholar of the region,

must count as one of the finest acts of collective self-imagination undertaken by a region's nationalist political elite in the wake of liberation from European and American colonialism. As with nationalism and nation-states, regions may be 'imagined' designed, constructed and defended (Acharya 2003: 24).

It is not my intention to privilege Northeast India's ties to Southeast Asia over its subcontinental ties except to note that the living within the boundaries of a modern territorial state has a powerful effect on making some ties seem more natural than others. However, there are slippages in the nineteenth and twentieth century efforts to naturalize the space of nation-states that become most apparent in border regions. Yet the claims to the continuity of historical ties with Southeast Asia on the part of some revisionist popular historians of Northeast India are not unproblematical. For instance, in recent years there has been a powerful movement of cultural revivalism among the Ahoms of Assam—the westernmost of the Tai-speaking peoples spread in mainland Southeast Asia. After witnessing the performance of a number of Ahom rituals in Assam the German scholar of Tai culture B.J. Terwiel wrote:

The leaders of the Ahoms, in their search for an Ahom identity, were thwarted by the loss of virtually all of the Southeast Asian culture, the people long ago having adopted the Assamese language and various variants of the Hindu religion. The old priestly castes, through the custodianship of old manuscripts and their ability to read old Ahom texts aloud, had created the impression that they were still fluent in Ahom. This exaggeration of their knowledge placed them in a difficult position, when, as a result of the exuberant growth of the political revivalist movement, there arose a strong demand for the resurrection of ancient state, community and private rituals. In response to this demand the priests did what they could, searching for clues in the annals, with the aid of dictionaries coining Ahom phrases, and, ... creating new ceremonial elements virtually out of thin air, thus producing a make-believe ancient ritual (Terwiel 2002: 22).

Yet, I would argue, our era of globalism presents opportunities for the region to get out of the 'territorial trap'[6] and relate to its transnational neighbours on the east culturally and economically. In the spirit of what political theorist Peter Breiner (while interpreting Karl Mannheim) calls 'the utopian impulse' to project possibility beyond a given reality as a 'discovery process of political projects that may later become possible and realistic,' I shall now spell out some of these opportunities (Breiner 2001: 4) and how it could be a way of imagining a different future for the region than what the counter-insurgency discourse could muster.

Regions, Transnationalism and Globalization

In his widely quoted, and perhaps equally widely criticized, remarks on the borderless world of the future Keniche Ohmae had said that the nation-state 'has become an unnatural, even dysfunctional, unit for organizing human activity .... It represents no genuine, shared community of economic interests; it defines no meaningful flows of economic activity. In fact, it overlooks the true linkages and synergies that exist' (Ohmae 1993: 78). The lines that matter on the global economic map, according to him, are those defining what he called 'region states'. Region states, according to him are natural economic zones. They may fall within a country or they may straddle the borders of two or more countries. Among the regions that illustrate his point are: Catalonia in Spain, Hong Kong and the adjacent areas of southern China, the Kansai region around Osaka in Japan and the area combining the Canadian province of British Columbia and the US state of Washington. In India regions like those around Bangalore and Hyderabad—the centres of India's software and pharmaceutical industries—might play a similar role in the global economy. Since Ohmae wrote those lines more than a decade ago it has been possible to build effective cross-border regions only in some areas; and even in those areas the demand for flexibility in border-crossings has been met not with generalized forms of easy and fast track border-crossings, but border-control practices that seek to combine flexibility for selected groups with rigidity for others.

The backdrop to these developments of course is what is commonly called globalization. It may be useful to distinguish two elements in globalization: (a) the communication revolution and its impact on the nature and scale of production and the resultant reconfiguration of economic space and (b) the phenomenon of de-territorialization and re-territorialization including the softening of national borders enabling the formation of transnational regions.

It barely needs to be repeated today that the revolution in technology leading to declining transport costs and the virtually free transmission of digitized information has dramatically reduced distances. Production costs under these conditions encourage the organization of manufacturing by globally dispersing operations to exploit differentials in wages or natural or other resource endowments. For instance a manufacturer in a developed country can choose to locate the labour-intensive parts of the production process in certain countries and capital-intensive parts in others. We in India have become familiar with the phenomenon of business process outsourcing by US and European corporations: airlines, banks, and other financial organizations, even health care providers have located their back offices and service centres in Bangalore, Delhi, and other Indian cities.

New technology facilitates this way of organizing production. For instance, a Japanese company producing computers can produce components like microchips and transistors in Japan and then send them for further assembly to Thailand, Malaysia or China. The finished product can be exported back to Japan or to markets elsewhere. Similarly it is common now for the automobile industry in Japan, US or Europe to buy parts made in factories in another country. Even in less technology intensive sectors such as the garment industry it is common for synthetic yarn to be produced in one country and for it to be exported to another country for the production of garments. Indeed trade in components as opposed to final products is now a growing proportion of the total world trade in manufactured goods. Many developing countries are beneficiaries of this new international division of labour. Countries like China and India are benefiting in more complex ways, in India's case notably because of its role as a global leader in information technology and a large skilled labour power ready to take advantage of the business process outsourcing by Western corporations.

Today's globalized production process depends on smooth and low cost transportation—goods have to be shipped by trucks, by train, by plane in an almost seamless manner. Furthermore, physical connectivity would have to be supplemented by good telecommunications connectivity. To put it simply, it is impossible to participate actively in the global economy without access to a good transportation and communication infrastructure. The synergy between different modes of communication is sometimes missed. Thus the cell phone or the Internet cannot be a substitute for a physical transportation infrastructure. Telephone or videoconferencing, for instance, are not substitutes for face-to-face business meetings but necessary supplements to them. Thus to participate fully in this globalized economy a place needs both good air connectivity and telecommunications connectivity. For instance, the computer, the telephone and the Internet may give a retailer in the US ready access to instantaneous data on trends in changing demand. Thus he can be ready to order a different line from his manufacturer in India in the middle of a season instead of waiting for the next season. But for that to happen the supplier and manufacturer would have to be located in places from where they can produce and ship very quickly and with full predictability to the markets where the demand is.

To facilitate this kind of globalized production some of the rigidities of political borders—tariffs, customs, and other restrictions—will have to go. Whether this really happens or not is another matter. But the pressures on borders often created during the colonial era and reinforced during the golden era of nation-states are clear.

As national economies respond to the pressures of globalization, in many parts of the world, notably in Europe, regions have emerged as a key level of governance, innovation, and policy-making. There is significant pressure for region building—a 'political project in which leaders, build up a territorial form of reference and forge a territorial system of action' (Keating 1999)—even when a region may lack long-standing cultural ties. Can Northeast India and its transnational neighbours forge such a territorial system of action?

Transnational Region Building: Potential Economic Dividends

What could a cross-border region-building project bring to Northeast India in terms of economic opportunities? The region today is known for its high incidence of poverty. 'Though the causes of poverty are deep and complex,' writes economist Sushil Khanna of the Institute of Management, Calcutta, referring to Northeast India as well as Nepal, Bangladesh and parts of eastern India, 'there is no doubt that the disruption of trade and commerce and communication due to the partition of the country, as well as India's import substitution strategy of industrialization and gradual erection of barriers to international trade, have disrupted economies that till 50 years ago were well integrated, and deprived the region of the gains from trade based on comparative advantage' (Khanna 2002: 3).

When national borders define economic space decisions about locating economic enterprises often work against border regions. This has been the source of some of Northeast India's past tensions with the Government of India. Borders tend to distort markets thanks to tariffs and other rigidities. Producers avoid locating industries near a border since trade barriers limit the market for goods and the area that supplies inputs. It is more rational to locate in an area that is closer to the core of the domestic market. The 'border effect' leads producers to locate industries away from international borders. In Northeast India we have heard arguments based on the logic of the border effect being made during controversies about the location of public enterprises. For instance Barauni was supposed to be a better location than Guwahati for concentrating refining capacity. That argument assumed that the market for the products of the refinery would be strictly limited to India and that one could not sell them in Bangladesh or Myanmar without tariffs and other restrictions that would increase the price for consumers in those countries.

But if one begins to imagine the economic integration of Northeast India with surrounding areas in neighbouring countries the calculations would obviously be different. Border regions will cease to be border regions in any meaningful economic sense. Economic integration could bring about a spurt of economic activities. The removal of trade barriers and harmonization of tariffs on third country products could make border regions attractive sites for investments once we take into account full access to new cross-border markets. Such effects are, of course, not inevitable. Yet the disappearance of the border effect is bound to open new economic opportunities.

Some of the spectacular examples of the impact of economic integration on border areas can be seen in North America. The border regions of northern Mexico have benefited enormously from the integration of Mexico's economy with that of the United States as a result of the North American Free Trade Agreement (NAFTA). There has been a manufacturing boom in northern Mexico as a result of NAFTA. It was not only the result of US companies moving south of the border to take advantage of low labour costs, but many Asian producers have also moved to the region in order to produce for the US market. To be sure, many negative effects of NAFTA are apparent in these areas as well. On the north the economies of Canadian provinces have become more strongly integrated to the US than before. The value of cross-border trade between Canadian provinces and the US now far exceeds inter-provincial trade within Canada. 'If Canada gradually breaks up,' wrote two Canadian newspaper columnists 'individual provinces may seek a Puerto Rico-style association with the US' (Lovewell and Westell 2003). Puerto Rico, of course, belongs to the United States, but it is not a constituent state of the US federation.

No one would claim that integration of Northeast India's economy with Bangladesh, Bhutan or Myanmar would immediately produce effects like the relocation of industries taking place in Mexico or Canada as a result of the market-power of the US economy. But when a natural economic region—in Keniche Ohmae's sense—is allowed to emerge without the constraints of national boundaries, the locational advantages and disadvantages are necessarily very different from those in a situation when border effects are in full force.

A Transnational Politics of Recognition?

Quite significantly, apart from economic opportunities, transnational region building can bring important dividends in terms of Northeast India's political troubles. As I have argued in Chapter 1, the politics of recognition (Taylor 1994) is a recurrent theme in the politics of ethnic militancy in Northeast India.

Inside the European Union today, those regional identities that were once seen as threats by European nation-states are flourishing. The Mastrich Treaty of 1993 establishes the EU's Committee of the Regions in order to give local and regional interests influence in EU decision-making. Some of the historically distinct forms of identities that animate regional politics in Europe are not unlike those that animate the militias of Northeast India. The European political landscape today is dotted by paradiplomacy—international activities on the part of regions and stateless nations. Thus there are more than 200 regional 'embassies' in Brussels that lobby the European Commission and network with each other. For national groups that straddle inter-state boundaries such as the Basque Country, Catalonia, Ireland or the Tyrol, the EU affords the opportunity to pool resources and pursue a transnational politics of recognition that has been able to compensate for their marginalization within nation-states.

Could not EU-style multi-level citizenship allow historic regions like Assam, Manipur, Nagalim, and Tripura to reclaim their identities through a transnational politics of recognition? Even limited cooperation between India and Myanmar can improve conditions in Northeast India. As I have argued in Chapter 5, it can make a difference in the current Naga peace process that could end one of the world's oldest armed conflicts.

How realistic is this scenario? Any consideration of its feasibility would have to address a number of obvious obstacles. I will turn to them later. But I would first like to show that India's Look East policy—the overtures since the 1990s toward Southeast Asian countries—holds promises of historic proportions for transnational region-building in the area.

The Look East Policy: Where is it Headed?

India's Look East policy began in the early 1990s during the government led by P.V. Naramsimha Rao. All subsequent governments have supported the policy and have built on it. 'ASEAN [Association of Southeast Asian Nations] and India,' said I.K. Gujral to an audience in Jakarta in 1996, when he was India's External Affairs Minister, 'are no awkward strangers, we have been neighbours and friends in time, space and existence for as long back as we can remember.' He also said, 'Our habits, customs and social mores, our myths and legends, the clothes we drape, the cuisine we savour, the art, craft and design that is our shared legacy, even the languages we speak—all bear testimony to this good neighbourliness.'

Every aspect of India's ethos, he said, reflects the 'footprints of South-East Asia.' But 'the forces of history and circumstances' had interrupted this relationship. Colonialism and the Cold War, he said 'drew artificial boundaries between us' (Gujral 1996).

These days key Indian foreign and defence policy strategists reject the category South Asia and hint at a natural connection between India and Southeast Asia. They regard South Asia as a category that is disconnected from India's history and civilization, geography and strategic imperatives. The emergence of the term 'South Asia,' says Jasjit Singh, Director of the Institute of Defence Studies and Analyses, reflects a 'Washington-centred worldview' that 'imagined a world where the Indian subcontinent simply disappeared at the edges of peripheral vision.' India's Andaman Islands, he reminds readers, are closer to Indonesia and Thailand than to the Indian mainland (J. Singh 2000: 48).

Economics has been a prime mover of India's Look East policy. India had ignored the Asian economic miracle in its early phases since the lessons of the export-oriented economies of a few small countries indulged by the West seemed inapplicable to an economy of India's size and ambition. That view however, was badly shaken by the emergence of China—its spectacular growth since the 1980s that is based on trade and a liberalized economy (Baru 2000: 15). 'If we want to truly get into the globalization bus,' an Indian business professional is quoted as saying, 'we must first try and get into the shuttle of ASEAN' (cited in *Manila Times* 2002). Perhaps India has had to confront the element of truth in Samuel Huntington's claim that 'Outside Japan and Korea the East Asian economy is basically a Chinese economy' (Huntington 1996: 170). While the English language may give Indian businesses many advantages in the global economy, it is not much help in making inroads into East Asia where a network of overseas Chinese firms and families spread across the region is central to the organization of business. Since the countries of ASEAN have had a long relationship with China, Indian businesses appear to be keen on establishing ties with businesses in Southeast Asia hoping that they could be intermediaries with Chinese officials and businessmen for Indian companies.

The Look East policy began paying off in 2002 when the ASEAN heads of government and the Indian prime minister met in a summit meeting in the Cambodean capital of Phnom Penh. Summit meetings with India will now take place after every annual meeting of ASEAN heads of government. ASEAN and India have agreed to work towards negotiating a free trade agreement in ten years. But bilateral free trade agreements between India and individual ASEAN countries such as Singapore and Thailand may be only a year away. 'India's Asian breakthrough'—the BBC headline for one of its reports on the Phnom Penh summit—is perhaps not an exaggeration.

There are a number of bi-lateral and multi-lateral agreements that provide the foundation for India's growing relations with Southeast Asia. Of the multi-lateral relations are the Ganga-Mekong Sub-region and the Bangladesh, India, Myanmar, Sri Lanka, Thailand Economic Cooperation [BIMST-EC]. There is also the Bangladesh-China-India-Myanmar Regional Economic Forum [BCIM Forum]—an exercise in second track diplomacy—that has its roots in the Kunming Initiative of 1999. Official statements by ASEAN and Indian leaders call for deeper integration of the economies of ASEAN and India in coming years.

Looked at from the perspective of the potential for cross-border region building between Northeast India and its eastern neighbours the most relevant bilateral relationship, of course, is India's relations with Myanmar. In a highly publicized event in 2001, the then External Affairs Minister, Jaswant Singh inaugurated the 160-km Tamu-Kalewa-Kalemyo road in Myanmar. The Rs 90-crore road built by India's Border Road Organization was India's gift to Myanmar. In his speech inaugurating the road Singh said that 'the natural movement of goods, people and services for the Northeast is not through Calcutta;' and he described the importance of 'opening up the natural outlet of the Northeast' (*Assam Tribune* 2001a). Myanmar's Construction Minister, Major-General Saw Tun said that the 'road will become a vital section of the designated Asian Highway running from Singapore to Istanbul passing through Myanmar and India' (*Hindu* 2001). In December 2003 the Foreign Ministers of Myanmar, Thailand and India met in Delhi to discuss the technical and funding issues for a 1,400-km transnational highway.

Let me now raise a few questions about the future direction of the Look East policy that would determine the opportunities for cross-border region building across India's eastern borders.

Maritime versus a Continental Orientation

Northeast Indians think of Southeast Asian countries as their neighbours. But in a maritime sense the east coast of India—Orissa, Andhra, or Tamilnadu—is also next-door to Southeast Asia. Indeed historically mainland India's ties with Southeast Asia have been more maritime than continental. The Indian Ocean region has seen maritime commercial ties for millennia. The kingdoms of the Andhra and the Orissa coasts had maritime contact with Indochina. Even from the west coast of India 'it is believed that around 600 A.D the Saka kings of Gujarat set sail and reached the west coast of Java' (Baru 2000: 12). At least one commentator attaches some significance to the fact that Naramsimha Rao—under whose leadership the Look East policy began—was the first Indian prime minister from peninsular India. He belongs to a place very close to the Coromondel coast, known for its maritime ties to Southeast Asia (Baru 2000: 14).

As it has been in the past, even in modern times it is cheaper and less troublesome for India to trade with Southeast Asia by sea rather than by land. The land route not only goes through a difficult physical terrain, there is a perception that the route is full of danger. It may be tempting therefore for India to build relationships with Southeast Asia that are primarily maritime rather than continentally oriented.

Downplaying the continental dimension, however, will have costs not only for the region-building project that interests me but also in terms of Indian's diplomatic ambitions. It is not accidental that the world's only superpower, the United States, is both a continental and a maritime power. It is because of this dual orientation that it succeeded the maritime British and gained superiority over the continental Russians and Germans (Wang 2000: 111). The eventual success of India's Look East policy will depend on India's ability to embrace both a maritime and a continental thrust in its Look East policy.

Towards a Continental Look East Policy:
A Seat at the Table for the Northeast

One way to ensure a continental orientation to the Look East policy would be to give a direct role to the Northeastern states. In 1999, when China brought together experts, scholars and business people from China, India, Myanmar, and Bangladesh to initiate a regional economic forum, it invited them to Kunming, the capital of Yunnan province. The venue underscored Chinese intention to take advantage of Yunnan's geographical location and of its cultural affinities with its neighbours across the border—and to restore Yunnan's historical role as a bridge to Southeast Asia and South Asia.

Yunnan is well on its way. The road, air and rail links between Yunnan and the rest of China and with its transnational neighbours are impressive. The Kunming-Vientiane road connects Yunnan to Laos. There is a rail link between Kunming and Hanoi. There are air routes connecting Kunming with Bangkok, Singapore, Kuala Lumpur, Hanoi, Yangon, and Vientiane. The Lancang-Mekong river route links China with Laos, Myanmar and Thailand. The Yunnan provincial government gives incentives to foreign investors in addition to those available in other parts of China. Kunming today is very much a pan-Asian international city. Thailand, Myanmar, Laos, and Vietnam have consulates in Kunming. Thus while Yunnan's provincial government plays a direct role in the institutions of the Greater Mekong Sub-region, there is little room for India's Northeastern states in the Mekong Ganga Cooperation forum or in BIMSTEC (Bangladesh, India, Myanmar, Sri Lanka, Thailand Economic Cooperation). Even at the level of public diplomacy, when it came to India's turn to host the Forum of Regional Economic Co-operation—created by the Kunming Initiative—the meeting took place in New Delhi and not in Guwahati, Shillong or Imphal.

This is no small irony. After all, it is India and not China that has a democratic and federal polity.

The Fears

What then is holding India back? There are a number of factors of which the first is the ambivalence of Indian decision-makers vis-à-vis China.

The China Syndrome

Jairam Ramesh has observed that when it comes to developing full-fledged economic ties with China, Indian attitudes have been 'schizophrenic'. On the one hand, Indian companies are aggressively looking for investment opportunities in China and bi-lateral trade with China is 'galloping'. On the other hand the Indian government shows 'remarkable ambivalence' about Chinese investments in India. We are 'prisoners of an old mindset,' he writes (Ramesh 2003).

In recent years China's expansive economy has drawn India's South Asian neighbours into its economic orbit. Not surprisingly this has made many Indians nervous. Myanmar's trade with both India and China has expanded since 1989 but the trade with China has grown much more rapidly than trade with India. Even China's trade with Bangladesh has exceeded India's by a small but significant margin (Garver and Prime 2002). Apart from the economic sphere Chinese influence in Myanmar in military and political terms has been phenomenal. Indeed it has led India to reassess its policy of opposing the military junta and supporting the movement for democracy led by Aung San Suu Kyi. The U-turn in India's policy towards Myanmar since 1993 however, is not only antithetical to India's proclaimed democratic values it may not even serve Indian interest in the long run.

The Kunming Initiative and the BCIM Forum that it gave rise to advocate regional cooperation on infrastructure development by the four countries. Rather than being involved with China multilaterally, official India however, appears to prefer regional organizations such as the Ganga-Mekong Sub-region and BIMST-EC that do not include China. At the same time India has sought to improve bi-lateral relations with China. Yet there is enormous potential for following up on the Kunming Initiative, especially the proposal to rebuild the Stilwell Road—the road from Ledo in Assam to the Myanmar Road that connects to Kunming—constructed with American money during World War II. 'Since Kunming is already connected with Hong Kong by an express highway,' writes economist Jayanta Gogoi, 'North East India, or for that matter India as a whole could establish direct road link with Hong Kong if the Stilwell Road is well developed.' Apparently only a short stretch of the road—about 100–120 miles from the border of Arunachal Pradesh to Myitkyina in Myanmar—needs rebuilding. Beyond Myitkyina the road is well developed all the way to Kunming. Given its route and the rail and road networks linking that part of the road to provinces of south and central Myanmar that borders Laos, Thailand, Malaysia and Singapore, the Stilwell Road, Gogoi believes, 'can connect North East India and the mainland with the entire South East Asian countries' (Gogoi 2003). At the moment however, the Indian Government seems less than enthusiastic about rebuilding the Stilwell Road. On the other hand there is significantly more interest in building the road to Thailand taking a more southern route away from the emerging Yunnan-Northern Myanmar-Southeast Asia corridor.

Indian moves will remain somewhat hesitant so long as it tries to put China at a distance and remain blind to the uncertainties inherent in the present political stalemate in Myanmar. It would seem reasonable that we prepare for a political transition from military rule in Myanmar: after all it is unlikely that the junta will hold on to power indefinitely. More synchronization between India's policies towards China, ASEAN, and Myanmar would facilitate a more robust and long-term continental orientation to the Look East policy. A Sino-Indian rapprochement is not out of the question. Such a rapprochement could energize the Kunming Initiative. Indo-Chinese cooperation on developing transportation infrastructure could link Northeast India to Yunnan as well as to the rest of Southeast Asia.

The Security Anxieties

Earlier, I have noted that India has been hesitant about projecting Northeast India in its Look East policy the way Chinese projects Yunnan. The reasons, of course, are understandable. But it is worth remembering that the ethnic diversity of Yunnan and Northeast India is not dissimilar. Yunnan's population, in Chinese official parlance, is made up of 26 ethnic nationalities. This is not very different from Northeast India's demographic profile. Yet the Chinese, at least in Yunnan, do not have to confront anything like the insurgencies that India does. That the political uncertainty in Northeast India has been a major factor in shaping India's Myanmar policy is quite apparent. Indeed arguably it is India's security anxieties—getting Myanmar to act against Northeast Indian insurgent groups that take shelter in Myanmar—rather than a desire to give the Look East policy a continental orientation that explains Indian policy towards Myanmar, especially the U-turn in its attitide toward the military regime. Security expert Bibhu Prasad Routray wrote an article looking at the potential effects of the road-building project between Northeast India and Thailand through Myanmar on northeastern insurgencies. He concluded the article with lukewarm support for the road-building project with ample caution about the need for heightened border control.

It's actually a case of the positive outweighing the negative. The prospects of human development through regional cooperation and inter-linkages of economies, nullifies the negative effects, which might occur as a result of encouragement to insurgency. Underdevelopment of the region will alienate the law-abiding lot and in turn will feed insurgency, the effects of which would be much greater than allowing few insurgents to pass through the highways. However, an effective monitoring set up must be put in place to prevent the misuse of the highway. In fact such a mechanism must form a part of the broad objective of sealing the porous border (Routray 2002).

As I argued in an article in a newspaper India appears doomed to pay a price in terms of its diplomatic agenda for a bumbling Northeast policy that forces it to keep the door to the region half-shut. 'By denying itself the use of its natural gateway, India is in effect scaling back its ambitions in Southeast Asia' (Baruah 2003).

To be sure the sources of the security anxieties are real. Apart from the China factor and the insurgencies, roads through Myanmar are sure to bring drugs, illegal migrants, infectious disease, and small arms more easily than before. Already there are signs that smuggling routes for drugs through the Golden Triangle have become more diversified because of the availability of new corridors. Improved roads are sure to worsen India's HIV/AIDS crisis. Yet one of the peculiar challenges of our global era, as I will explain later, is that old-fashioned notions of border control to obtain security may be a cure worse than the disease.

Towards a Robust Look East Policy

(a) Today there is a virtual boom in the construction of cross-national highways, road, rail and air corridors in the world—thanks to the interest of multilateral organizations and advanced industrial countries with a stake in the globalized economy. Apart from the pressures from the globalizing economy, geopolitical changes are also pushing the process. For instance barriers to the creation of pan-Asian and Eurasian land transport linkages have disappeared thanks to the end of the Cold War. While the Trans-Asian Railroad was first proposed during the 1960s it 'remained stillborn due to conflict, Cold War rivalries, and lack of economic rationale' (Jasparro 2003: 1).

The United Nations now has a landlocked developing countries (LLDCs) group. Currently headed by Laos, it addresses the transport problems of landlocked countries. Were Ohmae's 'region states' the order of the day, Northeast India surely would have been part of this grouping. The European Union has a project entitled the 'Silk Road of the 21st Century'. The United National Development Program, the World Bank, the Asian Development Bank and other international organizations are all trying to bring together donor countries, land-locked developing countries and transit developing countries on infrastructure development, trade facilitation and regional cooperation projects. One such cross border regional development project in our neighbourhood is the Greater Mekong Sub-regional Development project. It brings together Vietnam, Cambodia, Thailand, Myanmar, Laos, and China's Yunnan Province. Funded by Japan and the Asian Development Bank it too seeks to establish transnational transport networks in the region.

But so far as Myanmar is concerned, most multilateral aid has ceased after the violent crackdown on the democracy movement by the military rulers in 1988. Multilateral development assistance has dried up because of the economic sanctions imposed by the United States and the European Union. It is only China, India, and Thailand that now give bi-lateral assistance to Myanmar.

While India and Thailand, and China and Thailand have been cooperating on road-building projects through Myanmar, the three countries are not about to sit down together to plan road and rail networks. And given the sanctions regime in place, there are no multilateral organizations involved. Under these conditions there are clearly limits on the scope and ambition of the road-building projects that are being discussed. As Jayanta Gogoi says about Stilwell Road 'To develop the Stilwell Road into a Trans-Asian Express highway, a huge amount of capital expenditure would be necessary which is possible only through the co-operation of the countries involved and the international financial institutions' (Gogoi 2003).

But it is necessary to think beyond one or even two roads. Whether it is the Stilwell Road or another road, by itself it cannot be expected to create a cross-border region. The buzzword in the world of transportation these days is Intermodalism. The term highlights the growing emphasis on the integration of different transport systems—road, rail, and air. The quintessential item associated with Intermodal transport is perhaps the Intermodal container. These brightly coloured rectangular containers that come in standard sizes are the most common sight in major ports as well as in many highways and freight trains passing through areas that are tied to global production networks. The container has become so ubiquitous in international trade because the same container can be carried by road, rail, and sea. The world of Intermodal transportation will remain a distant dream if our debates do not go beyond the question of whether to build the Stilwell Road or not.

(b) The prospects of building a cross-border region linking Northeast India with its eastern neighbours become brighter if one imagines linking the Kunming Initiative with the Mekong-Ganga project. Sino-Indian rapproachement can bring benefits that can scarcely be imagined at present.

(c) It is essential to think beyond the present military regime in Myanmar. There is good opportunity for India to take a leadership role in coordinating international policy towards Myanmar. In the US and Europe there is growing recognition that the sanctions against Myanmar are not working. As US Burma expert David Steinberg has said,

There is no doubt in my mind that sanctions and other U.S. actions have intensified Burmese reliance on China to the detriment of U.S. strategic and national interests .... The U.S. sanctions regime may make both the Congress and the administration feel morally good, but it is most unlikely to achieve its objective, which is regime change. Sanctions succeed in further cutting off Burma, and making reliance on China more extreme. This is not in either the U.S. or Burmese national interests (Steinberg 2003).

India is in a good position to play a leadership role in facilitating a political transition in Myanmar in cooperation with other international actors. Once

Myanmar has a more stable government based on reconciliation between the military and the democratic forces under Aung San Suu Kyi's leadership and multilateral initiatives are in place India will not have to make policies based primarily on fears of Chinese gains in Myanmar.

(d) India should take more advantage of Northeast India's history and culture as a soft power resource. While talking about our shared cultural ties with Southeast Asia, we refer endlessly to Buddhism, Angkor Vat, and the Ramayana. But we do not talk about the Southeast Asian roots of the Tai Ahoms or the Khasis. We scarcely acknowledge Balinese Hinduism and art forms are probably closer to Manipur's than to those of the Hindi heartland. Yet in Southeast Asia itself there is growing awareness of Northeast India. Many northeast Indian cultural figures too are drawn eastwards. For instance there is keen interest in Thailand in the culture of the Tai Ahoms of Assam. Similarly, Tai-Ahom intellectuals in Assam are focusing on the cultures of their ethnic cousins in Southeast Asia.

The Tai-Ahoms or Ahoms are an offshoot of the Tai people who are called Shan in Myanmar, Thai in Thailand, Lao in Laos, Dai and Zhuang in China and Tay-Thai in Vietnam. Recent conferences in Thailand on the culture of the Tai people have routinely included papers on the Tai Ahoms by Thai scholars as well as by ethnic Tai-Ahom Assamese scholars. Thai official interest in the subject has been quite apparent. For instance Princess Galyani Vadhana not only inaugurated one of those conferences, she presided over all its sessions. The Ahoms are not the only people of Northeast India with a Southeast Asian connection. The Khasis of Meghalaya had pioneered rice farming in Vietnam's Red River delta before losing out to the Vietnamese. They then moved up the Red River across Myanmar into Yunnan before crossing into India. But to date the cultural ties between Northeast India and Southeast Asia remain completely untapped as soft power resource in India's Look East policy.

Conclusion

There have been two contradictory developments vis-à-vis regions in the era of globalization. At one level the significance of regions seems to be on decline as the result of cross-national flows of capital, people, ideas and images. On the other hand there is a resurgence of regions both in the academic writings on globalization and in the intellectual horizons of government officials, development experts, and corporate managers.

A significant way in which 'contemporary global capitalism is different from capitalism's earlier forms,' writes Tim Oakes, is that 'local cultural diversity and difference are no longer regarded as obstacles to capitalist development, but rather have become core features of the expansion of the commodity form' (Oakes 2000: 671). Coca Cola's description of itself as multi-local and not multinational is perhaps more than a cute slogan. It is an example of the increasing significance attached to regions and localities in modern business practices. In China, according to Oakes, the promotion of provincial identities has meant that provincial elites are trying to 'scale-up more local, place-based identities to match the discrete space within a provincial boundary, as well as rein in transprovincial regionalisms that detract from provincial coherence.' This is an example of the ability of the Chinese political process to adapt to 'global capital's imperatives of neoliberalism and reterritorialization.' In order to attract investments localities today have to compete with one another not only by offering attractive packages of 'political-economic incentives, including a disciplined labour force and a liberalized regulatory environment,' they also package themselves as 'attractive and dynamic' cultural regions. The process has produced what Oakes calls 'often tortuous constructions of "provincial culture" and "provincial identity," where diverse local practices are sometimes cobbled together in cumbersome ways, or erased altogether, in the interests of a "pan-local" identity' (Oakes 2000: 669–71).

In cultural terms transnational region building across India's eastern border might even be as tortuous as constructing provincial identities in China. In the Tai-Ahom revivalism in Assam today Terwiel found a 'pseudo-Ahom' language and 'pseudo-old Ahom rituals' playing an important role. 'Thwarted by the loss of virtually all of the Southeast Asian culture,' Ahom ritual expert, Terwiel writes, 'have filled the gaps in their knowledge by relying upon inspiration' (Terwiel 2002: 22, 23).[7]

Yet the constructed nature of historical continuity does not make the politics of culture and history in Northeast India any less potent. Indeed as Terwiel puts it 'the case of the Ahoms of Assam illustrates how important a lost heritage can be and how a people may yearn for its roots, how keen may be its urge to recover the past, and how it may channel these wishes and urges into a strong political movement' (Terwiel 2002: 22). I have argued that a transnational region across Indian eastern border could create the space for a transnational politics of recognition that could respond to these urges, apart from bringing about significant economic benefits.

Such a project, of course, cannot take off without powerful institutional patrons. Regions to be 'real' have to become what political geographer Anssi Paasi calls 'an established entity in the spatial structure' that is 'identified in political, economic, cultural, and administrative institutionalized practices and social consciousness, and is continually reproduced in these practices.' Paasi calls this process the institutionalization of regions (Paasi 2000: 6). It is not accidental that the contemporary examples of cross-border regions and of paradiplomacy come mostly from Europe. They have occurred under the firm roof and encouragement of the European Union. In the coming together of states into supranational formations if the EU has been a trailblazer, South Asia has been a laggard. Till recently the South Asia Association for Regional Cooperation [SAARC] has been paralysed by hostility between India and Pakistan and it has been capable of taking up only very marginal issues. It is hardly in a position to encourage the building of cross-border regions. In the case of the transnationalism of the kind that is outlined in this chapter, there is an added problem. Were SAARC suddenly to gather steam, it will have no impact on transnational relations across India's eastern borders. For that to happen we will have to look for acceleration of the current trends of India 'looking east' and of the countries of ASEAN looking west.

In terms of Indian policy in the foreseeable future security anxieties might stand in the way of a robust Look East policy that includes the vision of a transnational region. But a half-hearted attitude can do more harm than good. There are risks for sure. Yet in our era of globalism border control may be the wrong way to deal with them. It will only put border control agents on a collision course with the demands of a global economy. It is important to recognize that in a dynamic transnational economic region there will never be enough inspectors or sufficient hours of the day to inspect all cargo in any busy border crossing. To handle the security challenges, under these conditions, there will have to be a 'paradigm shift' in the way we think of border control. Rather than controls at international borders, security will have to be tightened within the transportation and logistics system so that the risk of anyone in the transportation chain serving as conduits for criminals or terrorists is reduced. Transparent systems for tracking regional and global commercial flows could allow 'virtual' audits of inbound traffic before it arrives. Increased intelligence and data managing capacities of border agents can ensure that inspectors would target only high-risk goods and individuals (Flynn 2000: 58). Only close, comprehensive, and enduring relationships with our trading partners will allow such a paradigm change in border control.

All of this clearly requires an approach that is bold and innovative rather than cautious. Let me end with the story of one of the world's most successful airlines. Few people in India know that the story of Hong Kong's Cathay Pacific Airways began in Assam during World War II. From 1942 to 1945, American and Chinese transport planes carried essential military supplies from Dinjan, Assam to Kunming, China. The planes had to fly over the Himalayan peaks and the route came to be known as the Hump. The treacherous route exacted a heavy human toll. For years after the war pilots had reported seeing metal debris of planes that had crashed over the Hump, shining in the sun over Northeast India, Myanmar, and Yunnan.

After the War, Roy Farrell and Sydney de Kantzow, two Hump pilots, cashed in their experience and reputation to found the Cathay Pacific Airways. The experience of flying between Assam and Yunnan gave them the idea of flying passenger and cargo flights in Asia. They named their airline Cathay Pacific: Cathay because it is the ancient name for China and Pacific embodied the ambition of the embryonic airline to fly across the Pacific Ocean some day. Taking a flight from Northeast India to East Asia today invariably means flying west to Delhi or Kolkata first. One can fly east to Hong Kong, Bangkok, Singapore or Tokyo only from one of those western cities. Six decades after the Dinjan-Kunming flights flying west to Kolkata or Delhi in order to go east feels like a time warp and more than just a trifle ridiculous.

Parhaps the dare devil spirit of Farrell and de Kantzow can be our inspiration 'A positive embrace of risk,' writes sociologist Anthony Giddens, 'is the very source of that energy which creates wealth in a modern economy. Risk is the mobilizing dynamic of a society bent on change, that wants to determine its own future rather than leaving it to religion, tradition, or the vagaries of nature' (Giddens 2000: 41–2). Traditional cultures did not need a concept of risk, nor did they have one. Risk, as Giddens explains, is not the same as hazard or danger (Giddens 2000: 40). Letting our insecurities stand in the way of a robust Look East policy amounts to abject traditionalist surrender to fear. Risk is about actively assessing hazards in relation to future possibilities. 'It comes into wide usage only in a society that is future-oriented—which sees the future precisely as a territory to be conquered of colonised' (Giddens, 2000: 40). If the Look East policy is to live up to its potential of becoming Northeast India's road to peace and prosperity we will have to face up to the risks that exist and actively assess and manage them. That would mean taking a long-term view and synchronizing our foreign policies towards China, Myanmar, ASEAN—as well as towards Bangladesh and Bhutan—and our domestic policies vis-à-vis Northeast India. Building roads can deliver results only if they are part of a comprehensive transnational region-building project informed by a long-term strategic vision.

On a more academic plane political scientists have been rather complicit with the 'territorial trap' (Agnew 1994: 53–80). But given the changing spatialities of our age our intellectual horizons must go beyond the national order of things.[8] We will have to be able to project possibilities beyond today's reality and imagine transnational regions of the future. While considering the stubborn economic and political problems of Northeast India—trapped in the geopolitics of the colonial and post-colonial order— it is possible today to look for transnational solutions. Even if they might seem unrealistic today they could become possible and realistic tomorrow.

Notes

[1] The chapter originally appeared as 'Between South and Southeast Asia: Northeast India and the Look East Policy', CENISEAS Papers 4, 2004, Centre for Northeast India, South and Southeast Asia Studies, Guwahati, India and certain parts have appeared in two Op-ed articles published in the *Indian Express* (12 December 2003) and the *Telegraph* (9 February 2004). Earlier versions of the argument were presented in my 50th Golden Jubilee Lecture to the Assam Branch of the Indian Institute of Public Administration in Guwahati in January 2004, the 20th Foundation Day Lecture of Arunachal University in Itanagar, Arunachal Pradesh in February 2003 and in a paper at the Arizona State University's symposium on Regions and Regional Consciousness in Temple, Arizona in March 2004.

[2] To be sure whether Vasco da Gama's discovery of the sea route had put the silk route out of business is a matter of some debate. Andre Gunder Frank, for instance, rejects the notion that Central Asia was marginalized by the discovery of sea routes. He argues that the trade in the region remained a major global economic force till much later (Frank 1992).

[3] The abbreviations stand respectively for the United Liberation Front of Assam, People's Liberation Army, National Democratic Front of Bodoland and Naga National Socialist Council.

[4] The Silk Road—it owes its name to the nineteenth century German geographer, Baron von Richthofen—should not be construed to mean that it was either a single trade route or that it was only silk that was traded along the road. The term refers to a network of trails that connected the western region of China through Central Asia to the

Mediterranean. Along the way, there were branch routes leading to other destinations and from where the Silk Road ended there were trade networks that carried goods to destinations in the Mediterranean world, Europe and Asia.

[5] I owe this phrase to Zilkia Janer. See Janer, 2003.

[6] I owe the phrase territorial trap to John Agnew (1994).

[7] Terwiel's account of the following episode during his field study in Assam is particularly interesting. "The first time I asked an Ahom priest to translate some Ahom, not in general terms but word-for-word, he reluctantly admitted that this was rather beyond his powers and suggested that I pour him a glass of whiskey, since that might help obtain divine inspiration. The whiskey did not have the desired effect, but it did remind the anthropologists of the frequent use of alcohol by religious specialists. May we assume, then, that alcohol and other stimulants are occasionally used to bridge gaps in the historical continuity?" (Terwiel 2002: 23).

[8] I borrow the phrase from Malkki 1996: 447.

References

Aamee. 1992. Report of a Seminar held on 9 February 1992. *Aamee* (Guwahati, Assam) 1: (March) Special Supplement.

Abdi, S.N.M. 1990. 'India, Burma Rebels Work on Breakaway Plan', *Illustrated Weekly of India*, Supplement to Magazine, December 15–16.

Acharya, Amitav. 2003. 'Southeast Asia: Imagining the Region', *Himal South Asian* (Kathmandu) 16 (1) (January): 24–9.

Agarwal, A. 1999. 'Mayhem in Arunachal', *Down to Earth* 7 (11) 31 October.

Agnew, John A. 1994 'The Territorial Trap: The Geographical Assumptions of International Relations Theory', *Review of International Political Economy* 1 (1) Spring: 53–80.

Ali, Syed Sajjad. 1998. 'The Reang Refugees', *Frontline* [Chennai] Vol. 15 (15) 31 July: 65–70. Available online at http://www.flonnet.com/fl1515/15150650.htm.

Amnesty International. 2000. *Persecuted for Challenging Injustice: Human Rights Defenders in India*. London: Amnesty International.

AMCTA. (All Manipur College Teachers Association). 2001. *Manipur Fact File*. Imphal, Manipur: All Manipur College Teachers Association.

Anderson, Benedict. 1983. *Imagined Communities*. London: Verso Press.

——— 1994. Personal Correspondence. 10 December.

Angami, Sakhrie, Azeto Sumi, N. Chakhesang, Moa Ao and Sekhosie. 2002. 'Genesis of Nagalim', 2 November. Available online: http://www.kuknalim.net/focus/2002/focusApr2002item1.html.

Appadurai, Arjun. 1990. 'Disjuncture and Difference in the Global Cultural Economy.' *Public Culture* 2 (2): 1–23.

Aris, M. 1979. *Bhutan: The Early History of a Himalayan Kingdom*. Warminster, U.K.: Aris and Philips.

———— 1986. *Sources for the History of Eastern Bhutan.* Vienna: Arbcitskreis fur Tibetische une Buddhistische Studien, Universitat Wien.

Asia Watch. 1993. 'No End in Sight: Human Rights Violation in Assam.' New York: Asia Watch.

Asom Sahitya Sabha Barshiki (Asom Sahitya Sabha Annual), Annual Sessions, 1964, 1967, 1969, 1970, 1971, 1972 and 1973.

Assam Tribune. 2001a. 'NE Access to SE Asia a Must: Jaswant', *Assam Tribune.* 15 February.

———— 2001b. 'Expectations Run High Ahead of Northeast CMs' Meet', 11 October.

———— 2000a. 'Arunachal's Developmental Vision', Editorial, *Assam Tribune.* 15 June.

———— 2000b. 'Extend Ceasefire, Nagaland Congress Urges Centre, NSCN Factions', *Assam Tribune* 21 July.

Bachelard, Gaston. 1964. *The Poetics of Space* (Maria Jolas transl.) New York: Orion Press.

Balibar, Etienne. 1991. 'The Nation Form History and Ideology', in Etienne Balibar and Immanuel Wallerstein (eds), *Race, Nation, Class: Ambiguous Identities.* London: Verso Press.

Barbora, Sanjay. 2004. 'Unquiet History, Unquiet Peoples: The 'Tribal Question' in Assam', Paper presented at workshop on 'Historiography of Northeast India: Critical Perspectives', Centre for Northeast India, South and Southeast Asian Studies and Department of History, Cotton College, Guwahati, 27 February.

———— 2002. 'Ethnic Politics and Land Use: Genesis of Conflicts in India's Northeast', *Economic and Political Weekly.* 37 (13) 30 March: 1285–92.

———— 2001. Personal Correspondence.

Barooah, Nirode K. 1990. *Gopinath Bardoloi, Indian Constitution and Cente-State Relations.* Guwahati: Publication Board, Assam.

Baru, Sanjaya. 2000. 'The Problem', *Seminar* (487) March: 12–17.

Baruah, Sanjib. 2003. 'Look East, but via the Northeast', *Indian Express* (New Delhi) 12 December.

———— 1999. *India Against Itself: Politics of Nationality in Assam.* New Delhi: Oxford University Press.

———— 1997. 'Cutting States to Size', *Seminar* (459) November: 27–30.

———— 1995. 'The Western Cultural Boundary of Assam', *Economic and Political Weekly*, Vol. 30 (44), 4 Nov. 2783–4.

Basu, N.K. 1970. *Assam in the Ahom Age.* Calcutta: Sanskrit Pustak Bhandar.

Baxi, Upendra. 2001. 'Saint Granville's Gospel', Review of Granville Austin, *Working a Democratic Constitution: The Indian Experience. Economic and Political Weekly*, 36 (11), 17 March: 921–30.

Bayart, Jean-Francois. 1986. 'African Civil Society', in Patrick Chabal (ed.), *Political Domination in Africa: Reflections on the Limits of Power*, Cambridge: Cambridge University Press.

Bhuyan, Nakul Chandra. 1967. Presidential Speech, Asom Sahitya Sabha, 34th Session, Dibrugarh, in Hari Prasad Neog (ed.), *Asom Sahitya Sabha Barshiki* (Asom Sahitya Sabha Annual), Jorhat, Assam: Asom Sahitya Sabha.

Bidwai, Praful. 1990. 'ULFA: Assam's Irrational Syndrome', *Sunday Times of India* (New Delhi) 23 December.

Bordoloi, B.N., (ed.). 1986. *Alienation of Tribal Land and Indebtedness*, Guwahati, India: Tribal Research Institute, Assam.

Bose, Manilal (ed.). 1979. *Historical and Constitutional Documents of Northeast India: 1824–1973*. Delhi: Concept Publishing Company.

Breiner, Peter. 2001. 'Max Weber Among the Exiles: The Weber-Mannheim Problem and the Launching of a Dynamic Political Science'. Unpublished Essays from the 'No Happy End' Workshop, Bard College, Annandale on Hudson, New York. February.

Burling, Robbins. 2003. 'The Tibeto-Burman Languages of Northeastern India', in Graham Thurgood and Randy LaPolla (eds), *The Sino-Tibetan Languages,* London: Curzon Press.

———— 1967. 'Tribesmen and Lowlanders in Assam' in Peter Kunstadter (ed.) *South Asian Tribes, Minorities and Nations*, Vol. 1, Princeton, N.J.: Princeton University Press.

Butler, John. 1978 [1855]. *Travels and Adventures in the Province of Assam*, Delhi: Vivek Publishers.

Census of India (various years). New Delhi: Government of India, Office of the Registrar General and Census Commissioner, India.

Cerny, Philip G. 1998. 'Neomedievalism, Civil Wars and the New Security Dilemma: Globalization as Durable Disorder', *Civil Wars* 1 (1) Spring: 36–64.

Chassie, Charles. 1999. *The Naga Imbroglio: A Personal Perspective*. Kohima, Nagaland: Standard Printers and Publishers.

Chaube, Shibanikinkar. 1973. *Hill Politics in North East India*. Bombay: Orient Longman.

Chaudhuri, Kalyan. 1999a. 'Congress (I) Sweep', *Frontline* 16 (22) November 5: 33.

———— 1999b. 'Militancy Unchecked'. *Frontline* 16 (26) December 24: 61–2.

Cohn, Bernard S. 1987. 'Networks and Centres in the Integration of Indian Civilization'. in *An Anthropologist among the Historians and Other Essays*. Delhi: Oxford University Press: 78–87.

Collier, Paul. 2001. 'Economic Causes of Civil Conflict and their Implications for Policy', in Chester A. Crocker et al. (eds) *Turbulent Peace: The Challenge of Managing International Conflict*. Washington D.C., United States Institute of Peace.

Connor, Walker. 1994. *Ethnonationalism: The Quest for Understanding*. Princeton, N.J.: Princeton University Press.

Cover, Robert. 1992. 'Nomos and Narrative' in *Narrative, Violence, and the Law: The Essays of Robert Cover*. Martha Minow, Michael Ryan and Austin Sarat (eds). Ann Arbor, MI: University of Michigan Press.

Dabi, Tanya. 1997. 'Growth and Functioning of Panchayati Raj in Arunachal Pradesh', in S. Dutta (ed.) *Studies in the History, Economy and Culture of Arunachal Pradesh*. Delhi: Himalayan Publisher: 228–35.

Das, Gurudas. 2002. 'Probable Options: Cementing the Fault-lines in Assam', in K.P.S. Gill and Ajai Sahni (eds), *Faultlines*. Vol. 11 New Delhi: Bulwark Books and the Institute of Conflict Management: 91–8.

Das, Samir Kumar. 2002. 'Ethnic Conflicts and Internal Security: A Plea for Reconstructing Civil Society in Assam', in K.P.S. Gill and Ajai Sahni (eds), *Faultlines*. Vol. 10 New Delhi: Bulwark Books and the Institute of Conflict Management: 37–58.

Das Gupta, Barun. 2000. 'Assam's Angst', *The Hindu* (Chennai), 28 May.

Deka Kanaksen. 1993. *Natun Purushe Juktir Adharot Natun Samaj Gorho'k* [Let the New Generation Build a New Society Founded on Reason]. Guwahati: Dispur Print House.

Dutta, Dilip Kumar. 1984. *Bhupen Hazarikar Geet Aru Jeevan Rath* [The Songs and Life of Bhupen Hazarika]. Calcutta: Sribhumi Publishing Company.

Dutta, Nandana. 2003. 'Identities in the Wake of Militancy', in Kailash C. Baral and Prafulla C. Kar (eds), *Identities: Local and Global*. Delhi: Pencraft International: 144–53.

Easter, Gerald. 2000. *Reconstructing the State: Personal Networks and Elite Identity in Soviet Russia*. New York: Cambridge University Press.

Eaton, Richard M.1997. 'Comparative History as World History: Religious Conversion in Modern India', *Journal of World History* 8 (2): 243–71.

Errington, Joseph. 2003. 'Getting Language Rights: The Rhetorics of Language Endangerment and Loss', *American Anthropologist* 105 (4): 723–32.

Escobar, A.1995. *Encountering Development*. Princeton: Princeton University Press.

Evans, Peter. 1995. *Embedded Autonomy: States and Industrial Transformation*. Princeton, N.J.: Princeton University Press.

Fearon, J.D. and D.D. Laitin. 2001. 'Sons of the Soil, Immigrants and Civil War'. Available online: http://www.stanford.edu/class/polisci313/papers/LaitinOct29.pdf.

Ferguson J. 1990. *The Anti-Politics Machine: 'Development', Depoliticization, and Bureaucratic Power in Lesotho*. New York: Cambridge University Press.

Flynn, Stephen E. 2000. 'Beyond Border Control', *Foreign Affairs* 79 (6) November–December: 57–68.

Frank, Andre Gunder. 1992. *The Centrality of Central Asia* (Comparative Asian Studies. 8) Amsterdam: VU University Press.

Freitag, Sandria B. 1989. *Collective Action and Community: Public Arenas and the Emergence of Communalism in North India*. Berkeley, CA: University of California Press.

Friedman, Jonathan. 2003. 'Globalizing Languages: Ideologies and Realities in the Contemporary Global System', *American Anthropologist* 105 (4): 744–52.

Fürer-Haimendorf, Christoph von. 1980. *A Himalayan Tribe: From Cattle to Cash*. Berkeley, CA: University of California Press.

——— 1976. *Return to The Naked Nagas*. New Delhi: Vikas Publishing House.

Gadgil, Madhav and Ramchandra Guha. 1993. *This Fissured Land: An Ecological History of India*. Delhi: Oxford University Press.

Galanter, M. 1984. *Competing Equalities*. Berkeley, CA: University of California Press.

Gangopadhyay, D.K. 1990. *Revenue Administration in Assam*. Dispur, Assam: Government of Assam.

Garver, John W. and Penelope B. Prime. 2002. 'China Wins the Race: A Comparison of Chinese and Indian Economic Development and the Geopolitical Consequences of China's "Win"' Working Paper no. 2002–19, Michael J. Cole College of Business, Kennesaw State University, Kennesaw, Georgia, USA.

Geertz, Clifford. 1973. *The Interpretation of Cultures*. New York: Basic Books.

Gellner, Ernest. 1983. *Nations and Nationalism*. Ithaca, N.Y.: Cornell University Press.

Ghose, Sanjoy. 1998. *Sanjoy's Assam: Diaries and Writings of Sanjoy Ghose* (Edited and with an afterword by Sumita Ghose). New Delhi: Penguin.

Ghurye, G.S. 1980 [1959]. *The Scheduled Tribes of India*. New Brunswick,N.J.: Transaction Books.

——— 1943. *The Aborigines—So Called—and Their Future*. Poona, Maharashtra: Gokhale Institute of Politics and Economics, Publication no, 11.

Giddens, Anthony. 2000. *Runaway World: How Globalization is Reshaping Our Lives*. New York: Routledge.

——— 1991. *Modernity and Self-Identity: Self and Society in the Late Modern Age* Stanford, CA: Stanford University Press.

Gill, K.P.S. 2001. 'Managing Northeast: More Foresight Needed'. *The Pioneer* (New Delhi), 30 June.

Gogoi, Jayanta Kumar. 2003. 'Border Trade in North East India', *Assam Tribune* 24 October.

Goswami, Jotin (ed.), 1971. *Asom Sahitya Sabha Barshiki* (Asom Sahitya Sabha Annual), Dhing, 37th Session. Jorhat, Assam: Asom Sahitya Sabha.

Government of Assam. 1928. *Report on the Land Revenue Settlement of the Kamrup District* [by S. P. Desai] Shillong: Assam Government Printing Press.

———— 1890. *Annual Report on the Administration of Land Revenue in Assam, 1889–90.* Shillong: Assam Secretariat Press

———— 1885. *Land Revenue Administration Report of the Assam Valley Districts, 1884–85.* Shillong: Assam Secretariat Press.

———— 1882. *Land Revenue Report of the Assam Valley Districts, 1881–82.* Shillong: Assam Secretariat Press.

———— 1878. *Report on the Administration of the Province of Assam, 1876–77.* Shillong: Assam Secretariat Press.

Government of India. 2001. Ministry of Small Scale Industry, *State Profile of Arunachal Pradesh (Under Annual Action Plan—2001–2002),* Guwahati, Assam: Small Industries Service Institute.

———— 2000. Press Information Bureau Archives, 'Scheme of Margin Money to Surrendered Militants', statement by I. D. Swami, Minister of Home Affairs.. Available online: http://pib.nic.in/archieve/lreleng/lyr2000/rdec2000/r13122000.html.

———— 1972. 'Armed Forces (Assam and Manipur) Special Powers (Amendment) Act—1972'. No. 7 of 1972 (April 5). Reprinted in *Where 'Peacekeepers' Have Declared War.*

Grassroots Options. 2000. 'Focus Report on Rural Indebtedness in Meghalaya', *Grassroots Options* [Shillong, Meghalaya]. 4 (1) Autumn.

Griffiths, Percival. 1967. *The History of the Indian Tea Industry.* London: Weidenfeld and Nicholson.

Guha, Amalendu. 1991. *Medieval and Early Colonial Assam: Society, Polity, Economy.* Calcutta: K.P. Bagchi and Company [On behalf of the Centre for Studies in the Social Sciences].

———— 1977. *Planter Raj to Swaraj: Freedom Struggle and Electoral Politics in Assam 1826–1947.* New Delhi: People's Publishing House

Guha, Ramchandra. 2001. *Savaging the Civilized: Verrier Elwin, His Tribals, and India.* New Delhi: Oxford University Press.

Gujral, I.K. 1996. 'Statement by His Excellency Mr. I.K. Gujral Minister of External Affairs and Water Resources of India'. First Meeting of the

ASEAN-Indian Joint Cooperation Committee, New Delhi, November 14–16, 1996. http://www.aseansec.org/4338.htm.

Handler, Richard. 1985. 'On Having a Culture: Nationalism and the Preservation of Quebec's Patrimoine', in George W. Stocking (ed.) *Objects and Others: Essays on Museums and Material Culture,* History of Anthropology, 3. Madison, WI: University of Wisconsin Press.

Hansen, Randall and Patrick Weil. 2001. 'Introduction: Citizenship, Immigration and Nationality: Towards a Convergence in Europe?' in Randall Hansen and Patrick Weil (eds), *Towards A European Nationality: Citizenship, Immigration and Nationality Law in the EU,* New York: Palgrave.

Hausmann, Ricardo. 2001. 'Prisoners of Geography', *Foreign Policy* (122) January-February: 45–53.

Havel, Vaclav. 1989. 'Letter to Gustav Husak, General Secretary of the Czechoslovak Communist Party', in Vaclav Havel (Jan Vladislav ed.) *Living in Truth.* London: Faber and Faber.

Hazarika, Bhupen. n.d. Cassette tapes available in markets in Assam.

Hazarika, Sanjoy, 2002.'Of the Nagas, Regionalism and Power', *The Statesman* (New Delhi) 27 April.

Hindu. 2001. 'India, Myanmar Road Opened', *The Hindu* (Chennai) 21 February.

Hirschman, Albert. 1981. *Essays in Trespassing: Economics to Politics and Beyond.* New York: Cambridge University Press.

Hopkinson, Henry. 1872. Memorandum to the Secretary to the Government of Bengal, Revenue Department, April 6 1872. [Assam Commissioner's File, 1867–73. File No. 219, 'Land Revenue Settlements and Land Question in Assam' of the Assam State Archive, Guwahati, Assam].

HRW (Human Right Watch). 2002. Annual Report. Available online: http://www.hrw.org/wr2k2/asia6.html.

———— 1995. Annual Report. Available online: http://www.hrw.org/reports/1995/WR95/ASIA–04.htm.

Huntington, Samuel P. 1996. *The Clash of Civilizations and the Remaking of World Order.* New York: Simon and Schuster.

Hutton, J.H., 1922. 'Introduction', in James Philip Mills, *The Lhota Nagas.* London: Macmillan and Company.

———— 1921. *The Angami Nagas, with Some Notes on Neighbouring Tribes.* London: Macmillan and Company.

ICM (Institute of Conflict Management). 2002. 'South Asia Terrorism Portal'. http://www.satp.org.

India Today. 1998. 'Equality Before the Law: Must the CBI seek the Governor's Sanction Before Prosecuting a Chief Minister?' *India Today* 23 (3) 19 January: 6.

_____ 1993. 'Assam: Losing Business', *India Today* 18 (14) 31 July: 86–7.

Iralu, Kaka D. 2000. *Nagaland and India: The Blood and the Tears*, Kohima, Nagaland: Kaka D. Iralu.

Jacobs, Julian, Alan MacFarlane, Sarah Harrison and Anita Herle. 1990. *The Nagas: The Hill People of Northeast India: Society, Culture and the Colonial Encounter.* London: Thames and Hudson.

Janer, Zilkia. 2003. 'The Failed Narratives of Northeast India: Reading Sujata Miri's *The Broken Circle*'. Paper presented at seminar on 'Narratives of North East India: Creativity, Tradition and Interpretation'. Women's College, Shillong, Meghalaya, 6 September.

Jasparro, Christopher. 2003. *Paved with Good Intentions? China's Regional Road and Rail Networks*. Honolulu, Hawaii: Asia-Pacific Center for Security Studies. http://www.apcss.org/Publications/APSSS/ChinaDebate/ChinaDebate_Jasparro.pdf.

Johnstone, James. 1971 [1896]. *Manipur and the Naga Hills*. Delhi: Vivek Publishing House (original title: *My Experiences in Manipur and the Naga Hills*. London: S. Low, Marston & Company), Delhi: Vivek Publishing House.

Kalita, Gauri Sankar. 2003. 'Of Mahanta, Deka and an Insensate Gogoi Govt.', *Sentinel* (Guwahati). 27 July.

Karmakar, Rahul. 2000. 'Words Replace Guns in Nagaland Again', *The Hindustan Times* (New Delhi). 1 November.

Karna, M.N. 1990. 'The Agrarian Scene', *Seminar* (366) February: 30–8.

Kashyap, Samudra Gupta. 1999. 'Mahanta in Fresh Trouble over Letters of Credit', *Indian Express.* 5 July.

Keating, Michael. 1999. 'Rethinking the Region: Institutions and Economic Development in Catalonia and Galicia'. Paper presented at the Workshop on Regionalism Revisited: Territorial Politics in an Age of Globalization. Mannheim, Germany. March.

Khanna, Sushil. 2002. 'Trade and Investment in the South Asia Subregion for Economic Cooperation: Barriers and Opportunities'. Unpublished Paper. Kolkata, India: Indian Institute of Management, Calcutta.

Kiely, R. 1999. 'The Last Refuge of the Noble Savage? A Critical Assessment of Post-Development Theory'. *The European Journal of Development Research* 11 (1): 30–55.

Kunstadter, Peter, (ed.). 1967. *Southeast Asian Tribes, Minorities and Nations.* Vol. 1, Princeton, N.J. Princeton University Press.

Kymlicka, W. and W. Norman. 2000. 'Introduction', in Kymlicka and Norman (eds), *Citizenship in Diverse Societies*. Oxford: Oxford University Press.

Lama, Mahendra P. 2000. 'Internal Displacement in India: Causes, Protection and Dilemmas', *Forced Migration Review:* 24–8 August.

Lavakare, Arvind. 1999. 'The Autonomy Virus', *Rediff on the Net*. 11 August. Available online at http://www.rediff.com/news/1999/aug/11arvind.htm.

Licklider, Roy. 1995. 'The Consequences of Negotiated Settlements in Civil Wars, 1945–93'. *American Political Science Review*. 89(3): 681–90.

Liebenthal, W. 1956. 'The Ancient Myanmar Road—A Legend?' *Journal of the Greater India Society*. XVI (1): 1–17.

Lintner, Bertil 1996. *Land of Jade: A Journey from India through Northern Burma to China*. Bangkok: White Orchid Press.

Linz, Juan L. 1978. *The Breakdown of Democratic Regimes*. Baltimore: Johns Hopkins University Press.

Little, P. and M. Painter. 1995. 'Discourse, Politics, and the Development Process: Reflections on Escobar's "Anthropology and the Development Encounter".' *American Ethnologist* 22 (3): 602–16.

Lovewell, Mark and Anthony Westell. 2003. 'Union—But What Kind?' *Globe and Mail* 14 October (Toronto).

Ludden, David 2003. *Where is Assam? Using Geographical History to Locate Current Social Realities*, (CENISEAS Papers 1) Guwahati, Assam: Centre for Northeast India, South and Southeast Asia Studies.

Mackenzie, Alexander. 2001 [1884]. *The North-East Frontier of India*. Delhi: Mittal Publications [Originally published as *History of the Relations of the Government with the Hill Tribes of the North-East Frontier of Bengal*. Calcutta: Home Department Press].

Malkki, Liisa. 1996. 'National Geographic: The Rooting of Peoples and the Territorialization of National Identity among Scholars and Refugees', in Geoff Eley and Ronald Grigor Suny (eds), *Becoming National: A Reader*, New York: Oxford University Press.

Manila Times. 2002. 'India Looks to ASEAN to Boost Investments', *Manila Times*. 2 November.

MASS (Manab Adhikar Sangram Samiti). 2002. *And Quiet Flows the Kopili* [A Fact-finding Report on Human Rights Violation in the Karbi Anglong District of Assam], Guwahati: Manab Adhikar Sangram Samiti.

McCloskey, Donald N. 1990. *If You are So Smart: The Narrative of Economic Enterprise*. Chicago: University of Chicago Press.

Mehta, Uday Singh. 1999. *Liberalism and Empire: India in British Liberal Thought*. New Delhi: Oxford University Press.

Miller, J. Innes. 1969. *The Spice Trade of the Roman Empire, 29 B.C. to A.D. 641*. Oxford: Clarendon Press.

Miri, M. 2002. 'Northeast: A Point of View' (A Public Lecture). Available online: http://www.manipuronline.com/Features/May2002/Northeast14_2.htm.

Misra, Udayon. 2000. *The Periphery Strikes Back: Challenges to the Nation-State in Assam and Nagaland*. Shimla: Indian Institute of Advanced Study.

_____ 1988. *North-East India: Quest for Identity*. Guwahati, Assam:Omsons Publications.

Mithi, M. 2001. Speech at the Meeting of the National Development Council, 1 September, New Delhi. Available online: http://planningcommission. nic.in/cmstat49/arunachal.htm.

Moffatt Mills, A.J. 1984 [1854]. *Report on the Province of Assam*. Guwahati, Assam: Publication Board, Assam.

Muehlebach, Amy. 2001. '"Making Place" at the United Nations: Indigenous Cultural Politics at the U.N. Working Group on Indigenous Populations', *Cultural Anthropology* 16 (3): 415–48.

Mukhim, Patricia. 2003. 'Victory to the People', *The Telegraph* (Guwahati) 19 August.

Murasing, Chandra Kanta. 2003. 'Forest–1987' (Jayanta Mahapatra's version of a poem in *Kokborok*, a Language of Tripura; translated by Bamapada Mukherjee), in Kynpham Sing Nongkyrih and Robin S. Ngangam (eds). *Anthology of Contemporary Poetry from the Northeast*. Shillong: NEHU (North Eastern Hill University) Publications, xii, 254.

Nath, Sunil. 2001. 'The Surrendered Insurgents of Assam'. *Himal South Asian* (Kathmandu) 14 (12) December: 20–3.

Nibedon, Nirmal. 1987. 'Foreword', in Dalle Namo, *The Prisoner from Nagaland*. Tuli, Nagaland: Dalle Namo.

Nongbri, Tiplut. 1998. 'Khasi Women and Matriliny: Transformations in Gender Relations'. Paper Presented at Conference on Indigenous Asia: Knowledge, Technology and Gender Relations. 1–4 December. Available online: http://gendevtech.ait.ac.th/indigenous/tiplut.html.

Norwegian Refugee Council. 2001. Profile of Internal Displacement: India. [Compilation of Information Available in the Global IDP Database of the Norwegian Refugee Council]. Geneva: Norwegian Refugee Council. Available at their website http://www.idpproject.org

NPCC (Nagaland Pradesh Congress Committee). 2000. *Bedrock of Naga Society*. Available on line: http://www.nenanews.com/ng10.htm.

NSCM–IM. (Naga National Socialist Council Faction led by Isaak Chisi Swu and Thuingaleh Muivah). 2002. Also available online: http://www.angelfire.com/mo/Nagaland/Background.html (2 November 2002).

O'Donnell, Guillermo. 1999. 'Polyarchies and the (Un) Rule of Law in Latin America: A Partial Conclusion', in Juan Mendez, Guillermo O'Donnell, and Paulo Sergio Pinheiro (eds), *The (Un)Rule of Law and the Underprivileged in Latin America*. Notre Dame, Indiana: University of Notre Dame Press: 303–37.

Oakes, Tim. 2000. 'China's Provincial Identities: Reviving Regionalism and Reinventing "Chineseness"', *Journal of Asian Studies* 59:3: 667–92.

Ohmae, Kenichi. 1993. 'The Rise of the Region State', *Foreign Affairs* 172 (2): 78–87.

Paasi, Anssi. 2000. 'Re-constructing Regions and Regional Identity', Nethur Lecture, 7 November. Nijmegen, The Netherlands.

Pareto, Vilfredo. 1942. *The Mind and Society*, Vol. 4, New York: Harcourt, Brace and Company: 1512–13, 1527.

Phukan, J.N. 1992. 'The Tai-Ahom Power of Assam', In H.K. Barpujari (ed.), *Comprehensive History of Assam*. Vol 1. Guwahati: Publication Board, Assam.

Pommaret, Francoise. 1999. 'Ancient Trade Partners: Bhutan, Cooch Bihar and Assam (18th–19th centuries)', *Journal Asiatique* 287: 285–303. (English translation is available online: http://www.bhutanstudies.org.bt/journal/vol2no1/v2n1ancienttrade.pdf).

Prabhakara, M.S. 2003. 'Crackdown in Bhutan', *Frontline* 21 (1) 3 January: 4–10.

_____ 1994. 'The Northeast Turmoil', *The Hindu* 16 June.

_____ 1993. 'The Mailed Fist', *Frontline*. 7 July.

_____ 1985. 'Still Largely Symbolic', *The Hindu* 13 February.

Puri, Harish K., Paramjit Singh Judge, Jagrup Singh Sekhon. 1999. *Terrorism in Punjab: Understanding Grassroots Reality*. New Delhi: Har-Anand Publications.

Ramesh, Jairam. 2003. 'Growing Ambivalence', *The Telegraph* (Kolkata) Available online: http://www.jairam-ramesh.com/articles/article_telegraph.html.

Rammohan, E.N. 2002. 'Manipur: A Degenerated Insurgency', in K.P.S. Gill and Ajai Sahni (eds), *Faultlines*. Vol. 11, New Delhi: Bulwark Books and the Institute of Conflict Management: 1–15.

Ratan, Khumajam. 2001. 'A Retrospective on June 18 Uprising', in *The Book of Selfless Sacrifice: A Tribute to the Martyrs of Manipur's Territorial Integrity Movement*. Imphal, Manipur: Publication Committee, Manipur Territorial Integrity Movement: 1–5.

Ray, Sohini. 2003. 'Boundary blurred? Folklore/Mythology, History and the Quest for an Alternative Geneology in Northeast India', unpublished manuscript. University of California, Irvine.

rediff.com. 2003. 'Tarun Gogoi Reluctant to have K.P.S. Gill as Assam Governor'. rediff.com. 25 April. Available online at: http://inhome.rediff.com/news/2003/apr/25assam.htm.

rediff.com. 1998. 'Alarming rise in killings spreads terror in Guwahati'. *rediff.com*. 18 November. Available online at http://www.rediff.com/news/1998/nov/18ass.htm.

Roberts, William. 1947. 'Observations on the Cultivation of the Tea Plant and the Manufacture of Tea', Appendix in H.A. Antrobus. *A History of the Jorehaut Tea Company Ltd., 1859–1946.* London: Tea and Rubber Mail.

Routray, Bibhu. 2002. 'The Indo-Myanmar-Thai Highway: Impact on Insurgency in India's Northeast', *Bharat Rakshak Monitor* Volume 5(3) November–December.

Rudolph, Lloyd I. and Susanne Hoeber Rudolph. 1985. 'The Subcontinental Empire and the Regional Kingdom in Indian State Formation', in Paul Wallace (ed.) *Region and Nation in India.* New Delhi: Oxford and IBH Publishing Co.: 40–59.

Rustomji, Nari. 1973. *Enchanted Frontiers: Sikkim, Bhutan and India's North-eastern Borderlands,* Calcutta: Oxford University Press.

Rybczynski, Witold. 1986. *Home: A Short History of an Idea.* New York: Viking: 26–8.

Sachs, Jeffrey D. 2002. Keynote address, Inaugural Urban Research Symposium, The World Bank, Washington D.C. 9 December. Available online: http://www.worldbank.org/urban/symposium2002/docs/pres-paper/pres-pdf/sachs.pdf.

——— 2000. 'Tropical Underdevelopment'. Center for International Development Working Paper 57, Cambridge, MA: Harvard University, December.

Sachs, W. (ed.). 1992. *The Development Dictionary: A Guide to Knowledge as Power* London: Zed Books.

Sachdeva, G. 2000. *Economy of the North East: Policy, Present Conditions and Future Possibilities.* New Delhi: Centre for Policy Research.

——— 1999. 'Rejuvenating the Northeastern Economy', *Oriental Times,* Guest Column 1 (34–5) 22 Jan–6 Feb. http://www.nenanews.com/OT%20Jan22–Feb. 6, 99/GuestC.htm.

Sahadevan, P. 2000. *Coping with Disorder: Strategies to End Internal Wars in South Asia.* Colombo, Sri Lanka: Regional Centre for Strategic Studies, Colombo Policy Studies Paper 17. Available online: http://www.rcss.org/publications/POLICY/ps-17-5.html 2 November.

SAHRDC (South Asia Human Rights Documentation Centre).1995. *Armed Forces Special Powers Act: A Study in National Security Tyranny.* New Delhi: South Asia Human Rights Documentation Centre. Available online: http://www.hri.ca/partners/sahrdc/armed/fulltext.shtml?

Said, Edward W. 1979. *Orientalism.* New York: Vintage Books.

Saigal, Krishnan. 1992. 'Federal Democracy and Pluralism in the North East', in Nirmal Mukarji and Balveer Arora (eds) *Federalism in India: Origins and Development.* New Delhi: Vikas Publishing House under the auspices of the Centre for Policy Research.

Saikia, Rajen. 2000. *Social and Economic History of Assam,* Manohar Press: New Delhi.

Scott, James C. 2000. 'Hill and Valley in Southeast Asia ... or why the State is the Enemy of the People who Move Around ... or ... why Civilizations Don't Climb Hills'. Paper submitted at symposium on Development and the Nation State. Washington University, St. Louis. Available online: http://www.artsci.wustl.edu/~symp2000/jscott.PDF.

Sentinel. 2003. 'Jamir Raps DAN Government for Ignoring Truce with NSCN (K)', *Sentinel* (Guwahati) 26 July.

_____ 2001a. 'Lohit Deuri, nine others held in extortion charges', *Sentinel,* 4 March.

_____ 2001b. 'Lucrative Surrenders', Editorial, *Sentinel.* 13 March.

_____ 1994. 'Army Kills Five Persons in Tinsukia District', *Sentinel,* 24 February.

_____ 1990 'ULFA wanted Rs 4 Crores', *Sentinel.* 21 December.

Sharma, Kalpana. 1990. 'The Killing Fields', *Times of India,* Sunday Review, 10 June.

Shimray, U.A. 2001. 'Ethnicity and Socio-Political Assertion', *Economic and Political Weekly*, 36(39): 3674–7.

Shridhar, Purabi. 2000. 'Report on Threat to Matrilineal System in Meghalaya', *Femina* [Mumbai]. 1 December.

Simon Memorandum. 1999 [1929]. 'Memorandum of the Naga Hills to the Statutory Commission on Constitutional Reforms (Simon Commission)', 10 January 1929, Appendix A in Chassie, 1999: 165–7.

Singh, B.P. 1987a. *The Problem of Change: A Study of Northeast India.* New Delhi: Oxford University Press.

_____ 1987b. 'North-East India: Demography, Culture and Identity Crisis', *Modern Asian Studies*, 21 (2): April: 257–82.

Singh, R.K. Ranjit. 1990. 'Emergent Ethnic Processes in Manipur: A Reappraisal', in B. Pakem, ed., *Nationality, Ethnicity and Cultural Identity in North-East India*. New Delhi: Omsons Publications: 33–251.

Singh, Jasjit. 2000. 'Our Eastern Neighbour', *Seminar.* (487) March: 48–50.

Sinha, S.K. 2002. 'Violence and Hope in India's Northeast', in K.P.S. Gill and Ajai Sahni (eds), *Faultlines.* Vol. 10 (January) New Delhi: Bulwark Books and the Institute of Conflict Management: 1–23.

Skocpol, Theda. 1996. 'Unravelling from Above', *The American Prospect*, 25 (March-April): 20–5.

_____ 1999. 'Civic Groups Fostered Citizenship and Political Engagement', *Public Affairs Report.* Berkeley, CA: Institute of Governmental Studies, 40 (3) May.

Sonntag, Selmak. 2002. 'Minority Language Politics in North India', in James W. Tollefson (ed.) *Language Policies in Education: Critical Issues.* Mahwah, New Jersey: Lawrence, Erlbaum Associates: 165–78.

Soyinka, W. 1999. 'The Federal Quest', *West Africa Review*, 1 (1). Available online: http://www.westafricareview.com/war/vol1.1/soyinka.pdf.

Steinberg, David I. 2003. 'China's Role in Southeast Asia', Testimony before US-China Economic and Security Review Commission, 4 December. Available online: http://www.uscc.gov/testimony/031204bios/steinberg.htm.

Suryanarayan, V. 2000. 'Prospects for a Bay of Bengal Community', *Seminar* (487) March: 58–62.

Suny, Ronald Grigor. 2001. 'Constructing Primordialism: Old Histories for New Nations'. Available online: http://www.dartmouth.edu/~crn/crn_papers/Suny3.pdf. (2 November 2002).

Tara, T. 2000. 'Dindu Miri: The Man who Came in From China', *The Assam Tribune*, 23 November.

Taylor, Charles. 1994. 'The Politics of Recognition', in Amy Gutman (ed.) *Multiculturalism: Examining the Politics of Recognition*. Princeton, NJ: Princeton University Press: 25–73.

Taylor, E. M. 1996. 'A Review of the Social Basic for Sustainable Development in Arunachal Pradesh', *Future Generations, India. Arunachal In-depth*. Available online: http://www.future.org/PAGES/5_INDIA/arunachal_bckgrnd_study.html.

Telegraph 2004a. 'Governor Slaps Spoilt-child Tag on Northeast', *Telegraph* (Guwahati) 14 February.

———— 2004b. 'Human Rights Panel Slams Mizoram Rights Record', *Telegraph* (Guwahati) 25 February.

Terwiel, B.J. 2002. 'Revivalism in Northeast India: A Case of the Ahoms', *Indian Journal of Tai Studies* (Institute of Tai Studies and Research, Moranhat, Assam) 2: March.

Thakur, D.D. 1991. Governor's Report to the President. March 20. In *News of North-East: A Monthly Compilation of Clippings*. Guwahati, Assam: Eastern Press Service. May.

Times of India. 2003. 'Rio Says Nagas Live in Arunachal Pradesh', *Times of India*, 29 July.

———— 2001a. 'NSCN Announces "Tax Break" For Industries', *Times of India* 28 February.

———— 2001b. 'Nagas Invite N-E Expert to Broker Peace', *Times of India* 20 June. (New Delhi).

———— 2001c. 'Instil sense of "Indianness" in Northeast: Advani', *Times of India*, 4 September.

———— 1999. 'Rehabilitation Package for N-E Insurgents Soon', *Times of India*, 24 January.

Tully, James, 1995. *Strange Multiplicity: Constitutionalism in an Age of Diversity*. Cambridge: Cambridge University Press.

ULFA [United Liberation Front of Assam]. 1979. Samyukta Mukti Bahini Asom, *Samyukta Mukti Bahini Asomor Dosom Protistha Dibos, Bishesh Procar Patra* [Tenth Foundation Day of ULFA, Special Publicity Pamphlet] 7 April. "Doi-kao-rong": United Liberation Front of Assam.

USCR (United States Committee for Refugees). 2000. 'Worldwide Refugee Information' *Country Report: India*. Available online: http://ww.refugees.org/world/countryrpt/scasia/india.htm.

van Schendel, Willem. 1995. 'The Invention of the "*Jummas*": State Formation and Ethnicity in Southeastern Bangladesh', in R.H. Barnes, Andrew Gray and Benedict Kingsbury (eds), *Indigenous Peoples of Asia*. Ann Arbor, MI: Association For Asian Studies: 121–44.

Verghese, B.G. 2001a. 'Unfinished Business in the Northeast: Pointers Towards Restructuring, Reform, Reconciliation and Resurgence', Seventh Kamal Kumari Memorial Lecture. Available online: http://www.freeindiamedia.com/economy/19_june_economy.htm.

_____ 2001b. 'End of Isolation', *The Hindustan Times* [New Delhi] 2 May.

_____ 1996. *India's Northeast Resurgent: Ethnicity, Insurgency, Governance, Development*. Delhi: Konark.

Vishwanathan, S. 2004. 'Shining Kitsch', *Himal South Asian* 17 (3–4): 6–8 March–April.

Walzer, Michael. 1995 [1992]. 'The New Tribalism: Notes on a Difficult Problem', in Omar Dahbour and Micheline R. Ishay (eds), *The Nationalism Reader*. Atlantic Highlands, N.J.: Humanities Press: 322–32. [Originally published in *Dissent*, Spring 1992: 164–71].

Wang, Gung Wu. 2000. *The Chinese Overseas: From Earthbound China to the Quest for Autonomy*. Cambridge, MA: Harvard University Press.

Where "Peacekeepers" Have Declared War. 1997. New Delhi: National Campaign Committee Against Militarization and Repeal of the Armed Forces (Special Powers) Act. April.

Winichakul, Thongchai. 1994. *Siam Mapped: A History of the Geo-Body of a Nation*. Honolulu: University of Hawaii Press.

Young, M. Crawford. 1976. *The Politics of Cultural Pluralism*. Madison: University of Wisconsin Press: 72.

Yunuo, Asoso. 1974. *The Rising Nagas: A Historical and Political Study*. Delhi: Vivek Publishing House.

Index